# Reports of Cases Decided in the Ecclesiastical Courts at Doctors' Commons

James Parker Deane, M. C. Merttins Swabey

BIBLIOLIFE

# REPORTS

OF

# CASES

DECIDED IN THE

# ECCLESIASTICAL COURTS

AT

## Doctors' Commons.

1855 TO 1857.

BY

JAMES PARKER DEANE, D.C.L.,

AND

M. C. MERTTINS SWABEY, D.C.L.,

IN CONTINUATION OF DR. ROBERTSON'S REPORTS.

LONDON:

WILDY & SONS, LINCOLN'S INN ARCHWAY, CAREY ST.,

LAW BOOKSELLERS AND PUBLISHERS.

DUBLIN:

HODGES & SMITH, GRAFTON STREET.

1858.

# PREFACE.

The first number of this volume, as far as page 265, was edited in 1856 by my friend Dr. Deane himself. Some weeks since he gave me the manuscripts, consisting chiefly of the judgments, which he had provided for the second number. I have freely used and added to these materials, in order to complete the volume, which brings the series of ecclesiastical reports to within a few weeks of the date when the jurisdiction of the Ecclesiastical Courts in matters testamentary and matrimonial was abolished by the 20 & 21 Vic. chapters 77 and 85. Though under these statutes the form of proceeding is very much varied, and the Court for Divorce and Matrimonial Causes wields an ampler authority than the Ecclesiastical Courts have, probably, ever exercised; yet, for principles which will be acted upon in a majority of instances, there can be little doubt that the series of reports, of which this is the concluding volume, will for many years to come furnish important precedents.

M. C. MERTTINS SWABEY,

Doctors' Commons.

*April* 30, 1858.

# TABLE

OF

# CASES REPORTED.

---

## A.

## B.

## C.

## D.

## E.

## S.

## T.

## W.

# REPORTS OF CASES

### ARGUED AND DETERMINED

#### IN THE

## ECCLESIASTICAL COURTS

##### AT

## Doctors' Commons.

### PREROGATIVE COURT OF CANTERBURY.

*In the goods of* JANE WEBB.

*On Motion.*

1855.

Nov. 7th.

JANE WEBB, on the 18th of March, wrote and signed her will, and on the 13th of May following she executed it, by acknowledging this signature in the presence of A. and B., both present at the same time; immediately after which B. left the room, and during her absence, but in the presence of the testatrix, A. subscribed the will as a witness. In a short time B. returned to the room, in which A. and the deceased still were, and B. then subscribed the will as a witness in the presence of the deceased and of A.

*Deane* moved for probate of the will.

The 1 Vic. c. 26, s. 9, does not, in terms, require that the witnesses shall subscribe in the presence of

Where the attesting witnesses subscribe the will in the presence of the testator, but not in the presence of each other, the execution is good under 1 Vic. c. 26, s. 9.

each other. It would appear from a passage in the report of *Casement* v. *Fulton*, 5 Mo. P. C. C. 140, that the Privy Council considered a joint presence requisite at the time of subscription ; but there is probably an error in that part of the report, for in a case which followed immediately afterwards (*Faulds* v. *Jackson*, 6 N. C. Supl. 1), their Lordships held the will to be well executed though the witnesses did not subscribe in the presence of each other. And in *Chodwick* v. *Palmer*, 12th of July, 1851, a case which has not been reported, Sir H. Jenner Fust, referring to this passage in *Casement* v. *Fulton*, said, " That dictum has not been acted upon and received as the true interpretation of the statute in this Court. Cases have occurred in which the witnesses have not signed in the presence of each other, yet the Court has decided that the statute was complied with." And he held the will in that case well executed, though the witnesses had not subscribed in the presence of each other.

SIR JOHN DODSON.

I was at first inclined to take a different view of this case, but upon the authority of *Chodwick* v. *Palmer*, I will grant this motion.

*Probate decreed.*

*In the goods of* WILLIAM JONES.

*On Motion.*

1855.

Nov. 7th.

WILLIAM JONES left a will which was drawn up from his instructions, and read over to him in the presence of J. and E. The deceased expressed his approval of it and signed his name at once, and before W., one of the subscribing witnesses, had come into the room; but when that witness came in, he still held the pen, and E., who had assisted the testator by holding a book on which the will was placed for him to sign, he being in bed, still held the book and the will in his hand. Immediately on W.'s entering the room E., in the presence and hearing of the deceased, said that the paper he held in his hand was the deceased's will, and asked W. to sign it, which he did in the presence of the deceased, who watched him in doing so. E. then wrote his name under that of W., upon which E. said to the deceased, " Will that do?" to which the deceased replied, " Yes." The deceased died the same day. The property left was under £100 in this country, and about £200 in Australia.

*Addams* moved for probate of the will as having been executed by a virtual acknowledgment of the signature by the deceased, in the presence of two witnesses.

Execution by the testator's acknowledgment of his signature.

1855.

Nov. 7th.

In the goods of
JONES.

SIR JOHN DODSON.

I think that, from the facts of the case, what was said and done by the testator amounted to such an acknowledgment as will satisfy the provisions of the Act of Parliament; but had the property not been so small, I should have directed the will to be propounded. Under the circumstances, however, I decree probate to the executor.

---

### In the goods of THOMAS OSBORNE.

1855.

Nov. 16th.

#### On Motion.

Probate of
several papers
(one written
after the death
of the testator)
granted as to-
gether con-
taining his will,
on proof of the
Law of the
Domicil.

THIS deceased was a natural-born British subject, but he had resided in Spain for many years, had married a Spanish woman, and continued to reside and carry on business there till his death. He was never naturalized as a Spaniard.

After his marriage, and when he had two children, he executed an instrument conferring on his wife the power of making and extending his will, instituted his then two children his heirs, and appointed his wife executrix. Subsequently, when he had five children, he executed, before the British Vice-Consul at Port St. Mary, a paper described on the face of it as a codicil to his will, appointing his wife executrix, and instructing her to dispose of his property among his five children.

After the death of the deceased, in February, 1854, the widow appeared before the Captain-General of the Province in which the deceased had resided, and produced a copy of the codicil, and prayed that the then five children might be declared heirs. The Captain-General having so decreed, she, in June, 1855, appeared before a notary at Port St. Mary, and, in accordance with the power, and the codicil, and the decree of the Captain-General, made and extended the will of the deceased, and thereby instituted the five children of the deceased as his heirs, and assumed the office of executrix of the will.

1855.

Nov. 16th.

In the goods of OSBORNE.

An affidavit of an advocate of the national tribunal of Spain was read, from which it appeared that by the law of Spain one person may, by an instrument in writing, direct another to make a will for him after his death, in conformity with the contents of such written instrument, and that the Captain-General of the Province had jurisdiction over the civil affairs of all foreigners resident therein; and the Court was moved to decree letters of administration, with the three papers (that is, the power, the codicil, and the extended will) annexed, to the attornies of the widow.

SIR JOHN DODSON.

The domicil should have been established by affidavit; but the long-continued residence in Spain is, in the circumstances of the case, sufficient to let in the law as stated by the affidavit which has been read. The administration may therefore go as now prayed.

*In the goods of* SIR JOSIAS HENRY STRACEY, BART., *and* DIANA STRACEY, *his wife*.

1855.

Dec. 3d.

Joint will.
Practice.

*On Motion.*

SIR J. H. STRACEY, and Diana Stracey, his wife, made a joint will, dated the 25th of April, 1850. Lady Stracey died in June, 1854; Sir J. H. Stracey died on the 6th of November, 1855, without having altered or revoked the will. The will was enclosed in a sealed envelope, endorsed in the handwriting of Lady Stracey, "The will of J. H. Stracey, Esq., 1850."

After her death, one of the daughters asked Sir J. H. S. whether the will was to be opened; he said, "No, not in his lifetime, as it might give rise to unpleasant feelings." Lady Stracey had a power of appointment by will over certain property; and Sir J. H. Stracey had, as survivor, a power of appointment over other property, independent of his general property.

The will commenced, "We, Josias Henry Stracey and Diana Stracey, do hereby declare this to be our last will; and after the payment of all our just debts and funeral expenses, we direct that all our monies," &c. Certain bequests were then given to their children; and there was an appointment of executors of "this our joint will." The attestation clause described the will to have been "signed by the said J. H. S. and D. S. in our presence, who, in their presence, &c., have hereunto affixed our signatures as witnesses to this their will."

*Deane* moved the Court to decree probate of the paper, as the last will and testament of Diana Stracey, to be granted to the executors, limited to all such personal estate and effects as she, the said D. S., had a right to appoint or dispose of ; also, to decree a special general probate of the said paper, as the last will and testament of Sir J. H. S., to the executors. *Hobson* v. *Blackburn*, 1 Add. 274, is adverse to *mutual* wills, but, if it has any bearing upon the present case, shows the validity of a *joint* will like the one now before the Court.

Sir John Dodson.

I think you are entitled to the prayer of your motion. *Hobson* v. *Blackburn*, when examined, is certainly not an authority against you. The paper should have been proved as the will of Lady Stracey upon her decease, but that cannot affect the right of the executors now.

1855.

Dec. 3d.

In the goods of Sir Josias Henry Stracey, and Diana Stracey, his wife.

---

Ewen *against* Franklin and Others.

*On admission of an Allegation.*

This case came before the Court upon the admission of an allegation propounding a paper as the last will and testament of James Stares, propounded by Mr. W. Ewen, and opposed by an executor under a prior will.

1855.

Dec. 3d.

A will regularly drawn up by a solicitor was signed by the testator and also by two witnesses in the margin of the first four sheets ; but in the fifth and last sheet the signature of the deceased alone appeared.—Held, that the witnesses had not subscribed the will.

1855.

Dec. 3d.

EWEN
*against*
FRANKLIN
and Others.

In April, 1846, the testator gave instructions to his solicitor, who accordingly prepared a will, which was read over to the testator, at the solicitor's office; but the testator declined to execute it there. The solicitor gave him full verbal instructions how to proceed, and made pencil marks indicating where the signatures of the testator and the witnesses should be placed. The will was written on five sheets of paper; at the bottom of each of the first four sheets appeared the testator's signature in ink, above his name, penciled beforehand by the solicitor; on the margin of each of the first four sheets appeared the subscriptions of the witnesses. On the fifth and last sheet was a testimonium clause, expressing the testator's intention of executing the paper by placing his name on each sheet, and his name and seal at the end. The testator's signature followed opposite a regular attestation clause; but the witnesses had not written their names on any part of the fifth sheet. Both witnesses were dead; and no other person, apparently, was present at the execution.

Declarations of the testator as to the execution, and that the death of the witnesses would make no difference, were pleaded in the allegation, the admission of which was opposed.

*Addams* and *Spinks,* for different parties, opposed the admission of the allegation.

*Jenner* and *Twiss contrà.*

SIR JOHN DODSON.

I think the signatures on the first sheets were intended merely to guard against other sheets being interpolated; that the testator's signature at the end of the paper is that which the Court must consider as intended to give validity to the whole instrument, and consequently that is the signature which ought to have been attested. In the *Goods of Chamney*, 1 Rob. 757, it clearly appeared that the signatures on the back of the paper were intended to attest the sole signature of the testator; whereas, in the present case, there is nothing even to show that the signatures in the margins were intended to attest that signature of the testator which alone would give effect to the paper as a will. I therefore reject the allegation propounding this paper.

*In the goods of* P. A. COOPER.

*On Motion.*

THE deceased directed that her will was "to take effect only in the event of my son Charles dying under the age of 21 years, and my daughter Sarah dying under that age and unmarried." She then went on to leave various legacies, disposed of the residue of her estate, and appointed C. G. her executor. The personal estate was under £200;

---

*Margin notes:*

1855.

Dec. 3d.

EWEN *against* FRANKLIN and Others.

1855.

Dec. 11th.

General Probate. Practice.

General probate decreed of a will intended "to take effect only in the event," &c.

1855.

Dec. 11th.

In the goods of
P. A. COOPER.

but in the event of the son dying under the age of 21 years, and the daughter dying under that age and unmarried, the deceased had a power, under her marriage settlement, to dispose of a certain amount of stock.   Both children were living.

Probate of the will, with such limitations as the Court should think fit, was moved for on behalf of the executor.

SIR JOHN DODSON decreed a general probate to the executor.

---

HERBERT *against* HERBERT.

*On admission of an Allegation.*

1855.

Dec. 14th.

1 Vic. c. 26, s.
11.   Actual
military
service.

THE deceased in this case died suddenly on the 16th of November, 1848.   He had written on the same day a letter to his brother in the following terms:—

"Jellundur, 16th November, 1848.
"MY DEAR GEORGE,
   "I have not heard from you for a long time, and being about to go to the Hills, sick, I write to give you a list of money, or rather a statement of my affairs, should anything happen to me during these

disturbed times. I intend that everything I have shall be yours, with the exception of £1000, which I purpose that John shall possess. My will I intend making over to George Hill, with whom I am staying. 1 have in this country, in Messrs. C. & Co.'s hands, 16,500 rupees in company's paper. I don't know the exact amount of last balance; I believe it was 250 or 260 rupees. I have paid 3350 rupees to the East India railway. I have not yet received last month's pay, 500 rupees, from Hodgson. I owe nothing in bills; and there are about 110 rupees in my boxes. I know not where to go or what to do in consequence of my regiment having gone on service, and also because I have been suddenly and unexpectedly relieved from the acting department I held at Hoosheropoore. John and my aunts can tell the amount of my property at home—indeed you know it pretty well. My wound pension is due from the 1st of August, 1847, until this time. I go before the medical committee to-day, so that the next time you hear from me will be from Simlah, in all probability.

"Your affectionate brother,

"R. A. HERBERT."

The allegation propounding this paper as the will of the deceased, pleaded that in January, 1848, he was ordered from his own regiment, the 46th, then stationed at Lahore, to join a Sikh regiment at Hoosheropoore, which he immediately did, with which regiment he remained till November, 1848; that during such time he was engaged in various skirmishes with the rebel troops of Rajah Shere

Sing, and that in the course of such services he was seriously injured in an arm which had been previously wounded; that during such time the deceased's own regiment was brigaded with the army on the Sutlej, and continued in active service until after his death; that the deceased left the Sikh regiment by order to rejoin his own regiment on the Sutlej on the 13th of November; that upon the urgent recommendation of the medical officer of the Sikh regiment, he, on his route to his own regiment, went to Jellundur, but little out of the direct road, to submit himself to the examination of a medical committee then sitting, in respect to the propriety or fitness of his immediately joining his own regiment, then in active service; that on the 15th of November he arrived at Jellundur, and stopped at a friend's house, to whom he expressed his intention of leaving his property, except £1000, to his brother George, and that he died on the 16th; and that the paper propounded was entitled to probate as the will of a soldier in actual military service, under 1 Vic. c. 26, s. 11.

*Sir J. D. Harding, Q.A.,* and *Twiss,* opposed the admission of this allegation—first, on the ground that the deceased was not shown to have been in actual military service; secondly, that the paper was not intended by the deceased as his will.

*Addams* and *Spinks contrà.*

Sir John Dodson.

The admission of this allegation has been opposed on two grounds: first, as to the paper itself, it has been argued that the language is not dispositive, but gives a mere list of property—is, in fact, a letter without the form or semblance of a will; and so far from proving final intention, points in fact to the making of another instrument as a will. But a deed poll, a deed of gift, a bond, a marriage settlement, letters, and so forth, have been held sufficient in form to be entitled to probate as testamentary papers, provided the deceased intended that any of them should operate after his death: *Wms. Exrs.* 73, 3d ed. It is true these were cases before the present Act, but the 11th section of that Act puts the wills of soldiers on the same footing as they previously stood; assuming, therefore, for the moment that the deceased was in actual military service, these cases are to the point. Looking next to the paper itself, I am clear that the deceased intended it to have effect after his death. This letter is very different from the paper in *The King's Proctor* v. *Daines*, 3 Hagg. 218, or that in *Torre* v. *Castle*, 1 Curt. 303. The second ground of opposition was, that actual military service was not shown by the facts pleaded. But I do not think so: the facts are much stronger than those either in *Drummond* v. *Parish*, 3 Curt. 522, where the testator was at Woolwich, or *In the Goods of Hill*, 4 N. C. 174, where he was on a tour of inspection at a time of perfect peace. And again: in *Bowles* v. *Jackson*, 1 Eccl. & Adm. Rep. 294, the deceased had been ordered to join the expedition, but he had not left home. In all those cases probate was refused. In the present case the deceased was on his way from one regiment to another, both of which were in actual military service. The allegation must consequently be admitted, when it has been

1855.

Dec. 14th.

HERBERT
*against*
HERBERT.

reformed, so that actual military service be distinctly pleaded.

(*Theakston* v. *Marson*, 4 Hagg. 297, was cited in argument, as well as the cases referred to in the judgment).

In the goods of EMMA HAKEWELL.

*On Motion.*

E. H. duly executed a will in February, 1847, in which was the following clause:—" As to all the rest and residue of my estate, property, and effects, not hereby or by any codicil in writing hereinafter by me especially bequeathed, it being my intention by a separate paper to allot my plate, I give and bequeath the same, subject to the payment," &c. She executed a codicil in January, 1851. After her death in November, 1855, there was found, with the will and codicil, a paper in the handwriting of the deceased, which began—" This is a codicil to my will dated 5th February, 1847, but which I do not wish to be proved at Doctors' Commons;" and ended, " And I confirm my will in all respects not altered thereby." By this unexecuted paper she gave and bequeathed, &c., and allotted her plate and pictures, among several legatees; it was dated

26th of April, 1847, and signed by the testatrix. The attesting witnesses to both will and codicil deposed that they saw nothing of this paper of the 26th of April at the execution of either will or codicil, nor was any paper attached to either of them. The codicil of 1851 confirmed the will only.

Probate of the will and codicil only, excluding the paper of February, 1847, was prayed on behalf of the executors named in the will. *Ferraris* v. *Hertford*, 3 Curt. 468; *Haynes* v. *Hill*, 13 Jur. 1058, were cited.

SIR JOHN DODSON granted the motion as prayed.

1856.

Jan. 13th.

In the goods of
EMMA
HAKEWELL.

---

BAYNES *against* HARRISON.

*On Motion.*

J. H., late of Glasgow, died in the month of August, 1853, a widower, and intestate, leaving R. H., an only son. At the time of the death of the deceased he was indebted to B. in the sum of £23 4s. After the death of the deceased that debt was assigned to A. A decree issued at A.'s instance, citing the son of the deceased, to accept or refuse letters of administration of the effects of the deceased, or show cause why the same should not be granted to A. on his giving the usual security. This decree was personally served on

1856.

Jan. 23d.

Creditor. Administration. After the death of an intestate, A. procured from B. an assignment of a debt due to B. by the intestate. Motion for administration to such assignee rejected.

1856.

Jan. 23d.

BAYNES
*against*
HARRISON.

R. H., who was a minor, on board the ship in which he was serving as an apprentice, in the presence of the mate of the said vessel. It appeared that all the parties were Scotch, and that a grant had been obtained in Scotland. The property in England consisted of the proceeds of a policy of insurance, amounting to the sum of £105. In the decree served on R. H., A. was described as a creditor, whilst he was in fact but an assignee of the debt.

Administration to be granted to A., as a creditor of the deceased, upon his giving the usual security, was moved for.

SIR JOHN DODSON rejected the motion, observing that the decree being invalid, there must be a fresh citation, and that it would be a dangerous practice to decree administration of an intestate's estate to a person who had bought up a debt after the death of that intestate, especially where, as in the case before him, the assets considerably exceeded the amount of the debt.

——

On a subsequent date the motion was granted on affidavit, stating that A. was also a creditor of the intestate, and had been chosen by the several creditors of the intestate as the person to obtain the administration for their benefit.

*In the goods of* D. MACKENZIE.

*On Motion.*

1856.

Feb. 8th.

Administration with the will annexed. Form of grant in Scotland varied as to the effects of the deceased in England.

THE deceased, a domiciled Scotchwoman, died in Scotland in the month of August, 1852. She left a will, in her own handwriting, signed by herself, but unattested, and without the appointment of an executor. By this will, after giving several general and specific legacies, the testatrix gave to her sister, for life, her money in the funds or in the bank, after payment of a legacy in the will mentioned; and, " After my sister's death, all to go to my nephew, George Jones." On the 3d of November, 1852, this will of the deceased was duly confirmed by the Commissary Depute of the Commissariat of Wigtown, in North Britain, at the instance of George Jones, to whom, as executor dative, *qua* legatee, and residuary legatee, full power was granted by the Court of the said Commissary Depute to administer the personal estate of the deceased in Scotland,—and Mr. George Jones was accordingly constituted the sole personal representative of the deceased in Scotland; but it was afterwards suggested that, according to the true construction of the will, Mr. Jones was not entitled, according to the law of England, to the general residue of the personal property of the deceased, and therefore not entitled, according to the ordinary practice of this Court, to the letters of administration with the will annexed. It had now become necessary, for the purpose of substantiating pro-ceedings in Chancery, that there should be a representative of the deceased in this country.

*Middleton* moved for administration with the will annexed to George Jones, as legatee substituted in the will, limited to the goods of the deceased within the Province of Canterbury, varying the character of the representative so as to make the proceedings conform to the law of this country. He cited *In the Goods of Read*, 1 Hagg. 474, where a similar course had been adopted, the deceased having died at Madras, and probate having been granted there to the widow, as sole legatee and constructive executrix; this Court would only decree administration with the will annexed to the widow, as the relict and the principal legatee, upon the usual security.

SIR JOHN DODSON.
Under the authority of the case cited, I feel no difficulty in granting this motion as prayed.

FOOT *against* STANTON.

1856.

Feb. 8th.

THIS was a cause of proving, in solemn form of law, the last will of Mary Ann Stanton, bearing date the 15th day of October, 1850, promoted by Honor Fry Foot, wife of John Foot, the sister and one of the next of kin of the deceased, against Henry Stanton, the sole executor named in the will.

Probate of will granted in the absence of proof of instructions or knowledge of contents, and the attesting witnesses not recollecting any of the circumstances of the execution of the will.

*Robinson* for the executor.

*Middleton* for the next of kin.

JUDGMENT.

SIR JOHN DODSON.

This paper is in due form. There is an attestation clause, and two witnesses have subscribed their names. The property is so small that I was in hopes the parties might have been induced to settle the whole matter out of Court; but as they will not do that, I must now give my opinion: The effect of the will is to give £19 19s. to Mrs. Wheeler, a sister of deceased; to Mrs. Foot, the party in the cause, £10; to Ellen and Martha Stanton, all the deceased's trinkets and jewellery; to Henry Stanton, party in this cause, £10, to be placed in his name in a savings' bank, in trust, for the children of another brother of the deceased, to accumulate till they are of age; to Henry Stanton, all furniture, linen, &c.; the residue to Henry

Stanton and Westcott Stanton, another brother of deceased; to appoint Henry Stanton sole executor, and to direct him to repay to deceased's brother-in-law, Henry Wheeler, all monies he may have expended for her use. It revokes all former wills. The whole property appears to be of the value of about £200. The will was propounded in a common *condidit,* on which three witnesses have been examined; Mr. Burke, a medical man; and Potto, in whose house the deceased was residing at the date of the will, and till her death—these were the two subscribing witnesses. Mr. Burke has no recollection whatever of the circumstances attending the execution of the will: in 1850 he was practising at Boxmoor and Hemel Hempstead, and was occasionally in attendance at Mr. Potto's house. When shown his subscription to the will, he has no doubt inferentially that it was so signed and subscribed as appears; he is acquainted with the formalities necessary for the execution of a will; his attendance on the deceased was not for the epileptic fits to which she was subject. The other witness, Potto, at whose house and in whose care deceased had been placed by her brother, on account of the epileptic fits from which she suffered, knows as little about the transaction. When Mr. Foot, on deceased's death, wrote to Potto to ask about any will, he received for answer: "I never signed any will for Miss Mary Ann Stanton, nor was she in a fit state of mind during the four years she resided with me to make a will." However Mr. Potto recognises his own subscription and that of Mr. Burke, and therefore has no doubt that whatever appears on the face of the

paper really took place. It is true that he can recollect no reading of the paper to the deceased, and
will not speak positively to her testamentary capacity; yet, there is nothing in his evidence to negative it, except at those times when she was actually
under the influence of a fit. The third witness,
Drew, was copying clerk in a solicitor's office, and
wrote out from a draft the paper now in question.
He speaks to the interlineation of £19 19s. as
made before it left his hands. There is no evidence
of any instructions given by the deceased. However, on the unopposed evidence of the subscribing
witnesses, I am of opinion that I must pronounce
for this will. I think Mrs. Foot was justified in
putting the executor on proof, and is entitled to
her costs.

1856.

Feb. 8th.

FOOT
against
STANTON.

DYCE SOMBRE *against* TROUP, SOLAROLI
(intervening), and
PRINSEP, and the HON. EAST INDIA COMPANY
(also intervening).

1856.

Jan. 26th.

Where insanity, though confined to certain one or more delusions, has once existed, and the evidence shows the deceased to have been instructed to conceal the continued existence of such delusion or delusions, and the evidence to prove perfect recovery of capacity is at least doubtful, the will made by a person so affected, though rational and rationally instructed and executed, is not entitled to probate. Costs.

THIS deceased died on the 1st day of July, 1851. He left a will dated the 25th of June, and a codicil dated the 13th of August, 1849.

On the 2d of July, 1851, a caveat was entered; and on the 5th of the same month an appearance was given for the widow of the deceased, alleging him to have died intestate, and praying administration. At the same time an appearance was also given for A. M. Troup, wife of J. R. Troup, alleging the deceased to have died without child or parent; that the said A. M. Troup was his natural and lawful sister, and one of his next of kin; and praying to be joined in the administration. And also, at the same time, an appearance was given for H. T. Prinsep; and he was alleged to be one of the executors named in a will of the deceased. On the 2d of September, 1851, the same proctor who had appeared for A. M. Troup intervened for G. Solaroli, wife of P. R. N. Solaroli (Baron Solaroli), and alleged her to be the natural and lawful sister of the deceased, and one of his next of kin. On the 7th of October, G. Solaroli was admitted by the proctor for the executor to be a contradictor to the will and codicil; and on the 7th of November, the interest of A. M. Troup was admitted.

On the 13th of December an appearance was given on behalf of the Honourable East India Company, as the residuary legatees in trust named in the will.

1856.

Jan. 20th.

DYCE
SOMBRE
*against*
TROUP,
SOLAROLI
(intervening),
and
PRINSEP,
and the
HON. EAST
INDIA
COMPANY
(also inter-
vening).

On the 16th of January the allegation on behalf of the executor propounding the will and codicil was brought in.

On the 4th of June, 1853, an allegation was brought in on behalf of the next of kin; and on the 7th of June, an allegation on behalf of the widow was also brought in. On the 30th of June additional articles to the allegation of the next of kin were brought in.

On the 21st of April, 1854, a further allegation was brought in on behalf of the executor; and on the 13th of October, a further allegation was brought in on behalf of the next of kin; but on the 17th this allegation was on consent subducted, and a new allegation brought in.

Upon these several pleadings 135 witnesses were examined in this country, in France, Belgium, and India. The proceedings and evidence, including a great number of exhibits, were contained in 1554 printed folio pages. There was also an octavo volume of 580 pages, published by the deceased in 1849, as a "refutation of the charges of lunacy brought against him in the Court of Chancery."

The case was argued for 19 days by

*Bayford* and *Phillimore* for the executor.

*Haggard* and *Robertson* for the East India Company.

Sir *J. D. Harding*, Q.A., and *Jenner*, for the widow.

*Twiss* and *Spinks* for the next of kin.

1856.

Jan. 26th.

Dyce
Sombre
*against*
Troup,
Solaroli
(intervening),
and
Prinsep,
and the
Hon. East
India
Company
(also inter-
vening).

## JUDGMENT.

### SIR JOHN DODSON.

The question in this case is as to the validity of the will and codicil of Mr. David Ochterlony Dyce Sombre, deceased—the will bearing date the 25th of June, 1849, and the codicil bearing date the 13th of August, in the same year. The deceased died on the 1st of July, 1851, at that time lodging in Davies Street, Berkeley Square, possessed of very large property.

The will and codicil are propounded by Henry Thoby Prinsep, one of the executors therein named —the two other executors, viz., the Honourable Mountstuart Elphinstone, and Sir Henry Miers Elliott, not being parties in the suit.

The will and codicil were opposed by the Honourable Mrs. Dyce Sombre, widow of the deceased; by Mrs. Troup, his lawful sister; and by the Baroness Solaroli, asserting herself also to be his lawful sister. The interest of the last-mentioned lady has not been confessed by Mr. Prinsep, on the alleged ground of her illegitimacy; but she has been admitted a contradictor to the will, and has appeared by her proctor and counsel. The East India Company have likewise intervened, with the intent of supporting the will and codicil, but have not thought it necessary to offer any allegation in the cause. The will and codicil are in due form, having been respectively prepared by a solicitor, and executed by the deceased in the presence of no less than three witnesses, all of them of the medical profession.

As to the contents of the will, it commences with a recital of the deceased having been appointed by her late Highness the Begum Somroo trustee under certain deeds and instruments for charitable purposes, and appoints under such trust the bishop or senior Roman Catholic priest at Sirdhana to be his successor. It then gives special instructions for his funeral—directs that his body shall be conveyed to Sirdhana, and there buried in the corner of the Christian burying-ground facing the south-east, and that there shall be placed over it a bronze cross, to be procured, if possible, at a certain place which he mentions, viz., at a certain manufactory at Berlin ; and his heart is to be enclosed in a silver case, with an inscription thereon, and to be buried separately from his body, in the room adjoining and leading into the sepulchre of the late Begum ; and tablets, with proper inscriptions, are to be placed both over his body and over his heart. It then directs the executors to attend to the erection of a monument to the late Begum, which was then preparing by the artist Tadolini, of Rome.

He then orders his executors to set apart out of his personal estate a sufficient sum to enable them to pay certain annuities, or rather, I should say, certain monthly payments; for although they are described as annuities in the will, yet it is proved, and is also admitted on the other side, that they were not intended to be annual payments, but that they were intended to be monthly payments. There was a misunderstanding in that respect between him and the solicitor by whom the will was drawn.

He then proceeds to enumerate the persons who were to receive those benefits. They are very numerous, and they seem to comprise a great number of persons who had received pensions from the

1856.

Jan. 26th.

DYCE SOMBRE against TROUP, SOLAROLI (intervening), and PRINSEP, and the HON. EAST INDIA COMPANY (also intervening).

1856.

Jan. 26th.

DYCE
SOMBRE
*against*
TROUP,
SOLAROLI
(intervening),
and
PRINSEP,
and the
HON. EAST
INDIA
COMPANY
(also inter-
vening).

Begum, and to whom he had himself made allow-
ances ; and that circumstance shows that he had a
very retentive memory at the time, that he was in
full possession of that faculty, and in that respect
it is clear that his capacity was good.

The will then goes on to give the interest of 20,000
rupees for life to Mrs. Troup, his sister, and if she have
any children, the principal is to go to them; otherwise it is to fall into the residue, and is afterwards
disposed of. He then makes certain other bequests
to Mrs. Reghelini, to Major Reghelini, and others.
He gives legacies to various persons, and, amongst
others, the sum of £1000 to the Honourable Meliora
Cotton, the daughter of Lord Combermere, who has
had a good deal to do with this case, and is one of
the witnesses examined in the cause. He then
gives £500 each to the two eldest daughters of Sir
Richard and Lady Jenkins, to Sir Charles Metcalfe
Ochterlony £2000, and to the eldest son of Colonel
Steuart the sum of £2000. The will then goes
on to give to each of the 24 directors of the Honourable East India Company, at the time of his
death, and also to the six directors who shall be
out of office by rotation, the sum of £1000 each,
in addition to the sums afterwards bequeathed to
the chairman and deputy chairman. It gives £5000
each to his three executors. It directs likewise
that the jewels, valued at £7000, shall be divided
equally amongst them at the decease of his wife.
He gives the palace at Delhi to Mrs. Troup for
life ; and then to her eldest and other sons, succes-
sively, in strict entail. And after other devises and
bequests, he gives the East India Company the old
palace at Sirdhana; and the residue of his real and

personal estate to the said Mountstuart Elphinstone, Henry Thoby Prinsep, and Sir Henry M.
Elliott, in trust, to pay debts and legacies, and to
invest 125,000 rupees, and apply the dividends for
the support of the blind, lame, or indigent, of Sirdhana, and to pay over the clear residue to the East
India Company, who are to set apart sufficient to
produce the annual sum of £2500—£1000, part
thereof, to be paid to the president of the Board of
Control, £1000 to the chairman of the Company,
and £500 to the deputy chairman.   The residue of
his estate to be applied for the endowment of an
institution to be called the Sombre College, for the
education of the higher classes of the natives of
India, without any distinction of religion.   Such is
the purport of the will.

The codicil seems merely to have been made for
the purpose of confirming the will, or to make it a
little more clear; but it makes no disposition whatever of any property.   Such are the contents of the
instruments now in question before the Court.

The opposition to these instruments, the will and
the codicil, is founded upon the averment that the
deceased was of unsound mind at the time when
they were prepared and executed; that he was labouring, not under any general kind of insanity,
but under that form of insanity which is usually
termed "monomania."   On the other hand, it is
contended that the deceased was at all times of perfectly sound mind, and that the supposed delusions
under which he is said to have laboured were not
of an insane character, but that they were attributable solely to Asiatic habits and manners, to the
feelings prevailing in India, and to his ignorance of

1856.

Jan. 26th.
___
DYCE
SOMBRE
*against*
TROUP,
SOLAROLI
(intervening),
and
PRINSEP,
and the
HON. EAST
INDIA
COMPANY
(also inter-
vening).

1856.

Jan. 26th.

DYCE
SOMBRE
against
TROUP,
SOLAROLI
(intervening),
and
PRINSEP,
and the
HON. EAST
INDIA
COMPANY
(also inter-
vening).

the customs and manners of this country; and that even upon the supposition that he had been of unsound mind at any particular time, he had entirely recovered from it previously to the execution of the will and the codicil, and that he was perfectly sane at those respective periods.

Before I enter upon the consideration of the particular delusions to which the deceased is alleged to have been subject, it may be convenient to see what are the principles which have been considered in these Courts applicable to cases of this description; and for this purpose, I think it will be necessary only to refer to the case of *Waring* v. *Waring,* which was decided by the Judicial Committee of the Privy Council, and which is reported in the sixth volume of Moore's Privy Council Cases. In that judgment reference is made to almost all the preceding cases; and being a decision of the Superior Court, I must take it as a binding authority, even if I entertained a different opinion upon the subject, which I, however, certainly do not. Lord Brougham, who delivered the very able judgment in that case, and which judgment was understood to have had the full concurrence and sanction of all the lords who sat upon that occasion, expressed himself in these words, which are to be found at page 348: "The principles which must govern a case of this description are sufficiently clear, and they may be regarded as well settled by the current of former decisions: indeed, they flow easily from considering the nature of the inquiry in which such cases engage us. The question being, whether the will was duly made by a person of sound mind or not, our inquiry of

course is, whether or not the party possessed his
faculties, and possessed them in a healthy state?
His mental powers may be still subsisting; no disease may have taken them away; and yet they may
have been affected with disease, and thus may not
have entitled their possessor to the appellation of a
person whose mind was sound. Again, the disease
affecting them may have been more or less general,
it may have extended over a greater or a less portion of the understanding; or rather we ought to
say, that it may have affected more or it may have
affected fewer of the mental faculties: for we must
keep always in view that which the inaccuracy of
ordinary language inclines us to forget, that the
mind is one and indivisible; that when we speak of
its different powers or faculties, as memory, imagination, consciousness, we speak metaphorically,
likening the mind to the body, as if it had members or compartments; whereas, in all accuracy of
speech, we mean to speak of the mind acting va-
riously, that is, remembering, fancying, reflecting—
the same mind in all these operations being the
agent. We therefore cannot, in any correctness
of language, speak of general or partial insanity;
but we may most accurately speak of the mind ex-
erting itself in consciousness without cloud or im-
perfection, but being morbid when it fancies; and
so its owner may have a diseased imagination; or
the imagination may not be diseased, and yet the
memory may be impaired, and its owner be said to
have lost his memory. In these cases we do not
mean that the mind has one faculty, as consciousness, sound,—while another, as memory or imagination, is diseased; but that the mind is sound when

1856.

Jan. 26th.

DYCE
SOMBRE
*against*
TROUP,
SOLAROLI
(intervening),
and
PRINSEP,
and the
HON. EAST
INDIA
COMPANY
(also inter-
vening).

1856.

Jan. 26th.

DYCE
SOMBRE
*against*
TROUP,
SOLAROLI
(intervening),
and
PRINSEP,
and the
HON. EAST
INDIA
COMPANY
(also inter-
vening).

reflecting on its own operations, and diseased when exercising the combination termed imagining, or casting the retrospect called recollecting. This view of the subject, though apparently simple and almost too unquestionable to require or even to justify a formal statement, is of considerable importance when we come to examine cases of what are called incorrectly 'partial insanity,' which would be better described by the phrase 'insanity,' or 'unsoundness,' always existing, though only occasionally manifest." That, Lord Brougham thinks, is the correct way of expressing the state where insanity always exists, but only occasionally and on certain subjects shows itself. "Nothing," he continues, "is more certain than the existence of mental disease of this description. Nay, by far the greater number of morbid cases belong to this class. They have acquired a name—the disease called familiarly, as well as by physicians, 'monomania,' on the supposition of its being confined, which it rarely is, to a single faculty or exercise of the mind: a person shall be of sound mind to all appearance upon all subjects save one or two, and on these he shall be subject to delusions, mistaking for realities the suggestions of his imagination; The disease here is said to be in the imagination that is, the patient's mind is morbid or unsound when it imagines, healthy and sound when it remembers. Nay, he may be of unsound mind when his imagination is employed on some subjects, in making some combinations, and sound when making others, or making one single kind of combination. Thus, he may not believe all his fancies to be realities, but only some or one; of such a person we usually predicate that he is of unsound mind only upon certain points. I have qualified the proposition thus on purpose; because if the being or essence which we term the mind is unsound on one subject, provided that unsoundness is at all times existing upon that subject, it is quite erroneous to suppose such a mind really sound on other subjects. It is only sound in appearance; for if the subject of the delusion be presented to it, the unsoundness which is manifested by believing in the suggestions of fancy, as if they were realities, would break out; consequently, it is as absurd to speak of this as a really sound mind (a mind sound when the subject of the delusion is not presented), as it would be to say that a person had not the gout because his attention being diverted from the pain by some more powerful sensation by which the person was affected, he for the moment was unconscious of his visitation. It follows from hence, that no confidence can be placed in the acts, or in any act, of a diseased mind, however apparently rational that act may appear to be, or may in reality be." He goes on further, using language of the same description, and very much to the same purport, and then considers what a delusion is, and what is a delusion which is an insane delusion, and which has been described as a belief of things as realities which exist only in the imagination of the patient. He then gives Dr. Willis's account with very much accuracy, which confirms the view which he had taken himself, and which, as I said before, had been taken by all the members of the Judicial Committee, for the judgment had their express sanction when Lord Brougham delivered it.

1856.

Jan. 26th.

DYCE SOMBRE *against* TROUP, SOLAROLI (intervening), and PRINSEP, and the HON. EAST INDIA COMPANY (also intervening).

1856.

Jan. 26th.

DYCE
SOMBRE
*against*
TROUP,
SOLAROLI
(intervening),
and
PRINSEP,
and the
HON. EAST
INDIA
COMPANY
(also inter-
vening).

We have to consider now a little of the history of the deceased, because, as I have before stated, it is asserted that he was not insane, that his imagination was not unsound, and that his conduct and behaviour were not the result and consequence of insanity, but proceeded merely from his Asiatic feelings, the manner in which he had been brought up, and the mode of thinking which prevailed in India; and that he was unused and unaccustomed to society in England, and to the ways and manners of Europeans.

The history of the deceased is this: He appears to have been born at Sirdhana, in the upper provinces of Bengal, in or about the year 1808, and to have been descended from ancestors some of whom were of European, and others of Asiatic origin. As to his exact pedigree, the parties are not agreed. Mr. Prinsep, the executor, alleges that Mr. George Alexander Dyce, the father of the deceased, was of Asiatic extraction; that he was for some time a colonel in the service, and an officer in the household of her Highness the Begum Sombre, or Somroo, who exercised a right of sovereignty over a certain portion of territory in the Upper Provinces of Hindostan; that his mother was the granddaughter of a General Sombre, who had been the husband of the Begum, or who cohabited with her as such, but who died in her lifetime; that General Sombre, by a previous marriage or cohabitation with a native Hindoo woman, had a son named Louis Balthazar Sombre, who was the father of Juliana Dyce, the mother of the deceased.

By Mrs. Dyce Sombre, the widow, it is denied that the father of the deceased was of Asiatic origin.

On the other hand, she asserts that he, that is, the father of the deceased, was the son of a British officer, a native of Scotland; and as regards the maternal side, that the mother of the deceased was Juliana Reinaud, the daughter of Louis Reinaud, by a Miss Lefevre; and that the said Louis Reinaud was the son, by a Rajpoot lady, of Walter Reinaud, who was a German by birth, surnamed Sombre, and who was the husband of the Begum.

Now, what may have been the very precise origin or pedigree of Mr. Dyce Sombre, it is perhaps not very easy to collect from these statements, or from the evidence given in the cause; but it cannot, I think, be of any great importance to determine whether European or Asiatic blood prevailed in his veins. It is more to the purpose to inquire how he was brought up, and by whom he was educated, and with whom he afterwards associated. Of this, I think, a very fair and satisfactory account is given by Dr. Drever, who was an intimate friend of the deceased, who knew him well in India, and who also knew him after his return to Europe. Dr. Drever says : " I became acquainted with David Ochterlony Dyce Sombre, the deceased in this cause, in the year 1829. I was then assistant surgeon to the 32d regiment of Bengal Native Infantry, at Meerut. The deceased was living with the Begum Somroo. I knew the father of the deceased, George Alexander Dyce, who had been in the employ of the Begum, but had left her service in disgrace. The mother of the deceased I never knew. The deceased was then about 21 years of age. His father

1856.

Jan. 26th.

DYCE
SOMBRE
against
TROUP,
SOLAROLI
(intervening),
and
PRINSEP,
and the
HON. EAST
INDIA
COMPANY
(also inter-
vening).

1856.

Jan. 26th.

DYCE
SOMBRE
*against*
TROUP,
SOLAROLI
(intervening),
and
PRINSEP,
and the
HON. EAST
INDIA
COMPANY
(also inter-
vening).

was a Protestant. I do not know it myself, but I have no doubt of the fact, that the deceased had been under the care of Mr. Fisher, a clergyman of the Church of England, who was still chaplain at Meerut. I was not on terms of intimacy with the family, but I knew his sons, who were in the same service with me. Meerut is twelve miles from Sirdhana. The deceased, while I knew him, always belonged to the Roman Catholic Church. He mixed in the society of the civil and military servants of the East India Company. They were frequently dining at the Begum's table, and the deceased was present. It is a large military station ; there were many English families; and when at her own place at Sirdhana, there was very good English society, male and female. The deceased had acquired their habits, and conducted himself at all times in a very becoming manner. Three years after I became acquainted with him, viz., in 1832—I was attached to the Begum's household, as her physician ; for four years I lived in her family, with the deceased, and we were then in daily intercourse. No person knew him so thoroughly as I did, and there was no one in whom he placed such entire confidence as in me. When going into society, the deceased dressed as an European— sometimes in plain clothes, at others in uniform, as a colonel in the Begum's service. For the opportunities he had, the manners of the deceased were very good. He lived altogether as an European. In regard to the treatment of women, it is to be remembered, that though the natives do not allow the females of their families to appear in society,

1856.

Jan. 26th.

DYCE
SOMBRE
*against*
TROUP,
SOLAROLI
(intervening),
and
PRINSEP,
and the
HON. EAST
INDIA
COMPANY
(also inter-
vening).

yet, meeting European ladies in society, they treat
them with great respect. In so far, there is no
difference between the conduct of Europeans and
natives; but the deceased showed a marked difference in another respect, viz., he had a native
woman with whom he cohabited, and although very
much attached to her, yet he never showed the
slightest jealousy of her, but allowed many of his
friends to visit her in the female apartments of the
Zenana. I frequently saw her, and unveiled. It
was in the palace of the Begum; she lived in one of
the apartments. His own disposition seemed to be
very gentle, mild, and forgiving; I never saw him
lose his temper; I have seen him under provocation, not disposed to take offence; and he was
unassuming, though frequently appearing and acting as the head of the establishment." Then he
goes on with an account of the continuance of his
acquaintance with the deceased till the period when
he departed for Calcutta, and afterwards he corresponded with him, and subsequently knew him in
England. The witness says that prior to the
deceased's embarkation for England, he sent the
witness his will. Such is the account given
by this gentleman, and from which it is to be
taken that the deceased certainly was cognisant to
a considerable degree of European manners; that
he associated with Europeans; that he had been
educated by a clergyman of the Church of England,
who was a married man, and who had a family,
one of his sons about the age of the deceased himself; that he afterwards became acquainted with
the officers and with their ladies, and others, who
visited the Begum; that he was in the habit of

1856.

Jan. 26th.

DYCE
SOMBRE
*against*
TROUP,
SOLAROLI
(intervening),
and
PRINSEP,
and the
HON. EAST
INDIA
COMPANY
(also inter-
vening).

going over to the military station where the officers were, and associating with them; and, therefore, that he was not altogether ignorant of European manners, though he was born in India; and I think that is the account which is pretty generally given by other witnesses who have been examined upon the point. There is a difference in some respects, in regard to his jealousy of women; because by some of them it is said that he never suffered anybody to see the women who were kept in the Zenana; but, according to Dr. Drever, he admitted his friends into the Zenana, who there saw the women, and unveiled. Now it is true that he can only mention, I think, one friend by whom they were visited besides himself, and that is a Captain Rogers; but to that extent they were admitted into the Zenana, and they did see the women. However, I think his manners were to be considered as partly Asiatic and partly European; that he was conversant both with the manners of Asia and those of Europe to a certain extent, and not so entirely ignorant of European manners as he has been described to be.

In 1836 her Highness the Begum died, and upon that occasion her will was proved in the Court at Calcutta. In October, 1836, the deceased quitted Sirdhana, to which he never returned. The Begum left him, as I before stated, and he became possessed, at her death, of a very large property. On quitting Sirdhana, he appears to have gone to Calcutta,—at least he was there about the month of January, 1837,—and to have remained there until August in that year, when he sailed for Singapore and Canton, in China, and returned to

Calcutta in February, 1838. He then embarked for England, and arrived at Bristol in August of that year. In September, 1840, he was married to the Honourable Mary Anne Jervis, the daughter of Lord St. Vincent. It appears that he had traveled upon the Continent for some time; that he had made proposals to her; that the marriage was broken off; that in consequence of a letter he received from her, he returned to this country, and the marriage took place between them, and they cohabited together after this marriage till about the month of March, 1843. At that time a separation took place between them, in consequence of the deceased having been put under restraint as a lunatic, at the Clarendon Hotel, and thence he was removed under the care of a keeper to Hanover Lodge, in the Regent's Park, at which place he continued for some time. In September, 1843, he was allowed to travel, for the benefit of his health, with Dr. Grant, who was to take care of him, and upon the 21st or 22d of September he escaped from Liverpool, and he arrived in Paris upon the 22d or the 23d of September.

With respect to this confinement and the insanity, the charge is that he became insane in 1842 or 1843, and that it was necessary to put him under restraint. On the other hand, it is said that he was not insane at that time; that he was not insane at any time; and Mr. Prinsep asserts, in his answers in the present suit, that he does not believe that the deceased was at any time insane. So the first question is, whether he was insane in 1842 and 1843, and especially

1856.

Jan. 26th.

DYCE SOMBRE against TROUP, SOLAROLI (intervening), and PRINSEP, and the HON. EAST INDIA COMPANY (also intervening).

1856.

Jan. 26th.
——
DYCE
SOMBRE
*against*
TROUP,
SOLAROLI
(intervening),
and
PRINSEP,
and the
HON. EAST
INDIA
COMPANY
(also inter-
vening).

in 1843, when he was put under restraint; and if it shall be established that he was insane at that time, the question will arise whether he had recovered from that insanity previous to the time of the execution of the will and the codicil. And the *onus probandi* must, in the first case, lie upon the party setting up the insanity, since every person must be presumed to be of sound mind till the contrary is shown. The question is, whether Mrs. Dyce Sombre has duly discharged herself of that duty; whether she has proved to the satisfaction of the Court that at this particular time, in 1842 and 1843, the deceased was of unsound mind?

The witnesses who have been produced to prove the insanity upon this occasion are several. Sarah Lake, who was the servant in attendance upon Mrs. Dyce Sombre, says: "I think it was in the year 1838 that I entered the service of Mrs. Dyce Sombre, then the Honourable Miss Jervis. I have lived with her ever since. The first occasion on which I noticed anything amiss in Mr. Dyce Sombre, the deceased, was on the way from Donnington Park to Lord St. Vincent's; that was in the year 1841." So that she carries it rather farther back; but that was the first time that she noticed anything extraordinary, and that was upon her return from Donnington Park, where they had been on a visit to the Marchioness of Hastings—that was in the month of May. "At Donnington, Mrs. Dyce Sombre came crying to me, in great distress, at what Mr. Dyce Sombre had been saying of her." "The next that I remarked extraordinary in him was in June of that year, at the Burlington Hotel. There I knew him to keep Mrs. Dyce Sombre in her room ·for as much, perhaps, as two hours, while he called her all sorts of names—a damned bitch, a person of improper character, worse than any woman that walked the streets," and so forth. We next come to a later period, which is rather more important. She says: "In 1842, at the Clarendon, I heard him charge her to her face with being guilty with Mr. M., with Mr. C. F., with Mr. F., with General V., with her own father." These are certainly most extraordinary charges to have been made against a lady: it is not a mere Asiatic suspicion of infidelity, but it is general infidelity, with a great number of people, and with her own father. However, it is said that this may still be consistent with Asiatic feelings— that incest between father and daughter is by no means an uncommon thing in India; and one of the learned physicians, to whose evidence I shall presently advert, says that even in England he has known very many cases of the kind. However, this is only the commencement of the charges which he makes : for they are not confined merely to those parties who are enumerated, but are made with respect to all manner of persons—the waiters, the tradesmen, anybody. The witness says : "I never heard him say that she had confessed it, but that her father had confessed it; that Lord St. Vincent had confessed it to him, Mr. Dyce Sombre. Now, surely that is not very consistent even with Asiatic manners in a person of sound mind. "He charged her many times, and in different words,

1856.

Jan. 26th.

Dyce Sombre against Troup, Solaroli (intervening), and Prinsep, and the Hon. East India Company (also intervening).

1856.

Jan. 26th.
——
DYCE
SOMBRE
*against*
TROUP,
SOLAROLI
(intervening),
and
PRINSEP,
and the
HON. EAST
INDIA
COMPANY
(also inter-
vening).

but what he said was always to the same effect, and that was, her being guilty of adultery with them. He charged her with having been guilty with Mr. M., in my room;" and so forth.

In this, to a certain extent, she is confirmed by a witness of the name of Roulin, who was the valet of Mr. Dyce Sombre at the time, and who speaks to the violent conduct of this gentleman towards his wife.

But, however, it does not rest merely upon these servants, because we have the evidence of the physicians by whom he was attended upon this occasion, and under whose authority he was put under restraint. Sir James Clark first knew him in the month of February, 1843. He says: "I was called in by another physician, since deceased." They were then at the Clarendon Hotel. "I continued to attend him at various places, from the end of February till the end of August," that is, in 1843, "when I left him, being obliged to be in attendance upon the Queen. I saw him at various times and places, as I shall have occasion to relate, till November, 1848, when I saw him for the last time." Then he goes on to say that he saw the deceased in Clarges Street, in June, 1844, and so forth; but that is not the point upon which we are now, which is confined to 1842 and 1843. "The deceased at all times manifested delusions respecting the infidelity of his wife. I knew it to be an insane delusion, from the nature of the accusations against her, and the reasons he assigned." Therefore, it is not merely that he was jealous of his wife; for jealousy, though unfounded, might not be any proof of insanity at all ; but the witness says he judges from the nature of the accusations against her and the reasons which the deceased assigned for them, "or rather from his inability to give any sound reason for it, or any rational account of his suspicion. One very manifest proof of its being an insane delusion, was his assertion that she had had connexion with her own father in Hyde Park in open day." So that it was not that which might exist in the mind of an Asiatic, that she had been guilty not only of adultery, but of incest; but his notion was that she had been guilty of adultery in Hyde Park in the open day, and with her own father. Certainly that is a strong instance of insanity, and I think that Sir James Clark is perfectly correct in describing that as an insane delusion. His evidence on this part concludes thus: "There were a variety of persons with whom he charged her, and not one sound reason could he at any time assign for his suspicions. On one occasion, indeed, he admitted that he might be wrong in his belief of her infidelity, but only as if he had been taught to say so—not at all as if the suspicion was abandoned, or the delusion at an end." That relates to an examination which took place at Mivart's Hotel in 1848, and the manner in which the deceased made the denial on that occasion must be afterwards looked at; the evidence given upon that occasion was taken by a short-hand writer and is now before the Court. There was another examination in 1844, and Sir J. Clark states not only the existence of the delusion as to adultery, but goes on to describe other matters which clearly show insanity. Referring to other

1856.

Jan. 26th.

Dyce Sombre against Troup, Solaroli (intervening), and Prinsep, and the Hon. East India Company (also intervening).

1856.

Jan. 26th.

Dyce
Sombre
*against*
Troup,
Solaroli
(intervening),
and
Prinsep,
and the
Hon. East
India
Company
(also inter-
vening).

delusions, he says: " On one occasion, on the 10th of April, 1843, the deceased said that he had that night seen the heavens open, and one of the spirits rise from his grave, and desire him to do one of three things: the first, he said, was too bad to men- tion, and he would not mention it ; the second was to kill a cat in a particular manner; and the third was to eat his own dirt.  He spoke of two spirits, one evil, the other good.  One had counselled him to throw Mrs. Dyce Sombre's ring (her marriage ring no doubt) into the fire.  I cannot speak to his talking to himself, or laughing aloud, &c.; it would not happen in my experience, because when I had done talking with him I left.   He was very restless, and his whole demeanour was such as to make it marvellous that any one could doubt his insanity."   I think from this statement it would be marvellous that any one could doubt it; because as to the truth of the statement there can be no doubt, since it is quite impossible to suppose that Sir James Clark would depose to facts untruly.   His opinion, like the opinion of any other man, might be wrong, but he could not depose to these facts untruly; he could have no interest in stating anything that was not perfectly correct.   He goes on to say that " on the 30th of March, in the same year, 1843, he had a consultation with Dr. Sutherland, Dr. Monro, and Dr. Conolly.  There were present also Lord St. Vincent, T. H. Parker, Esq., Mr. Edward Ricketts, and Mr. B. J. L. Frere.  That was held in his absence for the special purpose of deciding whether it was necessary to put Mr. Dyce Sombre under restraint, and it was decided that it ought to be effected immediately, provided that the consent of Mrs. Dyce Sombre could be obtained." It has rather been represented that she was a person eager to get this poor man placed under confinement; but the difficulty here was to get her to consent to it. The medical men and her father all thought that he was insane, and that it was necessary, even for her protection, that he should be placed under restraint, for that her life was in danger. Sir J. Clark, referring to the conduct of Mrs. Dyce Sombre, says: "She had hitherto expressed great reluctance to it. I saw her on the subject, and did strongly represent to her how indispensably necessary it was: she then gave her consent. Thereupon a certificate was signed by Dr. Conolly, Dr. Sutherland, and myself." Then he is placed under restraint, and Dr. Domier, a young physician, is selected to take care of him. The witness then deposes as to other instances of insanity about spirits; he says: "On the 10th of May, 1843, the deceased told me that his wife had acknowledged that her father had had connexion with her in Hyde Park in open day." Before, we had the confession of the father; now, we have her own confession: "On the 17th of May he told me that he was visited by a spirit every night; that the day before he had dined on what he called a 'state ball,' which consisted of some bread and apple (over which he had burnt some brandy) and a glass of porter. Being asked an explanation of this, he replied that he took that kind of dinner in order to stop the Queen's levee ; and he expressed surprise that the levee had notwithstanding taken place, adding that he should protest against it."

There is ample evidence of insanity here; but

1856.

Jan. 26th.

DYCE SOMBRE *against* TROUP, SOLAROLI (intervening), and PRINSEP, and the HON. EAST INDIA COMPANY (also intervening).

1856.

Jan. 26th.
———
DYCE
SOMBRE
*against*
TROUP,
SOLAROLI
(intervening),
and
PRINSEP,
and the
HON. EAST
INDIA
COMPANY
(also inter-
vening).

it is necessary also to advert to what he says upon the twentieth article, and it becomes necessary to advert to the particulars of the evidence which is given of the description of insanity; because I shall have to consider presently the examination which took place before certain physicians in Paris, who came to a very different conclusion from what Sir James Clark and the other medical men who attended the deceased in England, and who were consulted upon this case, did; a very different conclusion. Upon the twentieth article he says: "Whilst at Hanover Lodge, in the summer of 1843, he talked to me of the terms on which he was willing that his wife should return to him. These conditions were of such an extraordinary kind, that I requested him to put them in writing. Soon after, perhaps the next day—it may have been the next, he produced to me a paper in red ink, to be delivered to Mrs. Dyce Sombre, intimating that it contained the conditions for her return to him." A very different account is given by the deceased when he comes to mention the circumstance at Paris before the physicians there. Sir J. Clark identifies the contents of the paper, and says: "How and when I copied it, I cannot say. I have no recollection of that, or of having seen it after I sent it to Mr. Frere; but a copy of it I must have made, as I believe. I now speak to its contents from a copy in a paper before me, which is my own affidavit embodying it, and in which I am certain that it was correctly recited. The original was in the deceased's handwriting." He then says: "I know that by the 'A. B. of C.,' were meant and intended the Archbishop of Can-

terbury; by the letters 'E. J.' were meant and
intended the brother of Mrs. Dyce Sombre; by
' H. P.' were meant Hyde Park; and by the abbre-
viations ' Vis. Ct. St. V.' were meant the father of
Mrs. Dyce Sombre. That I know, because the
contents of the paper had been repeated to me by
the deceased by word of mouth. He talked them
over seriously, the names and place being mentioned by him at length. The paper was handed
to me by the deceased deliberately, as I have said,
as containing the conditions on which he would
receive back his wife. The paper was subscribed
with his own initials." The words of the paper
were these: " First—Let the A. B. of C. procure
and furnish every requisite for passing a pleasant
evening with a virgin of the same rank as the one
now lost. Second—Let Mr. E. J. produce another
lady to receive the extinguisher (of rank). Third—
Let there be a duel of three fires at the place in
H. P. Fourth—Let Vis. Ct. St. V. procure a roan
horse, well broke, for the occasion. Fifth—When
the ground has been consecrated with the duel, I
shall reconsecrate it with madame, and bring her
back home on the horse." This is indeed a most
extraordinary paper.

The other evidence, I think, of Sir James Clark
goes to the years 1844 and 1848; and I have
already cited quite sufficient with reference to the
year 1843; and Sir James Clark is confirmed in
all these circumstances by Dr. Monro, who attended the deceased, in February, 1843, at the
Clarendon, and, in July, 1843, at Hanover Lodge.
He says: " The main feature of his case was
delusion in respect to the infidelity of his wife.

1856.

Jan. 26th.

DYCE
SOMBRE
against
TROUP,
SOLAROLI
(intervening),
and
PRINSEP,
and the
HON. EAST
INDIA
COMPANY
(also inter-
vening).

1856.

Jan. 26th.

Dyce
Sombre
against
Troup,
Solaroli
(intervening),
and
Prinsep,
and the
Hon. East
India
Company
(also inter-
vening).

In July, 1843, it was very strongly marked, and wore a settled and determined character. It was pregnant with the seeds of much risk and danger to Mrs. Dyce Sombre, from the peculiar nature of the delusions under which he distinctly laboured with respect to her, and her supposed want of conjugal fidelity. The insane character of his suspicion was evidenced in his general accusation of incontinency with anybody and everybody; and the assertion that she had herself owned to having received men, from her own father down to shopmen. The delusion was fixed, as I have said, and was manifested by him on each of the occasions when I saw him in the years 1843 and 1844. I remember thinking that there was serious risk of his doing her some mischief when he was at the Clarendon Hotel in 1843." This witness attended the execution of the commission which was held to inquire into the state of the deceased's mind, and was examined, and so were Dr. Chambers, Dr. Elliotson, and others. And he speaks not only as to this insanity with respect to the infidelity of his wife, and the nature of that infidelity, but he also speaks to the belief which the deceased entertained, that he was likely to be poisoned, which is undoubtedly a very frequent attendant in diseases of this kind. He says, to the sixty-third article: " I find from my affidavit, but I do not depose from recollection, though I have no doubt of the fact, that in June, 1844, the deceased stated, as he had done before to my recollection, that pernicious things had been put into his food at the Clarendon and at Hanover Lodge. His meaning, in 1843, was, as I understood

1856.

Jan. 26th.

DYCE
SOMBRE
*against*
TROUP,
SOLAROLI
(intervening),
and
PRINSEP,
and the
HON. EAST
INDIA
COMPANY
(also inter
vening).

him, that such things were administered to him for the purpose of producing impotency." It does appear from the testimony of several other witnesses in the case, and from some of the entries in his own hand-writing, that he sometimes considered that his food was poisoned, and sometimes that pernicious drugs were put in to deprive him of the power of sexual intercourse.

Mr. M. has been examined, with whom the deceased supposed that his wife had committed adultery, but he seems to have had no intercourse with her to give any colour whatever to the suspicion; he merely, I think, on one occasion went to the same theatre, and went from one box to the other for a short period of time, and then they separated.

Of the other physicians, Mr. Martin says: "I was made aware of his delusions respecting his wife by his own communications, made to me personally when at Hanover Lodge. He then stated to me that his wife had been unfaithful to him, in that she had lived (for three days I think) with Sir F. B.; further, that he had seen her having sexual intercourse with soldiers of the Guards in the Regent's Park; and further, that she had had criminal intercourse with her father. At this time I became acquainted with Mrs. Dyce Sombre, I think by her signifying her wish to see me, with a view to her having a meeting with her husband. She accompanied me to Hanover Lodge, where I had previously prepared the deceased to expect her. They were together for perhaps half an hour alone, the door being left ajar in case of needful interference on my part, I remaining

1856.

Jan. 26th.

DYCE
SOMBRE
*against*
TROUP,
SOLAROLI
(intervening),
and
PRINSEP,
and the
HON. EAST
INDIA
COMPANY
(also inter-
vening).

in the passage. I saw their meeting. He shrank from her as from an object that was repulsive. His manner towards her appeared to me to be repulsive, certainly not cordial. At the conclusion of the interview, I was requested to enter the room, when the deceased declared to me in her presence, that his consenting to her wish to see her again should depend upon my calling out Sir F. B., and that the sooner the meeting was arranged the better." That was the way in which he was to be reconciled to his wife, though she had committed adultery with Sir F. B. ; that Mr. Martin was to call out Sir F. B. and to fight him, and then the husband and wife were to be reconciled. Now, this witness gives most important evidence, but it relates to other periods of time, viz., those of the examinations at Mivart's Hotel in 1848.

Dr. Conolly gives evidence to the same effect; and he speaks to the spirits, and the dining on apple and porter to prevent the levee. He says on the nineteenth article: "I have no more to say about the spirits. I remember his saying, on the occasion just deposed of, that he had dined upon an apple and some porter, I think for the purpose of preventing a levee; but my recollection of that is less distinct than of what passed on the same subject in June, 1844, when he was asked about it, and acknowledged that he had felt displeased that the levee had not been postponed. He complained also that the influence of the Duchess of Kent had been used against him." Dr. Elliotson, in his evidence, states that the deceased called upon him, and challenged him, and so forth, though he was quite a

stranger to him, and wanted him to give him something to make him have more intercourse with his
wife.

I think it is quite clear from this testimony of
these physicians, that in the year 1843 the deceased
was insane, and that he was incapable of making a
will, or doing any act whatever requiring thought,
and judgment, and reflection; for though he might
converse rationally upon ordinary subjects, yet the
fact of his having these insane delusions with respect to the infidelity of his wife, her committing
adultery in the open day with her own father,
with all manner of persons, with shopboys, with
the waiters of hotels, with the soldiers of the
Guards—his delivering the paper relating to the
Archbishop of Canterbury, and the mode that was
to be pursued to reconcile him to his wife—the existence of these delusions and strange fancies can
leave no doubt whatever that the deceased at this
time, in the year 1843, was of unsound mind, and
incapable of making his will. To all this I may
add, that there was the verdict of a jury in 1843,
finding that the deceased was of unsound mind, and
that he had been so from the preceding month of
October, 1842. The Court can, therefore, have no
hesitation whatever in considering that the deceased
was of unsound mind in the year 1843.

Then the question is, whether he had recovered
from that state of insanity.

The *onus probandi* that the deceased was of unsound mind, I have stated, lay, in the first instance,
upon the party alleging the insanity; but when
once the existence of that insanity has been esta-

1856.

Jan. 26th.

DYCE
SOMBRE
against
TROUP,
SOLAROLI
(intervening),
and
PRINSEP,
and the
HON. EAST
INDIA
COMPANY
(also inter-
vening).

1856.

Jan. 26th.

Dyce
Sombre
*against*
Troup,
Solaroli
(intervening),
and
Prinsep,
and the
Hon. East
India
Company
(also inter-
vening).

blished, as I think it undoubtedly has in the present case, then the *onus probandi* is shifted; then it
is necessary that the party setting up the recovery
from that insanity should satisfy the Court by distinct proof that their averments are well founded.

The deceased having been for some time at
Hanover Lodge, was permitted to travel; and about
the 9th September, 1843, he left Hanover Lodge,
under the care of Dr. Grant. He traveled about with
that gentleman; but on the 21st of that month,
while at Liverpool, he escaped from Dr. Grant, and
proceeded to Paris, and arrived there upon the 22d
or 23d of September. He was shortly followed
thither by Mr. Frere, who had been his solicitor,
and who was the solicitor of the committees of the
person. Mr. Frere took with him a keeper, and
upon his arrival in Paris, he made an application
to the English Ambassador, for the purpose of
having, through him, an application made to the
French authorities, that Mr. Dyce Sombre might be
delivered up and sent back to England. However,
it happened that the French authorities thought
that such was not a proper course to pursue, and
that it was not in conformity with the French law,
considering that they were bound to inquire into the
state of the deceased before they took that step; and
it was determined that an Investigation should take
place, and that an Inquisition should be held. Accordingly an Inquisition was held there, under the
direction of Monsieur Delessert, the Prefet of Police;
and it was attended by two or three physicians, who
were nominated by the French authorities for that
purpose. And it now becomes necessary to see

what the evidence before that Inquisition was, and what determination they came to with respect to the sanity of the deceased.

I should, however, first refer to an authority upon the subject of the mode of examination in France and in England; and I will now refer to a passage in Dr. Ray's *Medical Jurisprudence*, on the subject of the mode of examination which prevails in France.

He says, at page 246, and at section 268: "In England, and in this country, the choice of the means for establishing the existence of insanity when concealed, is left to individual sagacity. This, no doubt, is sufficient, where great practical acquaintance with insanity readily suggests the course best adapted to each particular case; but the great majority of medical men will feel the need of some system or order of proceeding that will simplify their inquiries, and render them more efficient. The French arrange their means into three general divisions or classes, which are made use of, each in succession, when the preceding class has failed of its object. They are called the *Interrogatory*, *Continued Observation*, and the *Inquest;* and as no better arrangement has ever been offered, it may be well to describe it; and it may be added, in passing, that it would materially conduce to our success in inquiries of this kind, if they were always pursued in the course here indicated." So that he approves of the French method, and he thinks that it would be well if applied in all cases. First, there is the Interrogatory; and he says that that "embraces only those means of information which are appli-

1856.

Jan. 26th.
——
DYCE
SOMBRE
*against*
TROUP,
SOLAROLI
(intervening),
and
PRINSEP,
and the
HON. EAST
INDIA
COMPANY
(also intervening).

1856.

Jan. 26th.

DYCE
SOMBRE
*against*
TROUP,
SOLAROLI
(intervening),
and
PRINSEP,
and the
HON. EAST
INDIA
COMPANY
(also inter-
vening).

cable in a personal interview with the patient.
After learning generally his moral and intellectual
character, his education and habits of living,
the duration and nature of his mental delusion (if
it can be ascertained from his acquaintances), and
the state of his relations to others, and after observing the expression of his countenance, his demeanour, and general appearance, we may proceed
to a direct examination of his case" (an examination of him upon Interrogatories). "He should be
led to speak of his relatives and friends;" and so
forth. He states the manner in which that examination should take place. Then, the next method
is that of Continued Observation, frequent personal
interviews, and constant watching, and inducing
the suspected persons to write letters and statements of their wrongs and grievances. The last is
the Inquest: "When the above means fail, our inquiries must take a wider range, and be directed to
the previous history of the patient, as made known
to us by the testimony of friends and relatives,"
and others. "For this purpose we consult his
writings;" and so forth. So that, first, they are to
interrogate the deceased; then, to consider his habits and manners, and to get information from
other persons as to these; and, likewise, to consult
any writings of his, if they can be obtained. Now,
unfortunately, these French physicians do not seem
to have had an opportunity of examining in all
these respects. They examined the deceased in the
form of Interrogatory; but it seems that they had
very little besides. They had a letter from Sir
James Clark, and that was all the instruction that

they had upon which this gentleman was examined by them.

1856.

Jan. 26th.

DYCE
SOMBRE
against
TROUP,
SOLAROLI
(intervening),
and
PRINSEP,
and the
HON. EAST
INDIA
COMPANY
(also inter-
vening).

The evidence given by Monsieur Delessert, the Prefet of Police, is this. He says: " On the 11th of October, 1843, the Commission appointed met in my office for the examination of Mr. Dyce Sombre. It was composed of myself, as President; Dr. Chermside, Physician to the English Embassy; Dr. Behier, one of the Physicians to the King of the French, and who, with Dr. Bouneau, was Physician Inspector of the Lunatic Asylums of this Department; Mr. Okey, English Lawyer, Counsel to the Embassy; and M. Jennesser, Commissioner of Police. There was present also M. Baron Solaroli." Those were the persons who were present on the occasion. He then goes on to say, in reference to the deceased: " He looked very quiet; his features did not indicate any agitation. I began by explaining the state of circumstances under which the Commission met, the asserted lunacy of the deceased on the part of Mrs. Dyce Sombre, and the denial of it by Mr. Dyce Sombre himself. I then asked Mr. Dyce Sombre to tell us the reasons of his having been placed under restraint. He answered immediately, with the assistance of M. de Conches and Mr. Okey as interpreters, that he arrived from India in 1838; that he had subsequently married Lord St. Vincent's daughter; that for two years and a half he had lived very amicably with her, but then some friends interfered officiously in their private affairs, before any quarrel took place. He then said, that in April, 1843, he was placed under restraint in his hotel, watched day and

1856.

Jan. 26th.

DYCE
SOMBRE
*against*
TROUP,
SOLAROLI
(intervening),
and
PRINSEP,
and the
HON. EAST
INDIA
COMPANY
(also inter-
vening).

night by servants during twelve days, and then desired to leave the house he lived in; that he refused; and then one day, when out in a carriage, he was pulled out of it and taken to another house in Regent Street, where he was kept without inquiry from the 11th of April to the 1st of July, when a legal inquiry took place. During all the time that this restraint lasted he saw only Sir James Clark; Papers placed in a sealed box had been taken from him and never given back; and that he had not been permitted to see a Solicitor, whose assistance he had requested." Now it is quite clear that those were untrue statements on the part of this gentleman, for he had not been refused the assistance of a Solicitor. He had been asked more than once whether he would have a Solicitor, but he declined to do so. He said there was a gentleman of the name of Cockerell whose advice he would take, and nobody else, but Mr. Cockerell was in India. This circumstance is mentioned by the Solicitor of the Committee; and it was also mentioned by Mr. Barlow, the commissioner, to him, that he might have the assistance of a Solicitor, but he declined it altogether. Monsieur Delessert continues: "He added, that in that house where he was so kept, the servants endeavoured to frighten him; they entered his bedroom suddenly when sleeping, placed themselves before the fire just to appear as phantoms" (that is the way in which he explains away the spirits); "that he was awakened by their proceedings, though not frightened." To the question to what person he attributed these proceedings, and his restraint, he answered that he

1856.

Jan. 26th.

DYCE
SOMBRE
*against*
TROUP,
SOLAROLI
(intervening),
and
PRINSEP,
and the
HON. EAST
INDIA
COMPANY
(also inter-
vening).

"did not know, except it were to the East India Company" (so that the East India Company was the occasion of all this), "against whom he had a lawsuit."

Then he is questioned as to the duel, and his answer is, that he did, by one of his friends, demand satisfaction of a person from whom he thought he had received provocation; but a letter of explanation having been addressed to him by the person, the matter ended. That is all that is said about the duels; yet, according to the evidence given, there can be no doubt of the fact that he had challenged a great number of persons; that he had sent challenges to several of the directors of the East India Company; and that he had called out, or challenged, various other persons.

Such is the account given by the Prefet. I come next to the account given in the Official Report. But I should state before I consider this, that it is laid down in that case to which I have already referred, the case of *Waring* v. *Waring*, that the account, and the statement, and the explanation of the parties themselves, cannot be received as sufficient, if they have any object whatever in view; that is, if they have an opportunity of imposing upon the parties who are examining them, and they have any object in view, they will deny that which they would otherwise have admitted; and that the insanity does not always come forth in the manner in which it was expected, because, generally speaking, if you touch the chord of insanity, it is immediately responded to, and then the parties betray themselves; but if they have any object in view—

1856.

Jan. 26th.
——
DYCE
SOMBRE
*against*
TROUP,
SOLAROLI
(intervening),
and
PRINSEP,
and the
HON. EAST
INDIA
COMPANY
(also inter-
vening).

for instance, escape from confinement—it is necessary to examine others, and to examine them
closely, in order to ascertain what the real state of
the case is.

Now, in the Official Report this is stated : " The
Prefet having then invited Mr. Dyce Sombre to
give him the history of the events which have
caused the sequestration of which he complained,
and from which he had escaped only by flight, the
latter answered by the interpretation of Messrs.
Okey & Feuillet: That he arrived from Calcutta
in London, on the 15th of February, 1838; that he
married the daughter of Lord St. Vincent, with
whom he has lived on the best understanding
during two years and a half; that, later, some
friends had improperly meddled in their affairs in a
manner which had caused such trouble as had never
been before between them. He says that, in the
month of April last, by order only of two Physicians, he was confined in his hotel, and guarded day
and night by servants ; that this lasted about twelve
days ; that, finally, he had been required to quit the
house he resided in, which he resisted; and that, at
last, one day, whilst he was taking a promenade, he
was violently pulled out of his carriage, and conducted into another house situated in Regent Street,
where he was watched over, without inquiry, from
the 11th of April till the 1st of July, the day when
the legal Inquiry took place. That during the
whole time while this detention lasted he only
saw the doctor, Sir James Clark, of whom he soli-
cited with earnestness, but in vain, the favour of a
public process." Now, he had seen many other

persons besides Sir James Clark — Dr. Monro and others had visited him ; and Sir Charles Trevelyan, who seems to have taken a deep interest in this case, and to have been very favourably inclined towa:ds Mr. Dyce Sombre, calls upon him in Regent's Park ; and Sir Charles Trevelyan is satisfied that at that time, when he so visited him, he was not of sound mind. However, this gentleman says that he was only visited by his Physician ; but it appears that his wife visited him during the time that he was in the Regent's Park ; " that papers which he had placed in a sealed box, and necessary for his defence, had not been delivered to him when he demanded them from Dr. Clark, to whom he had entrusted them ; finally, that he could not see an advocate, whose assistance he had required"—that Advocate being in India, and that being the reason that he could not see him ; and he was told that he was in India, and that he might have anybody else that he liked. He adds : " That in his house, the servants, no doubt in order to execute orders they had received, endeavoured to frighten him ; that they entered unexpectedly into his room whilst he was sleeping ; that they placed themselves before the chimney, in which there was a fire, in order to feign shadows ; that all this awakened, but did not frighten him." That is the explanation which he gives as to the spirits ; because he had told Sir James Clark and others that he was visited by a white spirit, and by a black spirit, and at another time, I think, by a blue spirit ; and that he had been visited formerly, in India, by spirits in the form of the letter T. But now, all this is to be reduced to the mere statement

1856.

Jan. 20th.

DYCE
SOMBRE
*against*
TROUP,
SOLAROLI
(intervening),
and
PRINSEP,
and the
HON. EAST
INDIA
COMPANY
(also intervening).

1856.

Jan. 29th.

Dyce
Sombre
against
Troup,
Solaroli
(intervening),
and
Prinsep,
and the
Hon. East
India
Company
(also inter-
vening).

that the servants attempted to frighten him, by getting between him and the fire when he was in bed, and that this was done for the purpose of alarming him, and making him think that they were spirits. But it appears that these gentlemen had nothing before them but the statement of the poor individual himself; they had no evidence except that letter to which I shall presently refer, viz., the letter from Sir James Clark, upon which he was examined. The report goes on to say: "The Prefet having asked him to what persons he thought he ought to attribute his sequestration, he replied : 'I am ignorant as to who could have provoked this act, somebody, however, who must have an interest in making me appear deranged; for whilst I was in this illegal manner detained, and two days before the legal inquiry, a physician, delegated by Sir James Clark, made me take a potion which gave me vertigo and giddiness—so much so, that I seemed to see the house turning over. Never before had I felt any similar thing, and never since this circumstance has it been renewed. This lasted three days; and it was under the influence of this draught that I appeared before the Commissioners of Inquiry. I do not know to whom to impute these facts, if not to the East India Company, against which I have instituted a process which has lasted seven years.'"

Now, certainly this is a most extraordinary statement upon the part of this gentleman. He directly charges Sir James Clark with sending another Physician to give him a potion which was to upset his understanding and affect his reason for the space of three days; and that, during this time, they brought him before the Commission of

Inquiry, and the consequence was that he was incarcerated. Surely, contrasting this statement of Mr. Dyce Sombre with the evidence of Sir James Clark and the evidence of all the other Physicians who have been examined, there is but one conclusion to be arrived at. For to suppose that Sir James Clark, or any other of those persons, had been guilty of such improper conduct, seems to me to be quite out of the question.

Then he is interrogated as to a challenge. "Interrogated regarding a challenge to fight a duel addressed by him to a person the name of whom was not asked, he said: 'Certainly I did address, by the intervention of a friend, a provocation to a person of whom I thought I had to complain; but a letter of explanation, which he addressed to me, appearing to me sufficient, this affair had no further consequences.'" These gentlemen think that, therefore, there was only a single duel: he was asked about *duelling*, and they think that there was only one occasion of this kind, and this is the explanation that he thought proper to give upon that occasion of one of his proceedings. It was an act of delicacy in this gentleman and of forbearance that he did not mention the person whom he called out, and with whom he was to have fought the duel. There is a total silence as to the challenges to the directors of the East India Company and the numerous other persons to whom he had sent challenges.

Then comes the paper with respect to Article 20, which is referred to in the examination of Sir James Clark. "The Prefet asked Mr. Dyce Sombre what had been his connexions with the Archbishop

1856.

Jan. 20th.

DYCE SOMBRE *against* TROUP, SOLAROLI (intervening), and PRINSEP, and the HON. EAST INDIA COMPANY (also intervening).

1856.

Jan. 26th.

DYCE
SOMBRE
*against*
TROUP,
SOLAROLI
(intervening),
and
PRINSEP,
and the
HON. EAST
INDIA
COMPANY
(also inter-
vening).

of Canterbury, and he explained them immediately, thus: 'On arriving from India, I was
bearer of a letter of recommendation from the
Bishop of Calcutta for the Archbishop of Canterbury. I saw him in order to give it to him, and
I found myself a second time in his presence at
the time of my marriage. It is to these two visits
only that my connexions with him are confined.'"
So that he confined his connexion with the Archbishop of Canterbury to those visits—one on his
arrival from India with a letter from the Bishop of
Calcutta, and the other to the time of his marriage.
Then he speaks thus: " 'Regarding this matter,
I ought to speak of a memorandum which I
am deprived of, in order to make a weapon of
it against me. During my detention, and for
amusing myself, I wrote some jokes of this sort;
I wrote, for instance, this among others: ' The
Archbishop of Canterbury should send me a
young girl '—a bad joke, perhaps, but which was
only for myself, and which should not have seen
the day. Dr. Clark has preserved this memorandum.' " He knew that the memorandum was preserved, and he knew that it had been sent, because
it had been sent with the letter of Dr. Clark to the
French authorities, those being all the instructions
which they had for the examination of Mr. Dyce
Sombre. But which account is the Court to take?
Is it to take the account of this gentleman, that
this was a scrap of paper which he had written for
his own amusement, that it was a mere fancy, and
that Dr. Clark had improperly possessed himself of
it? Or is the Court to give credence to the evidence
of Dr. Clark, that the deceased seriously and deli-

berately put this paper into his hand as a proposal, and that it should be carried into effect in the way which was described, and that in that manner a reconciliation should take place between himself and his wife? If Monsieur Delessert and the physicians of Paris had had Sir James Clark before them, they could have interrogated him upon the point, and would have heard the account which he could give of it, and they would not for a moment have given credence, as they appear to have done, to the statement of Mr. Dyce Sombre on this occasion. " The Prefet invited Colonel Dyce Sombre to relate to the Commission the particulars of his flight and of his arrival in France. Mr. Dyce Sombre said: ' I was required to travel for my health, always accompanied by a physician and three watching servants. I have been to Bath, then at Liverpool, where I was detained in a house. In this latter town I found an opportunity to escape. I took advantage of it; I escaped eight days after my arrival at Liverpool. I returned to London. I remained there two hours, and not finding any steamer going to France, where I wished to go, I took the railway, which conducted me to Southampton, where I embarked for Havre; from there I went to Paris, where I arrived without money, so that I was obliged to sell the watch of my valet-de-chambre, which I had taken with me in my flight, as well as a pair of diamond buttons for shirt-sleeves, and a gold pencil-case.' Interrogated by the Prefet with all caution which delicacy prescribes, but however with all the authority which his character of magistrate gives him, regarding his position in respect to his wife, Mr. Dyce Sombre answered

1856.

Jan. 26th.

DYCE
SOMBRE
*against*
TROUP,
SOLAROLI
(intervening),
and
PRINSEP,
and the
HON. EAST
INDIA
COMPANY
(also intervening).

1856.

Jan. 26th.

DYCE
SOMBRE
*against*
TROUP,
SOLAROLI
(intervening),
and
PRINSEP,
and the
HON. EAST
INDIA
COMPANY
(also inter-
vening).

that his relations with her were good; and in support of this assertion he gave to the Commission
the reading of a letter, dated the 6th of October,
1843, addressed to him by Lady Dyce Sombre, the
terms of which proved the good understanding."
Mrs. Dyce Sombre, who seems to have been a most
kind wife, was at all times writing most kind
letters, and seeing whether she could do anything
for his comfort or his convenience; he takes advantage of this, and he produces one of her letters
as if they were on good terms. But what was the
last interview between them? Why, according to
the evidence which the Court has recently adverted to, when she called upon him in the Regent's
Park, he withdrew from her as it were with a sort
of abhorrence, as if he could not bear her presence
in the room on the occasion. He now states, with
great calmness, that the relations between them
were very good, he having, up to that time,
charged her with having committed adultery with
all sorts of persons, including her own father.

The two other physicians who were present
on the occasion deposed pretty much to the same
effect as Monsieur Delessert has done. When he is
examined on interrogatories, Monsieur Delessert
says, on the thirty-second interrogatory: "I put
my questions in French, and they were translated
into English, as before deposed. The deceased was
not questioned as to any particular persons with
whom he had charged his wife with having criminal
intercourse. He was not questioned as to a charge
made against her by him of having had incestuous
connexion with her own father, or of having had
sexual intercourse with the lowest persons, both

before and after her marriage to him, and of having made a property of such conduct. The only question put to him on the subject of challenging to a duel, was that which I have mentioned. No name was introduced, none being contained in the letter of Sir James Clark." So that this was an exceedingly imperfect examination, for they had nobody to assist them even in interrogating, since they had nothing but this letter of Sir James Clark, and this paper about the Archbishop of Canterbury, which the deceased explained away as a joke. He represented that he had no charges to make against his wife; that they were upon the best terms; and that there was only one duel which had been likely to take place, and that was accommodated without resorting to violent means. And upon this evidence it was that Monsieur Delessert, Dr. Bouneau, and Dr. Behier, came to the conclusion that the deceased was of sound mind at that time. And, indeed, I think they rather came to the conclusion that he never was otherwise than of sound mind; because, when I look to the deposition of Dr. Behier, I find him saying: " I entered on the investigation with a strong belief that Mr. Dyce Sombre was a lunatic; but my opinion became completely changed. A letter was produced and read from Sir James Clark, suggesting the points of inquiry. The questions were proposed by Monsieur Delessert, having that letter in his hand; but the physicians suggested several as the inquiry proceeded. Monsieur Jennesser acted as secretary to the Commission for the civil portion of its members, and I took notes for the medical branch. I drew up the report

1856.

Jan. 26th.

DYCE
SOMBRE
against
TROUP,
SOLAROLI
(intervening),
and
PRINSEP,
and the
HON. EAST
INDIA
COMPANY
(also intervening).

1856.

Jan. 26th.

DYCE
SOMBRE
against
TROUP,
SOLAROLI
(intervening),
and
PRINSEP,
and the
HON. EAST
INDIA
COMPANY
(also inter-
vening).

which we made, the draft of which, as originally prepared by me, I hold in my hand. Every question received a satisfactory answer from Mr. Dyce Sombre. Several of them were delicate and difficult and embarrassing. He answered all with great calmness, giving many details when required. As the inquiry proceeded, I found that we had been led into error respecting him; but we continued it throughout, in order to leave no part of the case uninvestigated. I might have been troubled to suppress my feelings, as he did his, had I been subjected to the same trial. I did and do feel strong indignation at the manner in which it had been endeavoured, and successfully as it appeared in England, to make Mr. Dyce Sombre a lunatic." So that upon the mere statement of Mr. Dyce Sombre as to the manner in which he had been treated, and as to Dr. Clark's conduct to him, his getting a paper from him, and his giving him this potion, Dr. Behier thinks that he had been exceedingly ill-used, for he says that he felt very strong indignation at the manner in which he had been successfully made out a lunatic. " I thought, and I now think, him an oppressed man. The examination was conducted by Monsieur Delessert with great skill as well as kindness." I dare say it was from the very scanty materials that he had before him; and he says: " Agreeably to Sir James Clark's suggestion in his letter, the name of the Archbishop of Canterbury was mentioned. Monsieur Delessert having asked him a question accordingly, he voluntarily referred to a paper of which he gave us an account, very probably anticipating that it would be produced; he entered into it fully, and so as to have

1856.

Jan. 26th.

DYCE
SOMBRE
against
TROOP,
SOLAROLI
(intervening),
and
PRINSEP,
and the
HON. EAST
INDIA
COMPANY
(also inter-
vening).

an important bearing on my judgment respecting him." I have no doubt it had an important bearing upon Dr. Behier's mind. "Another circumstance struck me forcibly. When asked who had caused his confinement as a lunatic, he answered that he did not know. Was it Mrs. Dyce Sombre? He did not believe it of her, and so on; whereas it is observable with lunatics, that they have always some one on whom they fix as their enemy." But in the report drawn up by these gentlemen, it appears that he said that it was the East India Company. "One other circumstance I re-member—he was very moderate in his expression of feeling towards Sir James Clark. When asked about poison, and if he believed any one to have a design of it against him, he laughed at the suggestion —No, he had not; but he did think that, previous to his examination on the Commission in England something had been given to him, not to do him permanent injury, but to take effect upon him for the time; and he explained how his head had been affected by it;" that is, he explained it in the manner stated in the Report, which was drawn up by Dr. Behier himself. Dr. Behier is exceedingly indignant at the manner in which this gentleman is treated. Now, I say, if this Inquiry was conducted without Dr. Clark or any other witnesses being called to depose to the facts, without any of the writings of the deceased being before this Commis-sion, and without their having any opportunity of knowing anything except what is declared by the deceased himself, this examination, as matter of evidence, cannot be put in competition with the evidence which was shortly before taken

1856.

Jan. 26th.

DYCE
SOMBRE
*against*
TROUP,
SOLAROLI
(intervening),
and
PRINSEP,
and the
HON. EAST
INDIA
COMPANY
(also inter-
vening).

in England; and it cannot have the effect of proving that the deceased had entirely recovered from the insanity under which he had laboured; and much less should it have the effect of showing that he never laboured under any insane delusion whatever.

But, in truth, that this conduct of the deceased was for the purpose of concealment, and that he still entertained the same opinions as to his wife—that he still entertained them, even at this time, when in Paris — is to be found in the evidence of other witnesses, and in the conduct of the party during the time that he was at Paris; because, very shortly after this examination had taken place, we find, from the evidence of Mr. Okey, that he still entertained the same opinion as to the conduct of Mrs. Dyce Sombre. Mr. Okey speaks of the arrival of this gentleman at Paris, and the Solicitor, Mr. Frere ; and of the application which was made to have him delivered up; and, finally, of this inquisition being taken. Mr. Okey told him that he had received very kind letters from his wife, and the answer of the deceased was: " He did not doubt that his wife wrote fine sentimental letters, but her conduct towards him had been such, that it was impossible he could ever be reconciled to her again. Strangely at variance this declaration was with the continued preservation of her picture. In answer to my inquiry, what she had done so to excite him ? he replied, that she had put him in prison, for which he would never forgive her; also, that she had done things for which he had often threatened to cut off her little nose (which was a favourite expression with him). He added: 'I asked her to cover her face, as women do in my country, but she would not.' 'Do they?' I asked. 'Yes,' he said; 'my sister does.' Then he said: 'Her conduct when I was in prison, was most shameful; she used to lie about with men on the grass in the Regent's Park (Mr. Q. D. he named, and Sir F. B.) in the most indecent manner.'" This is directly after his examination at Paris, when he said that he was on the best terms with his wife. "When I told him that it was a delusion, he said it was not; he had complained to Sir James Clark about it. He proposed to leave their disputes to the Jockey Club at Paris." This is immediately after his examination, when he was conducting himself to the entire satisfaction of Monsieur Delessert and of Dr. Behier and of Dr. Bouneau, and satisfied them that he was of perfectly sound mind; but when his object is answered in that respect, immediately afterwards he repeats all those charges against his wife. " I replied, that it might be very well if Mrs. Dyce Sombre was a horse, instead of his wife. On one occasion he told me he was almost sorry he had not treated her as she deserved, and put her to a lingering death. I inquired what he meant. He said: 'You know she is a little woman; I could have thrown her over my knee, and rasped her back, and then broken it with the but-end of my pistol,' accompanying his words with the double action of scraping and then rapping, as representing both proceedings; upon which I told him that if he talked such mad stuff as that, I would give him up. On another occasion he said: 'Why does not the man take her; he is a rich man. I'll allow her

1856.

Jan. 26th.

DYCE SOMBRE against TROUP, SOLAROLI (intervening), and PRINSEP, and the HON. EAST INDIA COMPANY (also intervening).

1856.

Jan. 26th.

DYCE
SOMBRE
*against*
TROUP,
SOLAROLI
(intervening),
and
PRINSEP,
and the
HON. EAST
INDIA
COMPANY
(also inter-
vening).

a handsome sum, say three thousand a year; then she can go her way and I mine.' On another occasion he desired me to write to my half-brother, the late Colonel Gurwood, to remonstrate with the Duke of Wellington for inviting her to his parties." "It was as early as about the 6th or 7th of November, 1843, that this insanity broke out respecting his wife, and it continued from that time, whenever her name was mentioned, as long as I continued to see him, till June, 1849." So that here is the evidence of Mr. Okey, deposing to these conversations immediately after the examination at Paris, in which he makes these charges against his wife, and his desire to refer their disputes to the Jockey Club at Paris; he speaks of that and similar conversations from that time, as long as this gentleman knew him, and down to the month of June, 1849, that month of June being the very month in which the will which is in dispute in this cause was executed by the deceased.

But there is also the evidence of Mr. Q. D., who happened to be at Paris at the time when this gentleman arrived there, and when he underwent his examination. It was in October, 1843, that the examination took place before Monsieur Delessert. To the Twenty-fourth Article he says: "In the latter end of 1843 and beginning of 1844 I met the deceased in Paris frequently; I went to the play with him, and met him at the Tuilleries, as well as in private circles. He complained to me, at my first meeting him in Paris, that his fortune had been taken from him, and that he was not allowed enough to maintain him, and his wife was a party to it. He stated to me that it was a notorious fact that she was guilty of many infidelities. On my reasoning with him upon the impropriety and unreasonableness of such accusations, he stated that it was a matter of perfect notoriety that I and others were in a conspiracy to conceal the truth, that her father, Lord St. Vincent, had had con- nexion with her before her marriage. On my expressing indignant surprise at such a charge, he said it was quite true, and Sir James Clark would prove it." Now, again, this is directly after his examination at Paris that he makes these charges: he repeats them, and he says that there is a con- spiracy against him, and that he knew Mr. Q. D. was one of the conspirators ; and that Sir James Clark would prove the facts. Sir James Clark was to be his witness on this occasion, to prove that his wife had been guilty of all those infidelities; and I cannot help thinking that it was with the cunning which belongs to madmen, that, having an object in view at the time of his examination before Monsieur Delessert and the physicians, he concealed the opinion he entertained, which possessed him at the very time.

Now, Lord Brougham, in that Judgment to which I have before adverted, speaks of the manner in which insane persons will conceal insa- nity upon a particular occasion, when they have any object in view. He says that Dr. Willis on *Mental Derangement*, page 151, clearly states that men often mistake for a lucid interval the mere absence of the subject of delusion." Then he pro- ceeds to mention the well-known instance, which is reported in the State Trials, of the indictment of Dr. Munro by a person of the name of Wood, for ille-

1856.

Jan. 26th.

DYCE SOMBRE against TROUP, SOLAROLI (intervening), and PRINSEP, and the HON. EAST INDIA COMPANY (also inter- vening).

1856.

Jan. 26th.
———
DYCE
SOMBRE
*against*
TROUP,
SOLAROLI
(intervening),
and
PRINSEP,
and the
HON. EAST
INDIA
COMPANY
(also inter-
vening).

gally confining him when he was of sound mind; that upon the first examination in court upon the indictment, a question was put to him which immediately elicited his insanity; and then it was perfectly obvious to every one that Dr. Munro was justified in what he had done. But this person brought a second action, in which he again gave evidence, when it was found quite impossible to extract anything from him: they might mention to him the subject of his insanity, and try him in every possible way, but they could not elicit it from him in any way; and if they had not had an opportunity of calling in the short-hand writer who had taken notes of the evidence on the former trial, Dr. Munro must have been convicted of having illegally confined this person as a lunatic when he was of perfectly sound mind.

This is a remarkable instance of the manner in which lunatics will, upon particular occasions, and when they have a particular object to carry out, deceive the parties who examine them; and this power of concealment is admitted by all the physicians who have been examined both on one side and the other in this case—very skilful, able, and experienced physicians. They seem to think that though in their own case they could always detect insanity, yet that others are very frequently imposed upon. And I cannot help thinking that Monsieur Delessert and the two physicians who assisted him had so little means of examining and knowing what the real state of facts was, that they were deceived upon this occasion, and that the deceased entertained but hid from them the same insane opinions which he held when he was in England, and that this is

pretty clearly shown by the evidence of Mr. Okey
and of Mr. Quintin Dick almost immediately after
the examination had taken place.

Now such is the evidence in 1843. Then in
1844 there is very strong evidence to show that
the deceased was then insane; but I need not refer
to any particular evidence bearing upon that time.
But it should seem that this examination, which
took place in Paris, is not the only inquisition
which has been taken in foreign countries; for it
appears that the deceased, armed with this document from Paris, proceeds to St. Petersburg, and
there an examination likewise takes place at his instance. He produces before certain learned physicians there this acquittal from Paris; and he also
states that, owing to great misconduct in England
and to a bribed jury, he was there found to be an
insane person, and accordingly they are satisfied at
St. Petersburg that he was of sound mind.

Then the same sort of thing takes place at
Brussels, in the year 1845. Now at that time he
had entered into a treaty with a gentleman of the
name of Mahon, and he had contracted to pay Mr.
Mahon the sum of £10,000, provided he should,
by his exertions in obtaining evidence and procur-
ing physicians to certify to his sanity, obtain the
supersedeas of the Commission, and be put in possession of his property. Accordingly, an examination of the deceased took place at Brussels in 1845;
and it may be important to see what one or two of
those persons who so examined him state. Mr. Black-
wood is an English surgeon, resident at Brussels.
He says that in 1845 the deceased, referring to the
peculiar circumstances of his case, expressed a wish

1856.

Jan. 26th.

DYCE
SOMBRE
against
TROUP,
SOLAROLI
(intervening),
and
PRINSEP,
and the
HON. EAST
INDIA
COMPANY
(also inter-
vening).

1856.

Jan. 26th.

DYCE
SOMBRE
*against*
TROUP,
SOLAROLI
(intervening),
and
PRINSEP,
and the
HON. EAST
INDIA
COMPANY
(also inter-
vening).

to obtain a certificate, in order that the Commission of Lunacy in England might be superseded, and that he had already obtained a certificate of that kind at St. Petersburg. "Accordingly, on the 11th of June," he says, "I met Dr. Seutin in consultation, and we examined him together. On the 12th of June we again met, Mr. Mahon being then also present. On the next day, the 13th, I met Dr. Seutin again, the Advocate Theyssens being present for the purpose of legislation if wanted. The result was, that it was agreed to have a more extended and regular examination of the deceased, which took place accordingly on the 14th, Dr. Seutin having procured the attendance of Dr. Guislain, from Ghent ; Dr. Vleminckx, President of the Royal Academy of Medicine in Belgium and Director of the Military Hospitals ; and Dr. Crommelinck, proprietor of a lunatic asylum here ; Mr. Mahon and myself being also present." So that upon these examinations, and upon all subsequent examinations which have taken place, except those which have been conducted under the authority of the Lord Chancellor himself, Mr. Mahon was a constant attendant upon the physicians. He was the person who had made a contract with the deceased to give up his time, in order to procure medical men, and through their means to obtain a supersedeas of the Commission against him. "On the 16th of June there was a still further examination of the deceased, in the presence of the last-named persons, excepting Dr. Guislain. On every occasion the deceased was examined as carefully and closely as was possible to us, and on all points which we had reason to think most likely to make manifest a delusion, if any existed. I remember particularly that the report of his examination at Paris was here for our guidance," exactly as it had been at St. Petersburg. " There was no shrinking on his part from any point of inquiry, and no wilful omission on ours. His replies were prompt, collected, consistent, betraying no symptom of insanity or delusion. On the 14th, as I recollect, a certificate was signed by all of us as to the entire competency of the deceased to manage his affairs. That was Saturday; and we agreed to meet again on the Monday following, all but Dr. Guislain." So that they were all agreed upon this matter.

1856.

Jan. 26th.

DYCE
SOMBRE
against
TROUP,
SOLAROLI
(intervening),
and
PRINSEP,
and the
HON. EAST
INDIA
COMPANY
(also intervening).

But now let us see what this gentleman says in a later part of his examination. It is upon the eighth interrogatory. " I did not understand from the deceased that he had seen Lord Lyndhurst ; he spoke to me about his lordship repeatedly. At the time, or shortly afterwards, I could have fully complied with the direction to set forth what he told me concerning those interviews and concerning his lordship. All that I can now state specifically and distinctly is this : that he could have had his supersedeas and his divorce too, if only he would have bound himself to marry Lord Lyndhurst's daughter." Now really this is a most extraordinary thing to bring forward as an instance of the perfect sanity of this gentleman. They all testify to his being sane at this time ; they are assisted by Mr. Mahon; they have got this certificate from Paris, and one from St. Petersburg likewise; and yet this poor individual gravely tells them that he could have got his supersedeas, and that

1856.

Jan. 28th.

DYCE
SOMBRE
*against*
TROUP,
SOLAROLI
(intervening),
and
PRINSEP,
and the
HON. EAST
INDIA
COMPANY
(also inter-
vening).

he could have got his divorce too, if he would have married Lord Lyndhurst's daughter. It seems to me, therefore, that we cannot rely upon this testimony, which was so got up at Brussels by Mr. Mahon—who had a deep pecuniary interest on the occasion, and who placed the examination before the physicians—who was present upon the occasion, as we shall find that he was on all subsequent occasions when the examination of this gentleman was to take place. They certify to the perfect and entire capacity of the deceased at this time; and yet one of the persons who signs this certificate gives this account of what the deceased said about what would have been the case if he had consented to marry Lord Lyndhurst's daughter.

So much, then, for the foreign examinations. The one at Brussels was in 1845. Then, I think, in 1846 an examination takes place at Dover by Dr. Bright and Dr. Southey, under the authority of the Lord Chancellor. What Dr. Bright says is this: that under the direction of the Lord Chancellor he visited Mr. Dyce Sombre in Half Moon Street—that was in the month of June, 1844; and he visited him there in conjunction with other physicians. I think one or two of the physicians call it Clarges Street, but it is quite evident that they mean the same place. Sir James Clark and three or four others visited him in 1844, and they found him under insane delusions at that particular time, and each of them has been examined; two of them, I think, speak of their visits as if in Half Moon Street, and two others as if in Clarges Street;

but they speak of having visited him at the same time, and therefore there can be no doubt that that examination took place in the year 1844, in one or other of those streets, and under the authority of the Lord Chancellor; and they came to the conclusion, from conversation which they had with the deceased upon that occasion, that he was then insane. Dr. Bright says: "There were present Sir James Clark, Dr. Monro, Dr. Conolly, and my colleague, Dr. Southey. On the 24th of July following I saw the deceased in company with Dr. Southey at the house, and in the presence of Lord Lyndhurst, in George Street, Hanover Square. I saw him again on the 21st and three following days of September, 1846, at Dover, in company with Dr. Southey. Again, in August, 1847, at Brighton, on more days than one, certainly two, with Dr. Southey only." Then he says that he again saw him at Mivart's Hotel, in November, 1848. With regard to the examination at Dover, he finds him to be of unsound mind at that time, and so does Dr. Southey, who was present upon that occasion; and he so conducted himself as to leave no doubt upon their minds that he was labouring under a delusion at that particular time. It is quite clear, also, from the evidence of the two persons in whose house the deceased was lodging at that time, that he was in a state of insanity, because both the husband and the wife hear this gentleman walking about his own room talking to himself and saying: "Damn her; I will kill her; I will murder her; she shall be no wife of mine;" and conducting himself in that manner. And they

1856.

Jan. 26th.

DYCE SOMBRE against TROUP, SOLAROLI (intervening), and PRINSEP, and the HON. EAST INDIA COMPANY (also intervening).

1856.

Jan. 26th.

DYCE
SOMBRE
*against*
TROUP,
SOLAROLI
(intervening),
and
PRINSEP,
and the
HON. EAST
INDIA
COMPANY
(also inter-
vening).

speak of it so as to leave no doubt whatever that he meant his wife, during the time that such expressions were used.

I do not know that it is necessary to enter into the particulars of the evidence of these gentlemen at Dover, Dr. Bright and Dr. Southey, respecting what took place as to the deceased continuing to labour under delusions respecting his wife (to which they most distinctly depose), because, in a subsequent examination, in the year 1847, which took place at Brighton, when Mr. Dyce Sombre told them, or at least endeavoured to tell them, that he had got rid of those insane notions with respect to his wife, he distinctly admitted that it was since the time when he was at Dover; that he did entertain them at that time in Dover, viz., in 1846, at Dover; and that it was subsequent to that time (so he tells them at Brighton) that he had got rid of those notions. So that there is the admission of Mr. Dyce Sombre himself, that up to the year 1846, and at the time of the examination at Dover, he did entertain the same insane delusions as to the infidelity of his wife.

Now, with regard to what took place at the examination at Brighton, in the year 1847: Mr. Dyce Sombre came over from France for the purpose of being examined by Dr. Bright and Dr. Southey at Brighton, upon that occasion; and it is remarkable that upon his arrival at Dieppe, he there meets with Mr. Okey, and he tells him that he is going to England. He is asked the object of his visit, and he says it is to tell the Chancellor what a damned bitch his wife is; showing, therefore, that he entertained the same opinion at that time as he had done upon a previous occasion as to her infidelity. And yet when the physicians come to examine him, he tries to parry their questions, and says that he has got rid of that delusion; but this he does in such a way as to convince them that the delusion still prevails, for that is the opinion of Dr. Bright and of Dr. Southey; and they entertained no doubt whatever upon the subject, either when they saw him in Half Moon Street in 1844, or when they examined him at Dover in 1846, or at Brighton in the year 1847.

The Court has seen that Mr. Dyce Sombre had sufficient cunning of himself at that time to parry the examinations that were made of him, as he had done at Paris. But it is important to see whether that was not strongly advised and recommended; and whether it was not pressed upon him over and over again by Mr. Mahon and others, that he should conceal his delusion in this respect, that he had no chance of recovering his liberty unless he did conceal it, and unless he did state that that delusion had passed away. Over and over again is that caution given to him by Mr. Mahon and by many other persons; but it is given more especially and more emphatically by Lord and Lady C., who have taken an active part in this matter.

There is a letter from Lord C., which is dated in 1847; there are indeed earlier letters of the same kind, but this letter goes to the examinations which subsequently took place, namely, those in 1848, in December, and also in November, when he was examined by the Chancery physicians. Lord C.'s letter is to this effect: "You should

1856.

Jan. 26th.

DYCE
SOMBRE
against
TROUP,
SOLAROLI
(intervening),
and
PRINSEP,
and the
HON. EAST
INDIA
COMPANY
(also inter-
vening).

1856.

Jan. 26th.
———
Dyce
Sombre
*against*
Troup,
Solaroli
(intervening),
and
Prinsep,
and the
Hon. East
India
Company
(also inter-
vening).

come to Dieppe, and there wait till you get the permission to come over to Brighton, to be examined by Drs. Bright and Southey." So that he was preparing him for this very examination at Brighton. "If you answer their questions coolly, and in a few words, they must declare you to be in such a state as to render you quite fit to have your liberty and property, which, I think, have been so unjustly withheld from you. I hope when you are examined, that you will say as little as you possibly can about Mrs. D. S. You should, I think, say that whatever delusion you laboured under some time ago, it has left you." It is advice not only about what he is to conceal, but what he is to say. He is to be prepared for these examinations. He is to be crammed for them, as it is sometimes expressed: "You should, I think, say that whatever delusion you laboured under some time ago, it has left you, as you became divested of your eastern notions and feelings about women; and further, that there is no longer any danger of your being jealous of her" (not that you are convinced that you have been under error and under delusion), "inasmuch as you have lost all love, admiration, and affection for her, and that no power upon earth should induce you to live with or go near her again. You should say, also, that it is your wish to go to India for the benefit of your health, and in order to look into and arrange your affairs. Let me know on what day you will be at Dieppe. I will go down to Brighton when I hear that you are to be there." So that he is to go down and assist him upon this occasion. Now it so happens, I suppose, that he did not render him that assistance, that he was not there upon that occasion, because Mr. Dyce Sombre himself, when he is speaking of this examination, mentioning it in his book, says: "But what could I do when left by myself? I had nobody to support me, so that I was obliged to say what they would have me say." So that he did not conceal the delusion thoroughly and effectually upon that occasion; and the consequence was, that Dr. Bright and Dr. Southey reported in the manner which I have already stated. Afterwards, indeed, at the examination in December, 1848, he had that assistance, for he had Mr. Mahon there, who was present and assisting upon the occasion, and Mr. Prinsep was likewise present during part of that examination. He was called in when there was any difficulty; if there was any difficulty that wanted explanation, then Mr. Mahon and Mr. Prinsep were to give the explanation.

I have referred to the letter and the advice of my Lord C., who says that he will go down to Brighton upon the occasion and assist the deceased. Then we have a letter from Lady C., and that is to this effect: "Dear Colonel Sombre, I write to congratulate you on the happy turn your affairs have taken lately." She alludes to the use of his whole income. The last Chancellor refused to let him have the income of his whole property; he was allowed to have part of the income, but that was all. "I write to congratulate you upon the happy turn your affairs have taken lately; be assured that we feel most sincerely rejoiced at the prospect of your speedy release from constraint and persecution. Lord C. is most anxious that you should take his and Mr. Mahon's advice

1856.

Jan. 26th.

DYCE SOMBRE against TROUP, SOLAROLI (intervening), and PRINSEP, and the HON. EAST INDIA COMPANY (also intervening).

1856.

Jan. 26th.

DYCE
SOMBRE
*against*
TROUP.
SOLAROLI
(intervening),
and
PRINSEP,
and the
HON. EAST
INDIA
COMPANY
(also inter-
vening).

upon every point." That advice upon every point is, that he is to say that he gives up his delusions; that he no longer has any belief in them; that he does not think his wife has been guilty of the adultery with which he has charged her, and of incestuous intercourse with her father, and of connexion with the very numerous gentlemen who have been mentioned, who have utterly denied all appearance of it; and that he gives up his belief that she has had connexion with the waiters and with the common soldiers in Hyde Park in the open day. All that is to be abandoned. "Mr. M.," that is, Mr. Mahon, "is, I am sure, a trustworthy person, and seems to understand and feel for your position thoroughly. Now, my dear Sir, on your prudence in this emergency depends your fate through life. Guard every word and action; and whatever your opinions are," (not only whatever your delusions are, and you know they are, and you wilfully confess they are, and you are sure they are, but "whatever your opinions are",) "keep them to yourself, for there is no sort of comparison between the petty vengeance of expressing your suspicions and the far greater triumph of defeating your enemies now by your own liberation, and deferring to a later period the exposure of their evil intentions and unkindness towards you. No one will believe the possibility of any one having made the confessions you so often alluded to." That is, he had not only charged his wife with committing these acts of adultery and with this incestuous intercourse with her father, but he had declared that she had confessed those acts to him, and at another time that Lord St. Vincent had confessed his own crime to him. "No one will believe the possibility of any one having made the confessions you so often allude to, and I have heard from a person used to such transactions"—I really do not know what these transactions are, or who the person is with whom this lady associates—" I have heard from a person used to such transactions, that the object of making those confessions was to induce you to repeat them, and thus, by asserting what appeared impossible, to give this proof of insanity; for who could believe that such self-accusations were possible? And yet they were made with the object I just noticed. Trusting that you will be prudent, and above all things very quiet and abstemious, I wish you all the success you can desire for yourself;" and so forth. I think that this is a way of preparing a man to carry his point. He is recommended not to follow his own opinions, as, if he does, he will not get free. Therefore it is quite clear that it is in obedience to this pressing by Mr. Mahon, to this pressing by Lord C., and to this pressing by Lady C., that he says he gives up these delusions, though in fact he still entertains them.

Then there is another letter from my Lord C. in 1846: " I regret much that you will not take my advice, as well as that of Prinsep, &c.; indeed there is only one mode of proceeding, namely, that of signing the amended petition, which will lead to a final, and, I trust, satisfactory settlement of your unfortunate affairs. As to my speaking privately to the Lord Chancellor, it would be of no use to you, even if he would listen to me, which it would be irregular and improper for him to do. I have only to repeat (and for the last

1856.
Jan. 26th.

DYCE SOMBRE against TROUP, SOLAROLI (intervening), and PRINSEP, and the HON. EAST INDIA COMPANY (also intervening).

1856.

Jan. 26th.

DYCE
SOMBRE
*against*
TROUP,
SOLAROLI
(intervening),
and
PRINSEP,
and the
HON. EAST
INDIA
COMPANY
(also inter-
vening).

time) my recommendation to you to sign the amended petition without loss of time." This is the advice which is given by his lordship. He says in another letter: " Do not let anything irritate you, and when questioned by the Lord Chancellor, &c., avoid all remarks upon the past conduct of your wife, and say as little as possible upon the only subject that excites you." So that here is a preparation for these examinations by Mr. Mahon, by Lord C., and Lady C. ; and he is to follow the advice of Mr. Mahon and of Mr. Prinsep when he undergoes these examinations. However, in 1847, the examination at Brighton failed, as it had done before. Dr. Bright and Dr. Southey reported against the propriety of superseding the Commission, and the consequence was that it was not superseded.

Another petition is afterwards presented to the Lord Chancellor, in order that this matter might be again investigated, and whether the Commission might not be superseded. I think there are no less than six petitions to the Lord Chancellor to have this Commission superseded. I believe the sixth was not acted upon, Mr. Dyce Sombre having died.

After the examination to which I have adverted, by Sir James Clark and others at Mivart's Hotel, in November, 1848, there was an examination by physicians selected by Mr. Mahon—very eminent physicians, and whose character is entitled to great weight—namely, Dr. Paris, the President of the College of Physicians, and other very eminent men, who, no doubt, meant to depose, and have deposed, as far as their knowledge extended, to the facts of the case with great truth and propriety. But, first of all, it will be necessary to see what was the position of those physicians' who examined Mr. Dyce Sombre at Mivart's Hotel in November, in the year 1848, under the authority of the Court of Chancery. Those physicians are four in number—Sir James Clark, Dr. Bright, Dr. Southey, and Dr. Martin. I think Dr. Martin was selected by the deceased himself upon the occasion. Upon the forty-sixth and forty-seventh articles, as to the examinations at Mivart's Hotel in November, 1848, Sir James Clark says: "On the 1st, 2d, and 6th days of November, 1848, I was in attendance at Mivart's Hotel, and took part in the examination of the deceased, Dr. Bright, Dr. Southey, and Dr. Martin, being also present for the purpose of that examination. I signed a joint report as the result of the inquiry. I do not doubt that the minutes or exhibits now shown to me contain a correct account of what passed." And it is important that we should see those minutes, because, in point of fact, they contain the only information which was given to the physicians, Dr. Paris and others, as to the points to which they were to examine, except those other matters which might be suggested by Mr. Mahon and Mr. Prinsep, who were present upon the occasion. But as to the evidence of all that had taken place upon former occasions, of the nature of the charges, of his being visited by spirits, of his apprehensions of poison, and all the other subjects which have been adverted to, they do not seem to have had any information nor anything whatever laid before them, except what is to be derived from this examination and the report of what took place at

1856.

Jan. 26th.

DYCE SOMBRE against TROUP, SOLAROLI (intervening), and PRINSEP, and the HON. EAST INDIA COMPANY (also intervening).

G 2

1856.

Jan. 26th.

DYCE
SOMBRE
*against*
TROUP,
SOLAROLI
(intervening),
and
PRINSEP,
and the
HON. EAST
INDIA
COMPANY
(also inter-
vening).

Mivart's Hotel. " I was and am very decidedly of opinion that the deceased at that time continued to be of unsound mind. It is to be remembered that latterly he got more cautious than he had been at an earlier period, and so he fenced with the questions." And I think that this is the true description of the examination, when you come to look at the minutes which were taken down by the short-hand writer upon that occasion. He fenced with the questions, and he had been prepared to fence with them by the advice which had been given to him by Mr. Mahon, and by the strong recommendations of Lord and Lady C. He had been advised to conceal his sentiments in that respect. " He professed to have given up as a delusion the infidelities which he had charged upon his wife." They told him, Whatever your opinion is, you must give up that, for nobody will believe it—nobody will believe these impossibilities: that she has had connexion with her father, and that she has confessed it, and that the father has confessed it. " He professed to have given up, as a delusion, the infidelities which he had charged upon his wife, but he did not impress me with the idea that he was less under the power of the delusion. On the 1st of November, he stated that he must have been under delusions with regard to her; that he exonerated the physicians who gave their opinion on his state of mind, in 1843, and that the conclusion of the jury was just as far as respected her conduct. But on being asked whether he was satisfied that Mrs. Dyce Sombre having confessed her guilt was a delusion, his reply was, ' I believe she denies that.' " Now one of the other physicians, upon a former occasion (Dr. Conolly, I think), who has been examined, says that when he mentioned to the deceased his having given up this delusion, he immediately broke out and said, "Who the devil told you such a damned lie as that?" Therefore, upon this occasion he conceals his thoughts. He says, "I believe she denies that;" that is the way he answers it: he does not say, I was under a delusion; I confess that I was. I am very sorry that I made these charges against her. That indeed would have been the natural conduct of a man who had recovered from an insane delusion and had become a person of sound mind; but the answer is, "I believe she denies that." Then Sir James Clark says: "This reply, with several others, showed that he was by no means satisfied of her innocence. His belief in spirits he then denied, but he appeared to be capable of dissembling his delusions, and even of inventing stories to explain them. His manner, I often found, during all my attendance upon him, remarkably quiet and even self-possessed for ordinary purposes and subjects having no relation to his delusions." So these physicians say, upon other occasions, that he answered with great calmness. "On the subject of Madame Solaroli's illegitimacy, I must assume that the reasons assigned by him for knowing or believing in it were the offspring of his own mind, mere inventions, not only unfounded, but irrational. His manner appeared to me to indicate more caution, rather than less delusion." The impression, then, upon the mind of the witness was that he exhibited more caution; yet that upon these several points, and upon the point of the illegitimacy of Madame Solaroli, which is a point that did not arise till a later period of his

1856.

Jan. 26th.

DYCE SOMBRE *against* TROUP, SOLAROLI (Intervening), and PRINSEP, and the HON. EAST INDIA COMPANY (also intervening).

1856.

Jan. 26th.

DYCE
SOMBRE
*against*
TROUP,
SOLAROLI
(intervening),
and
PRINSEP,
and the
HON. EAST
INDIA
COMPANY
(also inter-
vening).

insanity, the deceased was insane. Then he goes on to say, that at that time Mr. Dyce Sombre considered that there had been something put into his food—not so much as a poison, perhaps, as to injure his procreative powers. That appears to have been the opinion which this poor man entertained—that sometimes it was for the purpose of poisoning him, and sometimes for the purpose of injuring his procreative powers. He believed that poison had been administered to him at the *Trois Freres Provenceaux*, where he had dined, at Paris: when he was ill at dinner, he thought that he had been poisoned. Again, Dr. Olliffe, who was examined on behalf of the executor to the sanity of the deceased, says that, upon one occasion, the deceased told him that the brandy had been poisoned, and Dr. Olliffe, to convince him to the contrary, drank some of it himself; the deceased was not satisfied, and Dr. Olliffe promised to take home some of it and analyse it, in order to prove that such was not the case. That he had a belief in poison is quite evident from the entry which he makes in his pocket-book or in his journal when he is at Naples; he considers that he has been poisoned there; " it is a remarkable thing, because it is exactly at the time and in the place" (he says) " that Baron Solaroli, at Venice, had told him that it would be so." So that it is quite clear that this delusion was going on at the time when he made that entry, and also when he published the book which must afterwards be referred to.

Dr. Bright, on the Fifty-sixth Article, referring to the examination at Brighton, says : " When urged to write or express regret at the pain that he must have caused his wife by his unfounded suspicions, he said he would not do so without consulting his lawyers; and that if he acted upon the impulse of his own heart and feelings, he should never obtain his freedom from the Court of Chancery." That is, that he never should give up that idea. Therefore, it was only in consequence of the advice which was given him, and which was so strongly urged upon him, that he feigned to give it up.

Dr. Southey, who had examined the deceased at Brighton and at other places, says: "On every occasion when I was in company with him, I firmly believe that he was labouring under delusions which rendered him of unsound mind. Viewed by itself, I might hesitate to consider his conduct towards the Baron Solaroli, of whom he spoke in very strongly opprobrious terms, as the offspring of insane delusion; but taken in connexion with other delusions, and with the inconsistent reasons by which he attempted to justify his opinions, I can attribute it only to insanity."

One and all of these medical persons who examined the deceased on the occasion—Sir James Clark, Dr. Bright, Dr. Southey, and Dr. Martin— came to the conclusion, in 1848, that he was of unsound mind. There is the evidence which was taken down on the occasion by a short-hand writer, who was admitted at the express request of Mr. Dyce Sombre himself. Probably he thought that he came fully prepared on this occasion, having received advice how to conduct himself, and he was prepared to make these admissions, so far as his state of insanity would allow him to do; and therefore, whatever his opinions might be, he was desirous that the evidence should be taken down,

1856.

Jan. 26th.

DYCE
SOMBRE
*against*
TROUP,
SOLAROLI
(intervening),
and
PRINSEP,
and the
HON. EAST
INDIA
COMPANY
(also intervening).

1856.

Jan. 26th.

DYCE
SOMBRE
*against*
TROUP,
SOLAROLI
(intervening),
and
PRINSEP,
and the
HON. EAST
INDIA
COMPANY
(also inter-
vening).

to show that he had given up those delusions. He
is examined; many of the questions do not seem
to be very important, or to elicit anything. "Up
to the period when we saw you at Dover, you were
labouring under certain delusions?" His answer is:
"I had just returned from St. Petersburg, where
I had been, and I had been reflecting on these
things; on my return from St. Petersburg, I remained some time at Brighton, and I thought a
great deal about these things. I went to Paris, and
from there I came to meet you at Dover. The
first day I saw you, I said that, having reflected
upon the disinterested opinion you gave on the
subject, my mind was quite clear that, whatever I
might have thought before, I must have been
labouring under delusions and acting on them."
In another place he says, I think, "I was obliged
to do it, for I was there by myself, and was obliged
to speak what they would have me say." The
next question is: "Therefore I wanted you to
state that in the presence of Sir. James Clark,
because that completely exonerates Sir James
Clark and all the medical men who saw you
in 1843; it exonerates them from the opinion
you suppose they gave?" He answers "Yes."
And then comes the question, "And it is your
own conviction that the jury were justified in
coming to the conclusion that you were of
unsound mind when they did come to that
conclusion?" The answer is, "As far as concerned Mrs. Dyce Sombre's conduct;" because
that, it had been told him, was the only point
which he had now to clear up; that if he would
but admit that that was a delusion, then he

would get his supersedeas; so his answer is: "As far as concerned Mrs. Dyce Sombre's conduct." "There was ground enough at that time to suppose you were of unsound mind, at the time the jury found that verdict?" "Yes." "Therefore you do not entertain any hostile feeling towards the persons who sued out that Commission?" "I have none; only it would have been better if I was not so much worried and annoyed about those things. If it had been left quietly to one or two physicians, I would not, perhaps, have had my mind so much annoyed and worked up about these different things. But there were too many examinations, I thought; and there was not only Sir James Clark, I believe in 1844, but there were not less than ten or twelve doctors, who examined me at different periods." "That was after the Commission?" "Yes." Further on he is asked: "You stated that once to Drs. Bright and Southey at Dover?" "Yes, that those were my impressions." So that he had those impressions upon him. "They were effaced somewhat during our interview; they were not in full existence at the time of our first interview?" "That is your report." "At the first interview you did not seem to be fully convinced of Mrs. Dyce Sombre's purity?" "That was in 1844." That was an admission at that time that he did not think her pure. "Did you see Count Nesselrode at St. Petersburg?" "Yes." "Had you any communication with him?" "I was in the steamer with him; like other people he talked on different subjects." Now before he had said that Count Nesselrode had told him of all these matters as to his wife. "I was in the same steamer with him; like other

1856.

Jan. 26th.

DYCE
SOMBRE
against
TROUP,
SOLAROLI
(intervening),
and
PRINSEP,
and the
HON. EAST
INDIA
COMPANY
(also intervening).

1856.

Jan. 20th.

DYCE
SOMBRE
*against*
TROUP,
SOLAROLI
(intervening),
and
PRINSEP,
and the
HON. EAST
INDIA
COMPANY
(also inter-
vening).

people, he talked on different subjects." "Concerning Mrs. Dyce Sombre, amongst others?" "He made some allusions to what the report was at the time." "Did he mention any particular person to you at the time?" "Not that I remember now." "Has that impression remained firmly on your mind ever since?" "Not since 1846." That was the time when he was at Dover; not since that time. "It has not remained?" "No." "You are not satisfied that it was a delusion before that period that you were labouring under?" "Certainly. What I have just been saying is, that when I came to Dover, it was with a firm mind to tell Dr. Southey and Dr. Bright, that after consideration I had come to the determination that I think I might have acted under delusions; that as I had no proof, the best thing for me was to consider it so. There was no proof of any guilt; but since then, as we are not of the same thinking, as our characters are not the same, why it is much better that there should be no talk or proposal of our living together again." Exactly what Lord Combermere told him to say. "Still your mind continued satisfied since 1846. You have not changed your mind?" "No." The delusion was that he had seen her himself having sexual intercourse in the Park with common soldiers and with a variety of people. Now he puts it that there is no evidence, and therefore it is best to give it up. "You are satisfied that the confession on the part of Mrs. Dyce Sombre of her guilt—you are satisfied that that was a delusion, and that she never did make such a confession." He does not answer, Yes, I am satisfied of that;

the answer is, " I believe she denies that." Why
that is exactly fencing with the question : " I
believe she denies that." Then the question is,
" Because she denied it, you disbelieve it? You
have that confidence in her veracity, that you
disbelieve it because she denies it?" " Yes; just
so." So that though he believed that he had seen
it with his own eyes, yet now he disbelieves it
merely because she says it is not so. " You think
that you must have been mistaken, and that she
was right?" " Yes." " To whom was the denial
made ?" " I do not know." He does not know to
whom the denial was made : he had never seen
Mrs. Dyce Sombre himself, excepting on two occasions, after the first removal from the Clarendon
Hotel. He had seen her once when he was in
Hanover Lodge, in the Regent's Park, and then he
shrank from her as something which he abhorred
and abominated. Then he sees her at Dr. Martin's,
in the year 1848, on the 10th of November, and the
very same thing takes place: he shrinks from her as
if he could not bear to go near her, or even bear
the sight of her. The examination proceeds: " Do
you remember the confession having been made to
you?" " I remember something of the kind." He
remembers the confession being made; but whether by Lord St. Vincent, or whether by his wife, he
does not say. " Would it not be more satisfactory to
your mind if the denial were made also in your
presence, and not to a second or third party?"
" As far as I am concerned, I am quite satisfied; I
would not wish to hear anything." " You would
not wish to see her, to hear her denial?" " It would
be no use." " Up to this time, you are quite

1856.

Jan. 26th.

DYCE
SOMBRE
against
TROUP,
SOLAROLI
(intervening),
and
PRINSEP,
and the
HON. EAST
INDIA
COMPANY
(also inter-
vening).

1856.

Jan. 26th.

DYCE
SOMBRE
*against*
TROUP,
SOLAROLI
(intervening),
and
PRINSEP,
and the
HON. EAST
INDIA
COMPANY
(also inter-
vening).

satisfied that Mrs. Dyce Sombre is quite innocent of all those charges?" "Yes." "And that it was all delusion, your speaking of her before?" "Yes." "And you were mistaken in supposing that she ever did confess?" "The impression on you and Dr. Bright was, that she was innocent, and I have no reason to disbelieve it. I have not seen any of those persons who ought to have been informed on the subject for some years now, and therefore I only go by what I hear." Now I cannot say that that is a candid admission and acknowledgment that he had been under a delusion, and that he was sorry for that delusion, and that he now saw his error. It appears to me that Sir James Clark and the other gentlemen have given a true account of this examination, that he is fencing with the questions. "Did she or not confess?" "You have told me that those were delusions, and I am satisfied with your opinion." That is what satisfies him. "You would rather take that than your own impression?" "After mature consideration, I think so—incompatibility of temper is the only fault." That is exactly according to the advice which had been given to him. He was told that, unless he did so, he never could recover his liberty. Then the question is put to him, "It is an affair rather of the heart and feelings. There is Lord St. Vincent—it was a terrible imputation upon him, having had incestuous intercourse with his daughter, that I should think you would be glad to have an opportunity of relieving him from as soon as you can?" What is the answer? "We have dropped all connexion." Not, I am very sorry for it, and I will make any apology for having made such a charge against him; I was insane at the time. " Does it·not pain you to have made such an atrocious accusation against your own father-in-law?" "I have no objection to saying that under the circumstances in which I was placed at the time, I am sorry that I accused him of this." Then the question is, " Knowing it to be unfounded?" and his reply is, " Hearing it to be unfounded." That is, you tell me so. I take your opinion, and I am ready to subscribe to it in that way. " I think you must know that it is unfounded. You must be satisfied that it was a perfect delusion. Of course one is anxious, for their sakes, that there should be as unequivocal a recantation as possible of such a charge; there ought to be a solemn disavowal?" "I do not know that I can say more than I have said." "Put it down on paper; you can do it when we are gone; you can say that you have a feeling of regret in having injured the feelings of Mrs. Dyce Sombre and Lord St. Vincent?" "I think it better not to mix Mrs. Dyce Sombre's affairs with her father's." " But they are mixed in the accusation?" "I am ready to express my sorrow. Lord St. Vincent can see that I am sorry for what I said at the time. As to my writing anything to Mrs. Dyce Sombre, that had better be left to the lawyers —there is Mr. Frere on her part, and Mr. Shadwell on mine." So that having made all these accusations against his wife of this incest and adultery, he makes no apology for it, but thinks that it had better be left to the lawyers—Mr. Shadwell on the one side, and Mr. Frere on the other. This is the tenor of the examination which takes place on that occasion. It goes further, but no importance

1856.

Jan. 26th.

DYCE SOMBRE against TROUP, SOLAROLI (intervening), and PRINSEP, and the HON. EAST INDIA COMPANY (also intervening).

1856.

Jan. 26th.

Dyce
Sombre
*against*
Troup,
Solaroli
(intervening),
and
Prinsep,
and the
Hon. East
India
Company
(also inter-
vening).

seems to me to arise upon the rest of the examination. There is a question about Lord Ward, and about his mistaking another person for Lord Ward. They ask him as to that, and he says that he had no doubt that it was the same Lord Ward. " There was no hesitation on my part that it was the same man." " You had no doubt that it was the same person that was introduced to you as Lord Ward at Lord Shrewsbury's?" " No." He met a man, who was not Lord Ward, at Rome, and he mistook him for him, and he engaged him for a certain sum of money to attend to his affairs, and to see that a statue, which was being prepared by Tadolini at Rome, was properly carried into effect. Then there is a question about Madame Solaroli, and Mr. Dyce Sombre says: " There was always some kind of mysteries and hints thrown out about it, that she was not really the child of my father's married wife, and Lord Metcalfe put it all at an end. He said to me when he was going away to America, ' The last proof I can give you of my regard for you, is to tell you what I know about her.' " It appears as if Lord Metcalfe told him that she was not his lawful sister.

This is the examination which takes place in November, 1848, after the preparation made for Mr. Dyce Sombre, by Lord C. and his lady, and Mr. Mahon; and I think it is not to be wondered at that he did not quite satisfy those physicians that those delusions had entirely passed from his mind. Upon this examination, too, it is to be observed that the advisers of Mr. Dyce Sombre did not think it necessary or proper to bring on his petition—it came before the Court at a later period—in the spring, I think, of the next year. But in December, 1848, an examination of a different kind takes place, an examination by Dr. Paris and several other very eminent physicians, who have given their opinion as to the perfect sanity of the deceased at that time; and undoubtedly, coming as it does from persons of their eminence, it is entitled to the greatest respect and to the greatest weight. It was in 1848 that Dr. Paris was applied to, and the application was made by Mr. Mahon—he was the grand conductor of these matters. He had entered into an engagement by which he was to receive a sum of no less than £10,000, if he succeeded in obtaining a supersedeas, and in obtaining the full possession of his property for Mr. Dyce Sombre, the deceased, by the 31st day of December, 1845. He did not succeed in this, as he fully expected to do; and notwithstanding this agreement, Mr. Mahon made an application to the deceased for payment, on account of the work and labour which had been done for him, though, according to the terms and tenor of the agreement, he was to have no reward whatever, unless he succeeded in his attempt. Mr. Dyce Sombre refused at first to make this payment, and the matter was agreed to be referred to arbitration. Mr. Prinsep was one of the referees, and Major Richardson was the other; and they decided that, though he had not been successful, yet it would be but fair and proper that he should be paid for the money which he had expended out of pocket, and also that he should have some remuneration for his work and labour. They accordingly awarded to him the sum which he had paid out of his

1856.

Jan. 2<sup>th</sup>.

DYCE SOMBRE against TROUP, SOLAROLI (intervening), and PRINSEP, and the HON. EAST INDIA COMPANY (also intervening).

1856.

Jan. 26th.

DYCE
SOMBRE
against
TROUP,
SOLAROLI
(intervening),
and
PRINSEP,
and the
HON. EAST
INDIA
COMPANY
(also inter-
vening).

pocket, and they made him an allowance at the rate of about £400 a year for the time during which he had been employed, that being the rate which a Mr. Warwick, who had been employed to attend upon the deceased in the first instance, under the authority of the Court of Chancery, had been allowed. The consequence was, that they awarded him the sum of £2,170 7s. 6d. But very shortly afterwards that agreement is renewed, and Mr. Mahon is to conduct the business again, and he is to receive the £10,000, less the £2170 7s. 6d., in case he is afterwards successful. And then this is the effort which he makes to get the opinion of these eminent men. Part of his business was to find medical men of eminence who would speak to the sanity of the testator.

Dr. Paris says: "In December, 1848, I was applied to by a Mr. Mahon, of whom I had no previous knowledge, to join with other physicians in examining into the state of the deceased's mind." And he goes on to say: "I suggested the addition of Dr. Mayo, who was called in accordingly. I had had put into my hands the opinion of Drs. Bright, Southey, Martin, and Sir James Clark." It appears that this was the note of the examination which I have referred to: "I saw the deceased once or twice alone, and five times in consultation with the other physicians at Mivart's Hotel. My visits were of three or four hours' duration. I had had put into my hands the opinion of Drs. Bright, Southey, Martin, and Sir James Clark. My first object was to satisfy myself as to the deceased's general deportment and condition of mind. To me that was quite satisfactory. It had none of the character of

1856.

Jan. 26th.
——
Dyce
Sombre
*against*
Troup,
Solaroli
(intervening),
and
Prinsep,
and the
Hon. East
India
Company
(also inter-
vening).

unnatural excitement or hallucination; his manner was tranquil, courteous, and gentlemanlike." It appears that such was his general character, and his general mode of conducting himself. Sir James Clark speaks of that; and also at Paris he seems to have conducted himself in the same tranquil and courteous manner. " The next object was to consider what had been communicated in the report of the physicians I have named, and the specific alleged delusions. The first was that of having seen and negotiated with Lord Ward at Rome for forwarding the monument to the memory of the Begum to India, when it was clearly established that Lord Ward was not in Rome at the time. Upon inquiry, we came to the conclusion that the deceased had either mistaken some other person for Lord Ward, or that a hoax had been played upon him." It is possible that it might have been so, though the deceased could not divest himself of the notion that it was the same person whom he had met as Lord Ward at Lord Shrewsbury's. He was acquainted with him in this country; he meets with him at Rome; he thinks that he is the same person; and he employs him, believing him to be Lord Ward. Then Dr. Paris goes on to say: " What at first sight appeared extraordinary, as to the idea of a person of Lord Ward's high station accepting such or any sum, is explicable on the consideration that the deceased was a foreigner. But he was mistaken as to the man; and when Lord Ward was shown to him in England, he at once admitted and never afterwards hesitated to acknowledge his mistake. His notion of the illegitimacy of Madame Solaroli had a foundation in fact. It may have been a mistake, but it was

VOL. I.                    H

1856.

Jan. 26th.
———
DYCE
SOMBRE
*against*
TROUP,
SOLAROLI
(intervening),
and
PRINSEP,
and the
HON. EAST
INDIA
COMPANY
(also inter-
vening).

not a creation of his own mind." Now we shall hear
the reason : " Major Bere, of his Majesty's Hussars,
affirmed that her illegitimacy was an admitted and
known fact." The other witnesses say that there
was a letter of Major Bere produced to show that
it was an admitted and acknowledged fact. But
what turns out to be the case when the genuine letter
of Major Bere is looked at? Why, that Major
Bere says that he cannot speak to that fact; his
words are—" which I cannot speak to." This makes
all the difference in the case. It shows how those
learned physicians were deceived upon that point.
There was this question as to insanity. I am not
saying now whether it was an insane delusion, or
whether it was not; but as to this delusion of the
Baroness Solaroli being illegitimate, Dr. Paris and
these gentlemen seem to consider that to be quite
cleared up, and that it was no fiction and no delusion
in the mind of the deceased, because it was asserted by
Major Bere that it was an admitted and known fact,
whereas Major Bere says no such thing. Major
Bere, on being asked to speak to it, says that he
cannot do so—" which I cannot do." " It has been
regarded," Dr. Paris deposes, " as strangely inconsistent that, under such a belief, he should have
permitted her to be called his lawful sister in the
instrument settling on her £20,000." Now undoubtedly he made a very large settlement upon
this lady, the Baroness Solaroli, after the Begum's
death. They were always brought up together.
Mrs. Troup is the admitted lawful sister of the
deceased; and the Baroness Solaroli was brought up
in the same manner in which Mrs. Troup was. She
was always admitted by the deceased himself to be

his lawful sister in India, because it was not till a late period—according to his own statement, and under his own hand—it was not till about the year 1846, that he took into his head this notion of the illegitimacy of the Baroness Solaroli. That is the time from which he dates it; and the only evidence that there is even as to any report of the Baroness Solaroli, while in India, being illegitimate, is to be found, I think, in the evidence of Mr. Craigie, who says that he heard it mentioned in common conversation there; but there is no other evidence whatever. Her Highness the Begum always treated her as the lawful sister; so did Captain and Mrs. Troup; and the Begum's expression is spoken to by Dr. Drever, when speaking of these two girls and of Mr. Dyce Sombre: "They are all out of one womb." Now Mr. Dyce Sombre does not at all doubt that the Baroness Solaroli was the child of his father, but he says that it was by a different mother. That is a strong expression of her Highness the Begum, that they all came out of the same womb. She treated the Baroness Solaroli precisely in the same manner as she treated Mrs. Troup, the other daughter; and when the marriage took place between the parties, she treated her in the same way; and though there was a difficulty with regard to the baptismal certificate of Madame Solaroli, that matter was cleared up to the satisfaction of the parties at the time. There is no doubt that she was married as the lawful daughter, as Mrs. Troup was. The Begum gave the Baroness Solaroli and Mrs. Troup rather unequal sums, I believe, but she gave each of them a pretty large sum upon their marriage; and after the death of her Highness the

1856.

Jan. 26th.

DYCE
SOMBRE
*against*
TROUP,
SOLAROLI
(intervening),
and
PRINSEP,
and the
HON. EAST
INDIA
COMPANY
(also intervening).

1856.

Jan. 26th.

DYCE
SOMBRE
*against*
TROUP,
SOLAROLI
(intervening),
and
PRINSEP,
and the
HON. EAST
INDIA
COMPANY
(also inter-
vening).

Begum, Mr. Dyce Sombre gives them still larger sums, so as to make them equal; for I think that the share which he gives to the Baroness Solaroli is larger than that which is given to Mrs. Troup. However, it was to put them upon an equality in that respect; and in the deed by which he conveys the property to her, she is described as his lawful sister throughout, and in that way she is treated and so considered by the deceased himself down to the year 1846. Then it is affected to be believed by him that she was illegitimate; and his assertions are most extraordinary in this respect. He says that this illegitimacy was communicated to him as a last act of favour by Sir Charles Metcalfe, before he left for Canada, and that is where he gets his information; but it does not appear that Sir Charles Metcalfe knew anything about it. According to the account of Mr. Prinsep himself, when he is interrogated upon it, he says what he heard from Sir Charles Metcalfe was, that the children he saw running about when he called on the Begum were presented to him as children of Colonel Dyce and the Chotee Begum; that the deceased was one of the children whom he saw running about when he called on the Begum, and so probably was Mrs. Troup. He could not say whether Madame Solaroli was or not : Mr. Prinsep presumes, because she was the younger. And this is interpreted into Mr. Dyce Sombre being right, and that Sir Charles Metcalfe confirmed that opinion. But how does he act? He does not give a certificate or anything in his own hand-writing to show that such was his belief, or that he had any notion of that kind. But what does Mr. Dyce Sombre say? Why that Sir Charles

1856.

Jan. 26th.

DYCE
SOMBRE
*against*
TROUP,
SOLAROLI
(intervening),
and
PRINSEP,
and the
HON. EAST
INDIA
COMPANY
(also inter-
vening).

Metcalfe, though he would not entrust him with a paper of that sort, sent it to my Lord John Russell; and that my Lord John Russell was in possession of this document, which would prove this part of the case; and he prints a letter in his publication, in the year 1849, about the time of his making his will. This letter is an application to Lord John Russell to give up this document, and a sort of hint that he shall have £1000 if he will do so, and this is in the handwriting of Mr. Dyce Sombre himself; there it is, "£1000" in the corner; and he makes this application for the paper which had been entrusted to Lord John Russell before Sir Charles Metcalfe sailed, in the imagination and according to the delusion of Mr. Dyce Sombre himself.

But to return to this examination. Dr. Paris says to the third interrogatory: "No one was present during the examination who was not professionally concerned in it." It turns out from the evidence of the other physicians, that when any difficulty arose, or anything required explanation, Mr. Mahon or Mr. Prinsep was called in. "No one was present during the examination who was not professionally concerned in it. I remember seeing a letter or letters upon the subject of the legitimacy of Madame Solaroli; that of Major Bere is the only one that I now distinctly remember. I think that in the course of the inquiry the statement in that letter was confirmed to us verbally by Mr. Prinsep." The statement was, that it was an admitted and well-known fact. Now I think Mr. Prinsep could hardly have done so; there must have been some mistake about that. He certainly, in his letter to

1856.

Jan. 26th.

Dyce
Sombre
*against*
Troup,
Solaroli
(Intervening),
and
Prinsep,
and the
Hon. East
India
Company
(also inter-
vening).

Mr. Dyce Sombre, says: "You are right in saying that that was Lord Metcalfe's impression." Here is this letter that is produced of Major Bere, where, as I stated before, it is quite the contrary. Bere says that he cannot bear witness to it. Dr. Paris says : "I think that in the course of the inquiry the statement in that letter was confirmed to us verbally by Mr. Prinsep. I think it probable that I did see the letter now shown to me at page 486 of the volume,* or rather the exhibit No. 1, but I have no recollection of it." He does not know whether he saw the letter or not. Now that letter, in this book which was shown to him, at page 486, No. 1, is not the letter of Major Bere. I presume that what did take place before these learned phy- sicians was that they said: "There is a letter of Major Bere, in which he says that it is an admitted and known fact." Whether it was the genuine letter, or whether it was this mutilated letter, so mutilated by Mr. Dyce Sombre himself, does not appear with sufficient accuracy, though I am in- clined to think, from a consideration of the evidence, that it was really the genuine letter which was upon the table at the time. Some of the medical gentle- men who have been examined say that there were certain letters and papers put upon the table, but beyond that they cannot speak to the handwriting.

Dr. Paris says, in another part of his evidence : " Lord C., in a letter to Mr. Mahon, distinctly states that the deceased was quite correct in saying that at Brighton, and he might also state

---

* This volume was "The Refutation" printed in Paris by Mr. Dyce Sombre, which was brought in as evidence, and is frequently referred to in the case.

upon other occasions, he, Lord C., strongly recommended him to be very circumspect in his conduct." I have read those letters, and I think they are well described. "With respect to his suspicion of the hostility of the East India Company, on the ground of his presumed pecuniary claims, I am satisfied from documents that such suspicions might be very naturally entertained in a sound mind. I have reason to believe it anything but a delusion. The indecency and grossly indelicate language with which the deceased is charged in his quarrel with General Ventura is not unconformable with Eastern manners. An undue weight has been given to a very gross Hindostanee phrase, used by General Ventura as expressive of his contempt; and by giving to it a literal translation, its true meaning has been unwittingly distorted." Well, but he must have taken the account here given by this gentleman, Mr. Dyce Sombre, upon the occasion. He had no opportunity of knowing what the evidence of General Ventura was upon the occasion. Is it a mere gross Hindostanee expression, or anything of that sort, that takes place? Such expressions were used, but, according to General Ventura, they came from Mr. Dyce Sombre, and not from him. But it does not rest, as Dr. Paris seems to suppose it does, upon a mere conversation between these parties, or upon the gross expressions which may have been used by either the one or the other of them; but it is an act of indecency which this poor gentleman commits at Brussels upon this occasion. There had been a previous rencontre at Baden-Baden, and afterwards at the railway station at Malines, and then some

1856.

Jan. 29th.

DYCE
SOMBRE
*against*
TROUP,
SOLAROLI
(intervening),
and
PRINSEP,
and the
HON. EAST
INDIA
COMPANY
(also intervening).

1856.

Jan. 26th.

Dyce
Sombre
*against*
Troup,
Solaroli
(Intervening),
and
Prinsep,
and the
Hon. East
India
Company
(also inter-
vening).

conversation takes place again at Brussels; it is in front of the hotel, where General Ventura and his wife and another lady are in a carriage; and in the presence of the landlady of the hotel Mr. Dyce Sombre comes up, he spits upon the carriage, and then he opens his dress and exposes his person to these ladies, and to all who are present. Therefore it does not resolve itself into a Hindostanee expression, or anything of the sort—it is the act of an insane man, for so I must consider him; because undoubtedly Mr. Dyce Sombre, had he been in his senses, having been brought up in a clergyman's family, having lived with officers, and having been some time in this country, must have known that it was not an act which he should have committed in Europe, and I apprehend that it was not an act that would have been committed in India or anywhere else: it does not arise from Asiatic feeling merely. An exhibition of this sort is made openly in the face of day, before the landlady, and before other persons who are assembled, and who might have been called to contradict General Ventura. Undoubtedly, I must give credence to General Ventura. I see no reason to discredit him whatever. He is a man whose character is entirely unimpeached; he is a man of high station; and he speaks to a fact which takes place in his presence. He acts upon it; he applies to the police; and the consequence is, that the police interfere.

Then, again, Dr. Paris, not knowing the whole facts of the case, refers to the statements as to the conduct of the deceased in the water-closet. That I do not dwell upon. I omit all the evidence both on the one side and on the other. I pass by that

which took place at Paris, where, undoubtedly, he
was received in good society, and where, undoubtedly, he may have conducted himself with great
propriety, because that is entirely consistent with
a case of monomania.  I put, likewise, out of sight
the conduct of Mr. Dyce Sombre in the profligate
life which he led with prostitutes of the lowest
description.  I do not think that either the one
is to be considered as proof of his having been of
sane mind, or the other of his having been under
an insane delusion.  Then Dr. Paris goes on to
speak as to his jealousy: " Born in a harem and
accustomed to its habits up to the thirtieth year of
his age—a period of life at which the opinions and
prejudices of early years are too deeply rooted to
be easily altered or corrected by subsequent changes
of residence or condition—jealousy of women is an
overwhelming passion in the Asiatic mind, and
evidently existed to an extreme degree in that of
the deceased, and will go far to explain, if not to pal-
liate in some degree, various acts of violence.  And
although there was nothing in the conduct of the
deceased's wife to excite a feeling of jealousy in a
well-educated European, yet it is conceivable that
a person circumstanced as the deceased, and to
which I have before alluded, might take an unjust
offence, and entertain suspicion, without falling
within the category of insanity."  Undoubtedly,
any person, whether an Asiatic or European, may
fall into an unfounded jealousy, and may entertain
suspicion that his wife is guilty without any sufficient foundation, or without any foundation, and yet
not be of unsound mind.  But how is that to apply
to a person who declares that his wife has been guilty

1856.

Jan. 26th.

DYCE
SOMBRE
*against*
THOUP,
SOLAROLI
(intervening),
and
PRINSEP,
and the
HON. EAST
INDIA
COMPANY
(also inter-
vening).

1856.

Jan. 26th.

DYCE
SOMBRE
*against*
TROUP,
SOLAROLI
(intervening),
and
PRINSEP,
and the
HON. EAST
INDIA
COMPANY
(also inter-
vening).

of incest with her own father before marriage; that she has lived with Sir F. B. (for which there is no foundation) for three weeks, or for three days, before the time of her marriage; that she was guilty of adultery with all the waiters in the Clarendon Hotel, and that she was guilty of the same crime with shopmen, and with soldiers, and with everybody, when there is no shadow of pretence for anything of the kind? That is a very different thing from merely considering this as a case of jealousy without sufficient foundation. It does not at all take it out of the category of insane delusions, whatever the opinion of Dr. Paris may be, because Dr. Paris did not know the extent of the delusion under which the deceased laboured.

As to the delusions having passed away, let us see what Lord C.'s own feeling was. " He answered," when Lord C. spoke to him, "more by a shake of the head than in words. He never would allow her innocence; he never yielded the belief that she had been unfaithful to him." Why, according to the evidence of Lord C. himself, who persuaded him to say that he had given up these delusions, he entertained them to the last moment of his life, and he never gave up the belief of her infidelity down to the latest period.

The other physicians depose very much to the same effect as Dr. Paris. Dr. Copland examines the deceased in 1848. He says that he was called to see him at Dover, in September, 1846. " That was at the suggestion to me of a Mr. Mahon, a stranger, whom I viewed in the light of an agent of the deceased; but exactly in what relation he stood to him I did not know, either then or at the more recent date of which I will now depose, December, 1848, when I again saw the deceased, at his request." Then he speaks of having had five private interviews with him, and of having read the reports of Drs. Bright and Southey, and the notes of the examination in November, 1848. He goes on to say: "My examination of the deceased was most searching, and calculated to test the character, notions, prejudices, temper, and disposition, as well as to determine the existence, of any insane delusion." He says: "The charge of an indecent fracas with General Ventura could no more be considered a sign of insanity, than a quarrel between other persons respecting any matter, topic, expression, &c., can be so considered." So that he regards it as a mere common quarrel between two persons; and that the circumstance is not to be considered as more indicating insanity than such a quarrel would do, omitting all mention of the indecent action of this gentleman. He says: "The most important delusion imputed to the deceased, is his belief in the infidelity of his wife; and this belief, when duly considered with reference to the circumstances in which he had been placed in early life, and in this country, when viewed in connexion with his origin, his education, his society in India, and the society in which he was thrown in this country, amounted in its most exalted form merely to an exaggerated form of jealousy." And a pretty exalted form it was, I think, considering the nature of the charges. He says: "First, the deceased was three-fourths a native Asiatic" (that is rather more than he is proved to have been) "and one-fourth an European by descent." I suppose Mr. Mahon

1856.

Jan. 26th.

DYCE SOMBRE against TROUP, SOLAROLI (intervening), and PRINSEP, and the HON. EAST INDIA COMPANY (also intervening).

1856.

Jan. 26th.

DYCE
SOMBRE
against
TROUP,
SOLAROLI
(Intervening),
and
PRINSEP,
and the
HON. EAST
INDIA
COMPANY
(also Inter-
vening).

or somebody told him so at that time. The deceased himself always insisted that he was an Englishman; and he said, though born in India, yet, from the blood which was in him, he had a right to be tried in an English Court and by Englishmen, and that he would not submit to the Indian Courts. "He was educated and lived among the higher class of native Indian society until he was 30 or upwards of 30 years of age." That is an incorrect account, again, which is given to this gentleman; it was not the case that he was educated by these people, and lived with them until he was thirty years of age. Dr. Copland says, as to the excitement of jealousy: "There may, too, have been circumstances arising out of the manners, bearing, and even conduct, of Mrs. Dyce Sombre, previously to and after marriage, which, although not admitting of an unfavourable construction in the society of this country, might yet have occasioned the most exaggerated jealousies in the mind of an Asiatic circumstanced as the deceased was from his birth up to his arrival in this country (soon after which period he became acquainted with his wife), jealousies which, however exaggerated and intense, would have nothing in common or to do with insanity, nor to be considered as any indication of unsoundness of mind. Much stress was laid on the fact of its being incestuous, but incest (and of that particular kind) is not so uncommon in India, or, as I regret to know, in this country." But with respect to all the other matters, his charges of the adultery of his wife in the open park, and his proposal of being restored to her through the means of the Archbishop of Canterbury selecting a virgin for him, and the other things which he demanded

—these, I think, can hardly be accounted for upon the plea of his being an Asiatic.

I believe the evidence of the other physicians all goes to the same effect. I do not think that they carry the matter any further; they are very eminent men. Dr. Paris is the President of the College of Physicians, and Dr. Mayo is a person certainly of very great eminence. They consider that the deceased was sane at the time. But then I say that they had not the whole matter before them. They had nothing but the examination which had taken place before the other physicians, in November, 1848, or, if they had, they had not a full account given them of all which had passed in the year 1843, and of the proposal about the Archbishop of Canterbury, and of all those matters. With respect to General Ventura, also, they think that it was only a quarrel between him and the deceased, like any common quarrel in the streets. They are not aware that Mr. Dyce Sombre unbuttoned his breeches and exposed his person in the manner in which he is represented to have done to those ladies, and in public. I cannot, then, consider that this testimony, given by these gentlemen, however eminent they are, and however much to be relied on as speaking the truth, is sufficient to upset the testimony of the witnesses who examined the deceased so shortly previously in the very preceding month of November—persons of equal skill, who were acquainted with the particular nature and the extent of his insanity, who knew what his prevailing opinions and his prevailing delusions were, examining him apart from Mr. Mahon and apart from Mr. Prinsep, and knowing all that had before passed. The con-

1856.

Jan. 26th.

DYCE SOMBRE against TROUP, SOLAROLI (intervening), and PRINSEP, and the HON. EAST INDIA COMPANY (also intervening).

1856.

Jan. 26th.

DYCE
SOMBRE
*against*
TROUP.
SOLAROLI
(intervening),
and
PRINSEP,
and the
HON. EAST
INDIA
COMPANY
(also inter-
vening).

clusion at which they arrived, I think, must be deemed to be the right conclusion; and I therefore hold that at this time, in the year 1848, in December as well as in November, 1848, the deceased continued to be labouring under insane delusions, though he attempted to conceal them, according to the advice which had been given him by Mr. Mahon, and by my Lord C. and Lady C. He could not bring his mind to say that these delusions had passed away—he fenced with the questions that were put to him. There was not a frank and free admission that he had been labouring under insane delusions, and that he was willing to do the best he could to make compensation for the injuries and for the calumnies which he had thrown upon respectable people during the time that he had been labouring under these delusions. I think it was merely for the purpose of deceiving, and for no other purpose, that he conducted himself cunningly, as he did.

So, again, as to the physicians who were attesting witnesses to the will; they are, I think, four in number. Three of them attested the will, and two of those same persons attested the codicil, with the addition of Dr. Sigmond, who was then brought in for the first time. Dr. Olliffe is a physician who seems to have known more of the deceased than most of them, and he is one of the attesting witnesses. They made a joint report between them. Dr. Sigmond is an English physician of some eminence, resident in Paris; he had seen Mr. Dyce Sombre in England, but had a very slight degree of acquaintance with him, and he was called in to be an attesting witness to this codicil. Dr. M'Carthy was the person who introduced him.

He went to the lodgings of the deceased, and he says: "Dr. M'Carthy introduced him to me, or me to him rather, as a previous acquaintance. Mr. Dyce Sombre recollected our former meeting, and spoke of the health of the prince. He then told me that he intended to publish a work on the treatment that he had received from the lawyers and persons calling themselves his friends." Now this is a most important introduction, I think, the introduction of this subject between the parties; because the first thing the deceased tells him is, that he intends in a publication to expose this matter; and that publication actually takes place very shortly after this, for it is in the month of August, 1849, the very same month in which the codicil is executed, that he publishes this refutation, which of itself affords pretty conclusive proof, I think, of the insanity of the deceased at the time when it was published. Dr. Sigmond goes on to say: "He spoke of this with great calmness of mind and apparent knowledge of the subject. He then told me that he had already made a will, to which he now wished to add a codicil. Dr. M'Carthy added: 'And it is proposed that you (I, that is) should witness it.' I said that after the conversation that had passed between them and myself, I should have no objection to sign it, if the deceased declared that he had duly considered the nature of the codicil, and that it was his own free will, uninfluenced by others. He said that as those who might have expected to benefit by his will had not behaved well to him, he had made such disposition of his property as he thought best. Some further conversation followed, in which the deceased referred to the instrument itself, as it lay

1856.

Jan. 26th.

DYCE
SOMBRE
*against*
TROUP,
SOLAROLI
(intervening),
and
PRINSEP,
and the
HON. EAST
INDIA
COMPANY
(also inter-
vening).

1856.

Jan. 26th.

DYCE
SOMBRE
*against*
TROUP,
SOLAROLI
(intervening),
and
PRINSEP,
and the
HON. EAST
INDIA
COMPANY
(also inter-
vening).

before him : he had brought it into the room with him, and was then sitting with it before him on the table. Dr. M'Carthy remarked that it had been made or prepared with great care, and from the deceased's own instructions. Mr. Dyce Sombre made some observation upon the seal, of which the wax impression was, as far as I recollect, already affixed. I was in earnest conversation with him, and possibly it might have been done then in my presence, but I do not remember it, or the lighting of a candle. It was then about the middle· of the day; the appointment had been made for twelve o'clock. The topics of conversation with me and the deceased were chiefly the book" (that is the refutation) "and the codicil, together with his reason for making the disposition contained in the codicil and the will." Upon the subject of the book, he says: "I have seen the book inquired of and shown to me. I have read parts of it. I forget when exactly it was, but some time in the year before ˙last (1850). I received from the deceased a message that a copy was left for me at Galignani's. I had heard him say, when he signed the codicil, that he was writing a life of himself, which I suppose might have reference to this volume. I gave him no advice as to not publishing it. I merely said that I thought it would be interesting for every one to know what he had to say upon his own case. I told him that whatever he did should be done with great temper and forbearance, for there were plenty of people ready to find fault. I have really no means of judging or giving any but a conjectural opinion on the subject of his delusions, real or alleged, having purposely avoided all inquiry into them. I have not read enough of the book." So that this gentleman will not undertake to depose either one way or the other. "I have really no means of judging or giving any but a conjectural opinion" as to the state of the deceased's mind. He says, that his opinion from what he saw on that particular occasion was, that at that time he was of sound mind; but as to his being sane or insane at other particular times, he says that he cannot give any but a conjectural opinion, and that he can say nothing whatever about it.

Dr. Olliffe is another person who subscribed this will. They all say that they believe the deceased to have been of sound mind, but Dr. Olliffe is a person who states that he was labouring under a delusion as to poison. He had attended him before when he was labouring under delusions, and he thought there was poison in the brandy, and he was not satisfied in that respect. Then he says: "What influenced me, I must confess—and as I believe the others also—was, that the act of the Lord Chancellor, in conceding to him the control of all that was available as income, was a virtual admission of his capability to make a will." Now that is what he goes upon, and he says he believes that the others went upon it also; that the Lord Chancellor, who at first allowed him only £4000 a-year, was induced afterwards, considering that his property had been managed well—that is, that the income had been well expended—to give him the whole of his income, but refused to give him the power over the fund. Dr. Olliffe says

1856.

Jan. 26th.

DYCE
SOMBRE
against
TROUP,
SOLAROLI
(intervening),
and
PRINSEP,
and the
HON. EAST
INDIA
COMPANY
(also intervening).

1856.

Jan. 26th.

Dyce
Sombre
*against*
Troup,
Solaroli
(intervening),
and
Prinsep,
and the
Hon. East
India
Company
(also inter-
vening).

that is what influenced him, and he believes that it
influenced the other physicians; that as the Chancellor thought he was sane enough to have the
management and expenditure of his own income,
he ought to be entrusted with the power of making
a will—that he was sane enough for that purpose.
But that would be contrary to all the principles
which are applicable to cases of this kind. A
person may have the power of managing his property to a certain extent exceedingly well, and of
spending his income, and yet be labouring under insane delusions. And if there is any insane delusion
whatever operating on the mind of the party, and
he still entertains any opinion founded on delusion,
he is, according to the law and practice of this
court, and all the decided cases, incapable of
making a will. Therefore Dr. Olliffe, founding his
opinion chiefly upon this circumstance of the deceased being intrusted with his income, and believing that the others do so too, detracts very
much from the weight which would otherwise be
attributable to the opinions of these learned persons. He goes on to say, not only that that is
what operated upon his mind, but he adds this:
" Had all then come to my knowledge of which I
have since been informed, I might have made a
more searching examination; but I was satisfied
with the inquiries I made in reference to what I
then knew, which included the reports of the physicians in England on either side, and the judgment of the Lord Chancellor in the spring of that
year." So that what he had before him——namely,
the examinations of the physicians——that is to say,
the examinations of the physicians on the one side

1856.

Jan. 26th.
____
DYCE
SOMBRE
*against*
TROUP,
SOLAROLI
(intervening),
and
PRINSEP,
and the
HON. EAST
INDIA
COMPANY
(also inter-
vening).

in November, 1848, and on the other side in December, 1848, and the decision of the Chancellor
as to the management by Mr. Dyce Sombre of his
property, and the circumstance of his being entrusted with the power over his own income,
induced him to attest the execution of this will.

I think one of the other physicians, instead of
speaking of the expenditure of the income, thinks
that the Lord Chancellor had given Mr. Dyce
Sombre the entire property, and the entire control
over it. However, undoubtedly the execution of
this will and of the codicil in the presence of those
four physicians, is a very important circumstance
in this matter.

But supposing these gentlemen thought, as no
doubt they did think, that Mr. Dyce Sombre was
in a sane state at the time of the execution of
this will, in June, 1849, and again in the month
of August, 1849, when he made this codicil, what
are we to say to the publication of the book,
"The Refutation," which took place very shortly
afterwards, which was in a state of preparation
at the very time at which this will and codicil
were executed? This "Refutation" was in progress
at the time, and the deceased was assisted in the
compilation and manufacture of it by a Mr. Mon-
tucci. According to many statements in that "Refutation," the deceased could hardly have been of
sound mind when he issued it. But take it only
as to the point respecting the Baroness Solaroli,
to which I have before adverted, which was one of
his recent insane delusions, supposing it to be an
insane delusion. He had always considered her
legitimate till the year 1846, and there was every

1856.

Jan. 26th.

Dyce
Sombre
*against*
Troup,
Solaroli
(intervening),
and
Prinsep,
and the
Hon. East
India
Company
(also inter-
vening).

reason to believe that she was so; but, forsooth, all at once the deceased takes it into his head that she is illegitimate, and in the book it is stated (though the fact was quite the contrary) that she had always been reputed to be illegitimate; but he says that all at once she is made to come out as a lawful sister, whereas she had always been reputed, until that time, as illegitimate. But when he comes to give an account of this illegitimacy, it is founded upon that which I have before mentioned —namely, the communication from Lord Metcalfe, before he left England, as a last mark of his favour to the deceased; and then there is this letter, which is left in the custody of Lord John Russell; and we have this poor insane person writing to Lord John Russell, and intimating that he may receive £1000, if he will produce the document. Lord John Russell can do nothing of the kind; and that matter drops to the ground.

Again, in this "Refutation" there is a republication and repetition about the poisoning, and a number of other things, and about his meeting with General Ventura at Kissengen and Brussels, in 1845; of Mr. Dyce Sombre's suspicions and quarrels with him, all of which, according to the evidence of his own valet, Roulin, had no foundation whatever in fact, because up to the latest moment (I am going back to the Clarendon Hotel now), after he had taken his wife down to her father's, Lord St. Vincent's, at Meaford, he returned to the Clarendon Hotel, and he desired to be called in the morning, in order that he might see his friend, General Ventura, off, who was going to India; and yet when General Ventura is gone, he takes it into his head that he has been committing adultery with his wife, he despatches a challenge after him. There is a second challenge; he assaults him at Baden-Baden; and finally there is the scene at Brussels to which I have already alluded.

Again, the deceased says that this "Refutation" is to be forwarded to everybody, and he has 1000 copies of it left in the lobbies of the House of Lords and the House of Commons. He writes to her Majesty the Queen upon the subject of his disputes with the East India Company. Of course he has a letter in reply, by command of her Majesty. But the whole train of these matters is repeated over again in this book, which is called "The Refutation," which is published immediately after the execution of the will and the codicil.

Therefore, under these circumstances, I can come to no other conclusion than that the deceased did, in the year 1843, labour under the various insane delusions which have been adverted to; and that those delusions, or at least many of them, had not passed away, but that he continued to entertain them at the time when he executed this will and codicil; and at a later period, when the book called the "Refutation" was issued for distribution by him. I make no mention of the other book, namely, the "Memoir," which he wrote against Baron Solaroli in three different languages, English, French, and Italian, and his going before him to every town, and distributing it at the different hotels, to prejudice Baron Solaroli. That appears to me an act of insanity in itself, looking at the charges contained in that "Memoir," because Baron Solaroli seems to have been a person of very high character. He

1856.

Jan. 26th.

DYCE
SOMBRE
*against*
TROUP,
SOLAROLI
(intervening),
and
PRINSEP,
and the
HON. EAST
INDIA
COMPANY
(also intervening).

1856.

Jan. 26th.

DYOB
SOMBRE
*against*
TROUP,
SOLAROLI
(intervening),
and
PRINSEP,
and the
HON. EAST
INDIA
COMPANY
(also inter-
vening).

bore a high commission in the army; he is now a member of the House of Representatives, or the Senate, in his own country, and he appears to stand very high in the estimation of all persons there. And yet these papers were distributed by this poor man, giving an account of the Baron Solaroli as if he was a person of the lowest extraction, and guilty of the gravest crimes; stating that he had been a cook in the service of the Marquis of Hertford, and that he had been guilty of murdering his own father, specifying the time and place, and making various other charges against him. Under all these circumstances, therefore, I can come to no other conclusion than that the deceased was labouring under insanity at the time in question, though he attempted to conceal it, according to the advice which he had received; that the delusion was still present in his mind; and consequently, according to the principles which prevail in these courts, and according to all the cases which were cited at the Bar, and most of which are referred to in the case which I have mentioned, namely, the case of *Waring* v. *Waring*, according to the principles there laid down, I must necessarily come to the conclusion, that this gentleman was incapable of making his will. I therefore must pronounce against the will and codicil.

With respect to the costs in this case, I must confess that I have found considerable difficulty; but I think that I should not discharge my duty with the firmness with which I ought, unless I were to condemn the parties in the costs of this suit. When I see how this poor man was prepared for the pur-

pose of undergoing his examinations—how he was
urged by various persons to conceal his thoughts—
not to give up his delusions, but to conceal them,
and to pretend that he had none remaining, in order
that he might pass his examination, might get his
supersedeas, and might recover the whole of his
property—when I see what has taken place with
regard to Mr. Mahon, and with respect to Mr.
Prinsep, though, undoubtedly, the letters which
were written by him were not precisely of the same
tenor, and I think not so blameable as those which
were written by my Lord Combermere and Lady
Combermere, urging the concealment of the delusion—I say, that I think, under all the circumstances of the case, I am bound to pronounce
against the will with costs.   I certainly should not
have thought of condemning the East India Company in the expenses which have been occasioned
by them with respect to this will.   It might, perhaps, have been their duty to have an investigation to see whether this will was well founded,
whether it was the act of a capable testator or not,
since the contents of it tended so much to the
benefit of the persons living within their jurisdiction and under their government.   But they
have thought proper to make altogether a common
case with the executor who has propounded the
will, and therefore I cannot well distinguish the
one from the other.   They have come to a mutual
agreement that the expenses are to be borne, if I
understand it rightly, by the East India Company;
they are the parties who are to bear them; and
this investigation would, probably, not have gone
on, or not have gone to this length, unless it had

1856.

Jan. 26th.

DYCE
SOMBRE
*against*
TROUP,
SOLAROLI
(intervening),
and
PRINSEP,
and the
HON. EAST
INDIA
COMPANY
(also inter
vening).

1856.

Jan. 26th.

DYCE
SOMBRE
*against*
TROUP,
SOLAROLI
(intervening),
and
PRINSEP,
and the
HON. EAST
INDIA
COMPANY
(also inter-
vening).

been for that understanding between the parties. I think, therefore, that I am bound to condemn the executor, and also the East India Company, in the costs of these proceedings. And I accordingly condemn those parties in costs.

———

This case was appealed, and on the 1st of July the Judicial Committee affirmed the sentence, pronouncing against the will and codicil; but varied the decree as to costs, giving no costs against the appellants (the Executor and East India Company), but allowing them one set of costs only, including the costs of the appeal.

# ARCHES COURT OF CANTERBURY.

## HUNT v. HUNT.

*Husband and wife—Adultery—Nonconsummation of the marriage—Medical evidence.*

1856.

Feb. 13th.

THIS was a cause of divorce by reason of adultery promoted by W. G. Hunt against his wife C. M. Hunt. The libel pleaded the marriage in January, 1845, consummation and cohabitation at different places till February, 1853; the commencement of a criminal intercourse in the summer of 1852 with M. B. P.; that in July, 1852, the wife and P. remained for one or two hours locked up alone in a private sitting-room, with the blinds down, at the Foley Arms at Malvern; in July and August, 1852, frequent visits by the wife alone to the lodgings of P. in Worcester, on all or most of which occasions the blinds of the room in which the parties were were pulled down; in September, 1852, visits by P. two or three times a week to the wife whilst staying alone for three weeks at the Belle Vue Hotel, Malvern, and his remaining there with her till 10 or 11 o'clock at night; that in December, 1852, the wife, accompanied by P., went to Oldbury, and remained locked up together in a sitting-room at the Talbot Inn with the blinds down; and the commission of adultery on each of such occasions; a verdict, and

A. and B. were married in 1845, and lived together till 1853. In a suit brought by A. against B. for adultery, B. pleaded her virginity, and recriminated. A. admitted that he had not consummated the marriage, and the medical evidence proved the virginity.—Held, that B. was not guilty of adultery, and was entitled to a separation from A. on the ground of his adultery, which was proved.

£50 damages. The libel also pleaded a letter from the wife to the husband, written at the time of separation, in which she admitted her attachment for P.

A responsive allegation was brought in on behalf of the wife, the 1st article of which pleaded as follows :—" Whereas it is pleaded in the 3d article of the libel given in and admitted in this cause on the part and behalf of W. G. H. that the said W. G. H. and C. M. H. his wife consummated their said marriage, and from and after the same lived and cohabited together as husband and wife at the several places and times therein mentioned; and whereas in the 4th, 6th, 7th, 8th, and 9th articles of the said libel it is pleaded that the said C. M. H. committed adultery at different times and places with a person therein set forth. Now, the same is therein falsely and untruly pleaded, for the party proponent expressly alleges and propounds that although the said W. G. H. and C. M. H. did from and after the said marriage live and cohabit together as husband and wife, yet that the said W. G. H. and C. M. H. never did in fact consummate their said marriage, and that the said C. M. H. now is a virgin, and hath never been carnally known by man, as will appear on inspection of her person by physicians, surgeons, and other competent persons," &c. The 2d article pleaded admissions by the husband to several persons that the marriage had never in fact been consummated. Several following articles pleaded the knowledge by the husband of the intimacy subsisting between the wife and P. ; the commission of adultery by the husband; and "that no evidence was taken in the action brought by the said W. G. H. against the said M. B. P. ;

that the verdict was for £50 nominal damages; that
the said M. B. P. was at the time in Mexico, and
had been at the time, as stated by his counsel, when
the said verdict was given, sent abroad by his relatives before the said action was brought; that the
said verdict was given by consent of the relations of
the said M. B. P., and that he was wholly unaware .
of the said verdict having been consented to.

This allegation was admitted after opposition.
The evidence of two medical men proved the first
article of the responsive allegation.   The facts
pleaded as to the wife's intimacy with and the visits
of and to P., as well as the circumstances alleged to
have occurred at the Foley Arms and the Talbot
Inn, were generally established, but there was no
proof of any single act of indecent familiarity.  The
adultery of the husband was established and admitted by his counsel.*

*Addams* and *Curteis* for the husband.

The facts proved against the wife, taken with her
admitted attachment to P., establish her adultery.
The evidence of virginity cannot be relied on, for
many cases show that those signs, upon which the
medical witnesses here rely, may exist, and yet
sexual intercourse have taken place.  To allow
such a defence would be not merely dangerous as a
precedent, but in the present case would enable the
wife to take advantage of her own wrong; she has
denied her person to her husband, and so been the
cause of the adultery he has committed.  The result

---

* An allegation exceptive to the testimony of one of the witnesses produced
to prove the husband's adultery was brought in, and after opposition admitted
on behalf of the wife, by whom the witness excepted to was produced.

of the case should be to pronounce for the divorce at the suit of the husband.

*Sir J. D. Harding,* Q.A., and *Deane,* for the wife.—The adultery of the husband having been admitted, the only question is whether the wife has been guilty. The circumstances are against her, but it is impossible to reconcile the medical evidence with the fact of her guilt. The case is not one of casual intercourse like those referred to in the argument for the husband, but of long continued intimacy and frequent opportunity. The husband admits he did not consummate the marriage, and the proved state of the wife is inconsistent with any other intercourse.

### JUDGMENT.

SIR JOHN DODSON.

The suit was commenced by the husband charging his wife with the commission of adultery, and praying a sentence of separation on that ground. A libel was given in by him, and upon that libel fifteen witnesses were examined. The wife denies her guilt, and she recriminates, and makes a charge of adultery against her husband. Upon her part an allegation was given in containing those averments, and fifteen witnesses were likewise examined upon that allegation. The guilt of the husband, so far as the commission of adultery is concerned, or rather, I should say, the commission of adultery by the husband, is admitted. I cannot, however, make any distinction between the fact of adultery and the guilt of that adultery; he is proved to have committed adultery, therefore there is an end to

1856.

Feb. 13th.

HUNT
v.
HUNT.

that part of the case, and it is wholly unnecessary to enter upon it. The only point the Court has to consider is, whether the wife has been guilty of adultery, or any such conduct as should bar her from the remedy which she now seeks at the hand of the Court, namely, that she may be separated from her husband on the ground of his adultery. The marriage took place on the 3d of January, 1845, and the parties cohabited together till February, 1853. The consummation of the marriage has been pleaded in this case by the husband in his libel. It is said that was a mere matter of form and a matter of course, and of no importance; that it was not expected it would be denied; but it is distinctly admitted by the counsel in the case arguing for the husband that that marriage never was consummated; indeed, it is proved by a conversation which the husband had with Mr. Hyde, whose testimony has been very much eulogised as a witness of truth. A similar admission is made to the two brothers-in-law—the brother-in-law of the husband as well as the brother-in-law of the wife; in point of fact, it is agreed by all parties, that though these persons were married in 1845, and were living together for a space of eight years, yet no sexual intercourse took place between them. I am sorry to say that in the answers of the husband there is not that distinct admission I should have expected, because, having pleaded that the marriage was consummated, he says in these answers that he entertains doubts on that subject, whilst it seems he entertained no doubt whatever when he conversed with Mr. Hyde and the other gentlemen whose names I have mentioned, and his counsel now entertain no doubt upon the subject.   The adultery of the wife is charged to have taken place with Mr. Portman first of all at Edgar Street, in the city of Worcester; it appears that he was visited there by Mrs. Hunt, and frequently visited.   It appears also from the testimony of the witnesses that it was not only Mrs. Hunt who visited him there, but she was occasionally attended by her mother or sister, and upon one occasion by her husband.   However, it is undoubtedly clear, from the evidence of two of the witnesses living nearly opposite, and also from the testimony of Miss Norris, who was the daughter of the person who kept the house, that Mrs. Hunt not unfrequently came there by herself and remained there for a very considerable time.   Mrs. Morris, the lady of the house, did not observe anything remarkable; she never found the door locked or anything of the kind; but the testimony of the two witnesses residing nearly opposite is, that they observed that this lady frequently went there, and on all occasions of her going there, whether morning or evening, whether the sun was on the windows or not, the blinds were pulled down; there they continued together a considerable time, and when the lady quitted the blinds were drawn up.   Now, certainly these are circumstances affording very great suspicion of misconduct between the parties.   I do not say they are conclusive evidence of adultery, or that they would be presumptive evidence of adultery, if standing by themselves; but there are other charges made, namely, of improper intercourse at the Foley Arms at Malvern, and the Belle Vue Hotel at Malvern, and also at the Talbot Inn, Oldbury.   It appears that Mr. Portman and this lady drove over to the Foley Arms at Malvern, and upon the same day Mr. Hunt, the husband, drove over a young lady who was staying on a visit with Mr. and Mrs. Hunt, and they all went to the Foley Arms. When they all arrived there the visitors' book was presented to Mr. Portman to inscribe the names, which is usual at that place; and he thereupon wrote down his name, and then the name of Mrs. Portman, in that book, as Mr. and Mrs. Portman, and also the name of this young lady. Whether Mrs. Hunt knew anything of this, or Mr. Hunt knew anything of it, does not appear. It is a matter of little importance; it was not pressed by counsel as having a forcible bearing on the question; it was a mere joke of a young man writing down " Mr. and Mrs. Portman," he having driven Mrs. Hunt there, and no unfavourable inference is to be derived from that. But it does appear that they were on another occasion alone together at that hotel, and upon that second occasion the door was found locked; that certainly is a strong ground of suspicion. And again : what is still stronger is, what took place at the Talbot Inn at Oldbury, for that is the last time they were detected acting in any clandestine manner. Upon this occasion Mr. Portman had driven her over in order to call on a gentleman, who had been his tutor, and who, it so happened, was not at home, and they proceeded to the Talbot. The only room that was unoccupied was one behind the bar, used as a coffee-room, or for more parties than one. They went into that room; the lady ordered some refreshment. After that they remained there; and there being occasion for the niece of the landlady to go to the room to get her umbrella, the door was found to be locked. There is no doubt they remained in the room with the door locked for a considerable time, for she is not the only person who deposes to that fact, she is confirmed by other witnesses. The room, when they come out, is found to be in a disordered state ; it is found that the blinds are drawn down ; but the learned counsel say that is nothing at all, it is common to draw down the blinds if the windows look, as those windows did, into the street or into a stable yard, and therefore no unfavourable inference is to be derived from that. It appears, likewise, that a pin from a lady's hair was found on the floor, or on a sofa in that room : this is said to be of common occurrence—not to be taken as proof against any particular lady. Again : as to the state of confusion in which the sofa is represented to have been found, it is said that it had a loose covering, and that any one sitting upon it would disorder it. The sofa was removed from the window, but it was urged there was nothing in that. Taking each of these circumstances separately, they do not amount to much ; but, taking them all together, when a young married woman goes with a young man to an inn, and the blinds are pulled down, the room is in confusion, the door is locked, and they are there for a considerable time, these circumstances offer a case of very strong suspicion. I do not say that they amount to more than presumption. But this is not the whole of the evidence, for there is other evidence in this case, and other most important evidence—that upon which I think I can place the most implicit reliance—the testimony given by

Dr. Farr, one of the most eminent physicians; and
by Dr. Frere, a man likewise of considerable eminence, who can have no interest in the case, and
who depose most positively, after an examination
of this lady, that she has never had sexual intercourse with man, that she is a virgin intact.  It
is said they have defined, and correctly defined,
in what complete sexual intercourse consists.
They both admit that there may be *quasi* sexual
intercourse, that pregnancy may take place notwithstanding there has not been this complete
sexual intercourse, notwithstanding the hymen may
not have been perforated, or not have been broken.
They give cases within their own knowledge in
which these matters have occurred, and they fully
confirm and fully admit the cases which are given
by Dr. Blundell, in his work on the subject.  But
they say that in this case not only is the hymen
unbroken, but that the condition of all the parts
satisfies them that sexual intercourse has never
taken place.  With respect to the husband, with
whom this lady cohabited for eight years, it is now
admitted there never was sexual intercourse with
him.  The conclusion necessarily is, however im-
prudent the wife may have been, however repre-
hensible her conduct may be and must be considered, that she has not been guilty of adultery.  I
do not enter into other parts of the case—into what
is called his connivance or encouragement.  I think
that was pressed against him rather more than is
necessary.  I am unwilling to enter upon this case,
either on the one side or the other, beyond what its
necessity requires.  I will state that I am of opinion
he has been guilty of adultery, and he has admitted

1856.
Feb. 13th.

HUNT
*v.*
HUNT.

it ; I am of opinion that she is not proved to have been guilty of adultery, that there never was sexual intercourse with man ; and upon these grounds I pronounce for the prayer of Mrs. Hunt.

# CONSISTORY COURT OF LONDON.

## LOWE *v.* LOWE.

### *Cruelty—Practice—Answers.*

THE libel of the wife in a cause of separation by reason of cruelty, pleaded certain acts of cruelty; and that the husband was only prevented from further violence by the interposition of A. L., their servant, who was present.

The answer denied the cruelty, and went on to allege that the said A. L. was evidently in collusion with the wife, and at hand and ready to witness her lying on the floor on the occasion when she falsely stated she had been knocked down by the respondent ; and that from a given time the wife had adopted a systematic course of provocation, evidently with the view to induce the respondent to act with violence towards her.

The libel further pleaded, that a summons having been obtained by the wife against the husband, the husband was convicted of the assault and fined. The answer admitted the conviction, and averred that the charge was supported by the grossest false swearing, and that the magistrates were not unanimous in giving their judgment.

*Addams* and *Spinks*, in objection to these answers. — The respondent cannot introduce the charges of evident collusion, and of the adoption of a systematic course of provocation; nor can he allege that the conviction was obtained by perjury, and that the magistrates were not unanimous.

*Sir J. D. Harding*, Q.A., and *Jenner*, *contrà*.

Dr. Lushington.
You have a right to say that the wife and her servant were acting in collusion; but you should not go on to say that the wife adopted a systematic course of provocation, because if you state in answer anything which you can prove, and do not prove it, the statement in the answer goes for nothing. You may however answer that you believe the conviction was obtained by false swearing, and that the magistrates were not unanimous.

DAVIDSON *v.* DAVIDSON.

1856.

May 17th.

Where there is proof of attachment, criminal intention, and opportunity, the presumption is, that adultery has been committed. Statements made in interrogatory are generally to be taken as admissions; and though a witness be in part discredited, yet where such witness is corroborated by circumstances or statements in interrogatory, the witness is to be relied on.

*Adultery—Attachment—Criminal intention—Opportunity—Interrogatories—Credit of witness.*

THIS was a cause of divorce by reason of adultery promoted by the husband against the wife. The libel pleaded the marriage on the 20th of February, 1855, and cohabitation till the 22d of May in the same year. That the wife had been partly educated in France, and there formed an acquaintance with a young Frenchman named E. Lalouette; that since leaving France she kept up a correspondence by letter with and had two portraits of him; that notwithstanding the great kindness shown by her husband to her, she treated him with indifference. That in May she induced her husband, much to his inconvenience and against his wishes, to take her for a short visit to Paris. That previous to leaving home for Paris she destroyed her papers, and packed up and took with her all her clothes, trinkets, books, and drawing-room ornaments. That when the time of their visit to Paris had expired, and the husband was obliged to return to England, she refused to return with him, alleging that she was a Roman Catholic at heart, and would not leave France before she was formally admitted a member of that church. That at daybreak of the 22d of May she accompanied

1856.

May 17th.

DAVIDSON
v.
DAVIDSON.

her husband to the station at Paris, and saw him leave by the train for Boulogne, parting with him with every expression of kindness. That Denman her maid remained with her, the husband having refused the wife's repeated suggestion that he should take Denman back to England with him. That immediately the husband left with the train, Lalouette joined the wife on the platform, and at noon of the same day called on and remained with her for about an hour in her apartment. The remaining material articles pleaded the facts occurring during the night of the 22d and morning of the 23d, which are fully stated in the judgment. The additional articles pleaded a correspondence in April, 1855, with the authorities of the Post Office respecting the missing halves of bank notes sent in a letter addressed to E. Lalouette, and a Mr. D'Alcorn acting under the directions of the wife. The receipt of foreign letters by the wife through D'Alcorn with envelopes initialed E. L., such envelopes having been made at a stationer's in London by the wife's orders, and the sending a writing-desk and her picture as a present to Lalouette in March and April, 1855.

No counterplea was given in on the part of the wife; but an allegation exceptive to the evidence of Denman was admitted on her behalf, pleading that whereas, in answer to the 13th interrogatory, the witness answered "That when Mrs. W., the ministrant's mother, arrived in Paris on the 29th of May, and I opened the door to her, she did, I think, say, the very first thing, ' Oh! Denman, tell me, is it as bad as we think?—is she guilty?' or something to that effect. I did not reply ' Comfort yourself, Madam, she is not guilty.' No; I am sure I did not. I will

venture to swear that I never told the ministrant
that those were my very words." She hath therein
knowingly, &c., for that she did reply in those very
words. And that whereas, in answer to the 18th
interrogatory, the witness answered, "I have not
expressed to Mr. and Mrs. W., the father and mother
of the ministrant, my belief that she is innocent of
the charge of adultery. I have never expressed that
belief to them. I have only told them, as near as I
could, everything as it occurred, the same as near as
possible as I have in my evidence, but never expressed
to them the belief interrogate." She hath therein
knowingly, &c., repeated expressions on several occasions of the witness's belief in the innocence of the
wife being pleaded in contradiction. This allegation
was admitted after opposition.—See *post* page 167.

*Addams* and *Bayford* for the husband.

*Twiss* and *Spinks,* for the wife, contended that
there was no evidence of adultery except that given
by Denman ; that she was a single witness, and discredited. And they cited *Rix* v. *Rix*, 3 Hagg. 74;
*Hamerton* v. *Hamerton*, 2 Hagg. 8 ; *Simmons* v.
*Simmons*, 5 N. C. 347; *Evans* v. *Evans*, 1 Rob.
165.

JUDGMENT.

DR. LUSHINGTON.

In the course of the argument addressed to the
Court in this case, two or three questions of law
were mooted, and before I proceed to the evidence
in the case, I think it may be expedient to dispose

of them, though indeed, according to my own judgment, the case must be determined by very simple
considerations ; whether or not criminal intention
is proved, and whether or not there was adequate
opportunity for the parties to have indulged that
criminal intention.

Now, I apprehend, that with regard to the proof
of adultery, the doctrine has long been settled.  It
is not necessary to prove, that the adultery with
which a party is charged should have occurred at
any particular time or place.  The Court must be
satisfied that a criminal attachment subsisted between the parties, and that opportunities occurred
when the intercourse in which it is satisfied the
parties intended to indulge, might with ordinary
facility have taken place.  Ocular proof, as was
said by Sir George Hay, in *Rix* v. *Rix*, is very
seldom to be procured; almost every case is a case
of presumptive proof, though such proof varies in
every possible shape and degree.  There was a case,
of which I am not aware there is any printed report,
in which this question was very greatly discussed.
I mean the case of *Trotter* v. *Trotter*, which occurred
before my time, and which, when I first came to
this profession, was frequently mentioned.

Now, in the case of *Hamerton* v. *Hamerton*,
which has been so much discussed in argument, Sir
John Nicholl said, it is true that the law does not
require direct evidence of the very fact, committed
at a specific time and place—repeating almost the
very words of Sir George Hay—but it does require to
be satisfied that actual adultery has been committed.
And I entirely accede to this doctrine.  It is, in
other words, that no proof of criminal intention

1856.

May 17th.

DAVIDSON
*v.*
DAVIDSON.

will suffice, the parties must be placed in a condition, as to opportunity, when such criminal attachment may be indulged.

To understand the judgment in *Hamerton* v.
*Hamerton*, it must be borne in mind that the suit
commenced in the Consistorial Court of Gloucester,
and the libel was there admitted, and so framed
that Sir John Nicholl said, as to the most important
part of it, that it was impossible for the party
charged to defend herself.

In fact the case of *Hamerton* v. *Hamerton* was
this—very different from what this is represented
to be on the face of it—there was conclusive proof
of criminal intention on the part of Mr. Bushe, the
alleged adulterer, there was less stringent proof
with regard to the feelings of Mrs. Hamerton, and
there was no satisfactory proof of opportunity at
all. One opportunity was alleged to have taken
place at Cheltenham, at the house of Mrs. Matthews.
That case wholly failed, because it was admitted on
all hands that Mrs. Matthews was a woman of irreproachable character, that she was in the condition
of a mother or guardian to Mrs. Hamerton; and
the only interview that took place was in the
drawing-room in the middle of the day.

With regard to the parties being brought together
at any other place, the evidence wholly failed. It
had been alleged that Mr. Bushe had taken a house,
which he certainly had taken, with a view of carrying on criminal intercourse, but there was no proof
that Mrs. Hamerton was there. With regard to
Paris, the same observations may be made, for the
evidence only went to this, that Mrs. Hamerton
was seen coming from that house on one occasion,

and three or four hours afterwards Mr. Bushe was seen coming out, without anything like evidence to show that the parties had ever been in the house together. Therefore, I say, I adhere to the doctrine which was promulged in that case. I approve of Sir John Nicholls' judgment when he required further proof.

1856.

May 17th.

DAVIDSON
v.
DAVIDSON.

But the circumstances of that case are not only of course different, but, as I shall have occasion to show in the course of further examination, wholly and altogether distinct.

Reference was made to the rules which prevail, I lament to say, in this Court as to the effect to be attributed to the evidence of a single witness. I am very clearly of opinion that the circumstances of this case do not admit of the reception of such an argument; for I apprehend that it has been held, even in these courts, on many occasions, that the evidence of a single witness, as to a particular fact, might be sufficient to establish that fact, if there was adminicular and corroborative testimony; of what kind may be matter of argument. However, to prevent misconception, I will make a few observations on this topic.

With respect to the case of *Simmons* v. *Simmons*, which was decided by myself, I must observe, that it was one of very great peculiarity, the whole question being hinged on the supposed commission of adultery at a particular time and place. Lucy Peacock, who cohabited with Mr. Simmons, deposed that the connexion did take place ; but there were no circumstances whatever, either admitted or proved, legally speaking, corroborative of her evidence. The existence of a prior intercourse discontinued was not evidence of a particular renewal; and more especially, as interviews were proved to have taken place for a totally different purpose, namely, the maintenance of a child, which had been the fruit of loose intercourse with her antecedent to the marriage. What was wanted in that case was, proof of a continued attachment; and there was not the least evidence to show that the intercourse which had been abandoned was likely to be revived.

As the law has not been altered, I must abide by the law as laid down by the Court of Arches. I did so abide in determining myself in that divorce; I acted under the constraint of a superior court, and against my own judgment; I said so at the time; and I should now act on the law as it stands, if I found circumstances admitted of its applicability; and I should do so even though the result might be, as in the case of *Evans* v. *Evans*, decided by Sir Herbert Jenner Fust, that a court of common law gave a verdict of £500 and an ecclesiastical Court dismissed the wife; the consequence of which might be, that the husband might be compelled to take her back, notwithstanding the verdict.

When I come to examine the particulars of this case, I shall be able to show what appears to me to be a very essential distinction between this case and that of *Simmons* v. *Simmons*.

There was another point adverted to, which might, under the circumstances, be one of considerable difficulty; I allude to the question, how far interrogatories can or ought to be taken as admissions.

It has been said, that I must not take facts admitted in the interrogatories without the colour put upon them. To this I cannot give my assent, at least to the full extent to which it has been carried. I conceive that where interrogatories have been put, I must first look to the evidence of the witness to whom the interrogatory has been administered, and that such answer, in the first instance, is the best evidence. Next, I must enquire, whether the interrogatory was framed for the purpose of trying the credit of a witness, and that only, or as a *bonâ fide* admission of a fact, in accordance with the rest of the evidence, and only so admitted for the chance of an experiment, for the purpose of putting a different construction upon it.

I cannot adventure upon a general rule; the Court must judge in each case, as I believe to be the practice in other courts of justice. There is only one other case, to the best of my recollection, in which this point has ever been mooted : that case was decided by myself, and consequently is no authority for me to rely upon; it was twenty-four or twenty-five years ago; that was *Story* v. *Story.* In that case I had no hesitation in assuming as proved the facts stated in the interrogatories. I have since referred to the interrogatories in that case in the original depositions. I find in pencil the observations which I made at that time on these interrogatories. I need not read them all; but my observations were, such interrogatories as these, by implication, necessarily admit the general facts. Again, on the ninth interrogatory, the question was asked, how a man was dressed when he was found under the bed by a lady, a witness, and who was the single witness in the case. This appeared to be an admission that the man was so found, and to

1856.

May 17th.

DAVIDSON
v.
DAVIDSON.

assist the main evidence in the case. There were many interrogatories of the same kind, but I had no hesitation in dealing with these as admissions—from the desperate condition in which the party pleading was placed—for there was the very strongest evidence of the witness having found him in the middle of the night, and concealed under the bed of the person charged with adultery; however, no doubt, under these circumstances, it would seem advisable to run many risks in order to get rid of the evidence. I need not occupy time in going into that case.

I now proceed to the facts of this case. It is clear, beyond all doubt, that one of the most important considerations to which I have to direct my attention is, the credit to be given to Ann Denman; but I must consider how far that credit is impeached—how far her statements are shown to be consistent with probability, and with the other admitted facts and circumstances.

Now, her credit has been attacked in several ways: First, by the exceptive allegation; secondly, by showing she is contradicted by one of the witnesses who has deposed to a declaration denied by Denman; thirdly, by her own letter; and fourthly, by alleged contradictions in her own evidence.

Now, I mean to consider these objections briefly in the order stated.

The exceptive allegation does not contradict any of the facts pleaded, nor any of the facts given in evidence—not one. That allegation is confined to a contradiction of certain declarations deposed to by Ann Denman, and is framed for the sole purpose of discrediting her testimony—not to show she had deposed erroneously as to any fact or circum-

1856.

May 17th.

DAVIDSON
v.
DAVIDSON.

stance, but in order to show that the Court ought not to give credit to the statements which she has made.

Now, admitting for a moment the whole evidence of Mr. and Mrs. W. to be correct, it would still be a question how far it should discredit Ann Denman, whether she was not to be believed as to the facts deposed to. As a general principle, the doctrine of *falsa in uno falsa in omnibus* has not, as I believe, prevailed in any of our courts; that in particular cases the evidence of a witness, proved to have sworn falsely and wilfully also, may be wholly rejected I doubt not, but each case stands on its own particular circumstances. The question I have to consider is, whether this witness is, to use a short phrase, so perjured in some particulars that she is to be wholly discredited as to all other matters. This will depend on several considerations, and more especially whether she is confirmed directly or indirectly by other evidence in the cause.

It appears that Mr. and Mrs. W. did give credit to Ann Denman's statement of facts; they continued her in their service; they were anxious that no opposition should be made by their daughter to this suit. I think that the letter of August 28, 1855, goes further. To that letter I must refer: "Dear "Frederick, I am sorry to trouble you with this, but "we are very anxious to know about what time in "November Katherine's unfortunate case is likely "to come on, and if it is likely to come out in the "public papers at once. I am told these matters "take a long time to settle; if such is the case, and "you think it wont come on till after Christmas, we "could then remain here till that time. My reason "for asking is," so and so "is expecting her confine-

"ment the end of November, and she expects to "come here at that time ; but as we wish to be away "during this dreadful trial, I shall arrange my future "movements according to your letter.  Can you "suggest anything to me that I might in any way "check her opposition to the suit, and by that means "prevent publicity and cruel exposure to both "families?"

Now, it is perfectly obvious that when this letter was written, which is August the 28th in that year, Mr. and Mrs. W. were anxious and desirous that no opposition should be made by their daughter to this suit.  According to the statement in his evidence, which I need not refer to again, he says, " I "was willing and desirous all along, very much so, "that the producent should not be an opposing "party, at least not actively so, to the ministrant's "suit against the producent. I was so, because being "satisfied from Denman's repeated statements to us "that she was innocent of any criminality, I looked "forward to a reconciliation between the parties ; "and I thought that her refraining from offering any "active opposition to his suit would best promote "that result.   It is only in consequence of its ap- "pearing by Denman's evidence, when it was pub- "lished, that she stated respecting my daughter "what, according to her (Denman's) own pre- "vious statements to us, we have every reason "to believe to be false, that we have been obliged "to come forward in opposition to that evidence. "We could not stand aloof when we had reason to "believe that there was false evidence against "her tending to prove her guilty—when we be- "lieved, and, from the statements of the very

1856.

May 17th.

DAVIDSON
v.
DAVIDSON.

" party who had given that evidence, had reason
" to believe her innocent."

Now this is a most extraordinary statement,
whilst Mr. W. believed the evidence of Ann
Denman, taking it to be such as he has represented
it to be, that Mrs. Davidson was entirely innocent
of the great offence, so long he withdraws from all
opposition to the suit commenced for the purpose of
proving she was guilty of adultery, and Mr. Davidson obtaining a divorce. It does appear to me most
strange, that a father, convinced of the innocence of
his daughter, by the declarations of this witness,
should, at the very time when he is expressing his
belief of that innocence, say, " Can you not furnish any means whereby I can assist in putting
a check to these very unhappy proceedings for
both families." His opinion is now shaken—why?
because he says that he finds that Ann Denman,
as to her declarations to him and Mrs. W., has
sworn falsely. I must say here, it is not a little
singular that Mr. W. should have acted in the
manner I have stated. If Denman did make the
declarations to which he has sworn, and he did
believe them, I can scarcely believe it possible that
he could have advised, or been a party to the with-
drawment of all opposition to this suit, and leave a
daughter, whom he believed innocent, undefended
and unprotected in such a suit. I will not dwell
upon this.

I must confess that I can place no very great
reliance upon evidence which appears to me so
wholly inconsistent, and so contrary to all probability; but, looking at the evidence of Denman herself, I should think it is very likely that she may

have expressed herself in very doubtful terms as to
the guilt or innocence of Mrs. Davidson, I think that
she, not having had ocular demonstration of the fact,
may have stated, though we have not the terms in
which she did express it, a doubt as to whether the
offence was committed. I apprehend she did not
choose to draw a direct conclusion as to guilt, and
that she expressed herself accordingly, and it may
be she went still further. She now denies that she
declared that Mrs. Davidson was innocent of the
fact. I believe the truth to be, that Denman did
use ambiguous expressions; that they are now represented by Mr. and Mrs. W. to be stronger
affirmations of innocence than they really were, or
than they themselves believed them to have been;
and that Denman has swayed from the strict truth
in denying them altogether, instead of admitting
them in a mitigated form. That I believe to be the
truth.

Now then, it is, I think, clear that Denman did
make a similar, or somewhat similar, declaration of
innocence to the witness Carr, and that she has now
denied such declaration generally; but I concur in
thinking that the question was not fairly put to Ann
Denman, and that according to all rule, as well as
all reason, the question ought to have been put
more specifically, whether she did not make a particular declaration in such terms to such and such
a particular person at such a time, and in such
a place.

With respect to the letter in Denman's handwriting, it may be expedient that I refer to the
words of it—the terms in which it is expressed.
It is not necessary to go through the whole of

1856.

May 17th.

DAVIDSON
v.
DAVIDSON.

the letter, it relates to many things which are irrelevant to the issue in the cause. "I know "you are kept short of money. The dear Pets "I have not seen yet, but when I do, I will "kiss them for you. Do, my dear Mrs. David- "son, keep up as well as you can, there is one "above who knows you are innocent, and will, "if you look to Him, protect you through all "your trouble." Now, I think it is impossible to deny that this is a strong declaration of Mrs. Davidson's innocence, the witness has admitted that she did write that letter, as far as it is admitted, it is inconsistent with the evidence now given, it operates against her credit; but she has not denied writing it, and therefore she is not to be charged with false swearing in that respect. I think, therefore, that I must consider that this letter is in strong contradiction of what she has now sworn in the course of her evidence; and I shall deal with this case, and with her evidence accordingly.

Lastly, there are alleged contradictions in the long evidence which she has given. Now, these I do not attempt to notice in detail. They were very properly brought forward by the learned counsel in great and minute detail, every circumstance importing the pettiest contradiction, in evidence of this great length, was brought under the notice of the Court. I do not attempt to look at them minutely, but I shall give my opinion as to their general effect.

I will now state what is the result of the consideration of all these circumstances, and of the whole evidence of Ann Denman. According to my opinion, Ann Denman has not been actuated by any malicious determination falsely to accuse Mrs. Davidson; that as to the commission of the offence itself, her mind and opinion has fluctuated because actual guilt was a conclusion to be drawn, and was not a visible fact. That she has made declarations importing innocence, or rather negativing knowledge of guilt. That she has most imprudently, and without due regard to the obligation of her oath, denied such declarations, and that, consequently, her credit is to some degree affected, and it becomes especially the duty of the Court to see that the main facts deposed to by her are, as far as the case will admit, supported by probability, and other facts not denied. In truth, this is the great point of the case, to ascertain the credit of Ann Denman. It is a most remarkable feature in this case, that the general statement made by this witness is not impugned. Some statements, of which I doubt the importance, have been questioned; but the stress of the attack has been upon the conclusions drawn by the witness, and not upon the facts deposed to by her.

I say, in my view of this case, it will not be necessary to travel minutely through the whole of the evidence. I think that the conclusion I am to draw, whatever it may be, must be drawn from facts which have scarcely been made matter of dispute, and not from circumstances, the truth of which has furnished so large a field for argument.

It was contended by the counsel for Mr. Davidson, that there was a deliberate plan on the part of Mrs. Davidson to abandon her home in the Regent's Park when she went to Paris, and to throw herself

1856.

May 17th.

DAVIDSON
v.
DAVIDSON.

into the arms of Mr. Emile Lalouette. It appears to me also unnecessary to trace all the circumstances from which that inference is drawn; the course I shall pursue is, to trace the origin and continuance of the attachment to Mr. Lalouette, and, as intimately connected therewith, her conduct during her married life. It is from this source that the evidence of criminal intention, if it existed at all, must be drawn.

I see nothing particular in the state of Mr. W.'s family that should induce me to adopt the suggestion that this lady was peculiarly disposed from circumstances to form a romantic though innocent attachment; nor do I see why Mrs. Davidson should be in any extraordinary degree the victim of girlish fancies. She, it is true, is one of a large family of daughters; but not, as far as appears, brought up or educated as a recluse.

The period and circumstances under which Mrs. Davidson's acquaintance with Mr. Lalouette originated are wrapped in some obscurity. Mrs. W. deposes that about a twelvemonth, more or less, before her daughter's marriage, she discovered a letter and a portrait in her possession, and about the same time she received a letter cautioning her against going abroad, as Miss W. was about to elope with a young Frenchman. Strange to say that of the circumstances connected with these letters, she has now a very indistinct recollection. I must say I think they were calculated to make a much more permanent impression, taking the deposition of the witness herself. I do not collect more specific information from Mr. W.'s evidence; according to his account, the matter ended in a reprimand and the return of the picture. This is said to have been a twelvemonth before the marriage. Of what may have passed in the interval there is no evidence; but in October or November preceding the marriage, which took place in February, 1855, the precise period matters not, about this time, we find that Miss W. was carrying on a clandestine correspondence with Mr. D'Alcorn, a music seller, for he states that the letters he wrote to her were addressed to Miss W., at Mr. Beidermann's, at Newnton, and not to her father's house; and through the assistance of this person, so clandestinely carried on, she forwarded her letters to this Mr. Lalouette, then residing in the Rue de la Paix, at Paris.

I think it necessary to refer to the letter, which is the letter written by this lady, that is annexed to the additional articles. This is it— " I have enclosed a letter for France, which " I should feel extremely obliged to you if " you would post for me as soon as you con- " veniently can. I have enclosed 1s. for you " to get a 10d. stamp to put on it for me. " You must pardon the trouble I have given, " but having within the last few days fallen a " victim to injustice and severity, I am not allowed " to do anything without the interference of " others. My letters are all read before I re- " ceive them, and all I write is also pryed into." To what injustice, to what severity this letter refers, the Court has no means of judging. If I am to trust the evidence in this case, it could not have referred—I repeat, if I am to trust that evidence — to the former discovery of the inter-

1856.

May 17th.

DAVIDSON
v.
DAVIDSON.

course that had taken place—the letter between Miss W. and Mr. Lalouette, but it refers to something else. "I must, therefore, beg you "never to mention having received this letter, "and if ever you have occasion to write again, "let it be as few words as possible. You can "write me a few lines to tell me you have "received this, and also that I am forgiven for "the liberty I have taken, to the address I have "enclosed; enclose the letter to me in that sealed, "and write For Miss W. on it. The stamps for "the music shall be sent to-morrow, I shall not "be allowed to do so, but some one else will. "I expect I may have to live in London in a "few months; should such be the case, you "shall find me a better customer than I have "been yet. I may probably live in town after "I am married, at all events some part of the "year. I must beg you to preserve the strictest "secresy, and never allude to this letter." Now, perhaps, erroneously, the Court, when it first read this letter, and having no information before it as to the commencement of the attachment between Mr. Davidson and Miss W., was inclined to think it must necessarily have referred to that attachment; and, I think, for the most obvious reason, because the lady speaks of going to reside in London, and speaks of being about to be married, or rather, she says, after I am married, at all events. Now it turns out, according to the argument of counsel, that this had no reference to any acquaintance between Mr. Davidson and Miss W. at all, it was either a pure invention of the lady to curry favour with Mr.

D'Alcorn, or it must have adverted to somebody else. These are matters of minor importance. The important point of the letter is, that in October or November, according to the representation of the parents, the intercourse having been broken off, as they believed a year before, we find the correspondence carried on, and that two or three months before the marriage. It is conclusive proof, and it would be a mere waste of time to comment upon it.

Now the marriage takes place in February, and what follows? I proceed with Mr. D'Alcorn's evidence—the box and the portrait, and a conversation which fixes the matter to Mr. Lalouette. Now this has taken place very shortly before the visit to Paris, not an unimportant date. In March preceding money was forwarded to this gentleman. I need not trouble myself, after stating these facts, with going into the evidence as to the box and the desk. Here is, in fact, undeniable proof of the continuance of this connexion immediately after the marriage, or nearly immediately after the marriage with Mr. Davidson, and carried on up to the very last moment of time.

I must slightly advert to the conduct of Mr. Davidson after the marriage. That Mr. Davidson was kind, affectionate, and indulgent to a fault, is the evidence of all of Mrs. Davidson's nearest relatives. Now what return does Mrs. Davidson make? An utter disregard of all the duties which, by her marriage vow, and by every tie of gratitude, she was bound to discharge; and to such an extent does she carry her misconduct, that she is the subject of just and severe reprehension from her own father. Towards her husband, she shows not a

1856.

May 17th.

DAVIDSON
v.
DAVIDSON.

spark of affection, regard, or just deference. To him she is cold and heartless, and what is the cause of all this? Can it be other than a disgraceful attachment, commenced before marriage, and shamelessly carried on afterwards. This is the state of things when the visit to Paris takes place. I shall not prolong this judgment by discussing the preparation for this visit, or the quantity of things taken, or the letters burnt, or the intended duration of the visit; that is no part of my judgment; though it may be perfectly true, that all this was a preconcerted plan, it is no part of my judgment, and is not the fact or circumstance on which I intend to rely. They go to Paris, the week expires, Mr. Davidson is compelled by his professional engagements to return to London, Mrs. Davidson refuses to accompany him. Now what is the excuse for this gross act of disobedience, this acknowledged breach of all duty. Surely there must have been some very powerful motive, some extraordinary strong feeling in operation, to induce so unjustifiable a resolution as that of deserting her husband, with whom she had cohabited but four months; no ordinary cause could possibly account for this; a husband, too, who had proved himself so devoted to her and so dedicated to the promotion of her happiness. I repeat, there must have been some powerful cause to work such an effect. What is a powerful cause? A criminal attachment, sad experience shows, can sever the strongest ties by which God and man can consecrate the marriage union.

To avoid this solution, this probable explanation, probable, because of all the circumstances I have already mentioned, Mrs. Davidson invents, and her counsel, in the distress to which they were driven, adopt the explanation, that religious obligations were at the bottom of the whole affair, and that a regard for conscience has dictated a step apparently so much at variance with all conscience. Mrs. Davidson appears in the new character of a Roman Catholic.

Now, I admit the motive to be strong enough, if the religious conviction is established. I am well aware that bonds the most sacred may be readily broken asunder, in the manner suggested. I deny not, that a violation of the marriage vow, the separation from a kind and affectionate husband, may be brought about by a conversion to that faith; but I must have strong proof of the reality of such conversion; I must be convinced that the assumption of such character is not a pretext put forth for the occasion, but a *bonâ fide* abandonment of a former faith, and the sincere adoption of another church.

But what are the proofs of this great and all-important change? The lady's own letter. I have not one word of any previous attachment to the Roman Catholic faith; I have not a single syllable from any of the witnesses of this lady intending to become a professor of that religion. It bursts out in the shape of the lady's own letter, the letter E to which I now refer. This is that extraordinary letter which this lady wrote on the 24th of May, Mr. Davidson having then left Paris and proceeded to England :—"My dear Madgwick, I hope you " arrived home safely without being very ill in " crossing. The rain must have calmed the sea, " I think. I am expecting to hear from you " every day to know what arrangements you

" have made. I do not see that these rooms we
" have are quite the right sort for me, the *entre-*
" *sole* is not quite the proper place for a lady,
" which I did not know when I took them.
" There is a very nice little apartment in the
" same house on the 4 *ieme étage* which is let at
" the rate of £18 a month ; it is very much
" better than this, and not so public, being higher
" up. I could go into it from Saturday or Sun-
" day, if you have no objection, or I could look
" out elsewhere, for I do not think this one is
" the right one for me ; but the other is just the
" one you would like, very private, and clean and
" comfortable. Write, and tell me what you
" think ; I also must have a servant, and no time
" should be lost. She must be French, and one
" of my own choosing." I will come to that
presently. " I do not think I am bound to
" submit to be kept in the custody of any one."
And that also : " and if you choose to part with
" me you cannot force me to be your prisoner.
" I never shall change my determination of being
" a Roman Catholic, and as soon I can I shall be
" received into the church." So the lady was not
a Roman Catholic at this time, she was only
bringing up for that extraordinary change at
that period. " Now, from force of circumstances,
" I am a member of none ; I cannot buy even a
" prayer book, but you must not think that poverty
" can make me change ; no, never !" Now, this is
the first intimation we have, in this letter, ever
breaking forth of her determination to become
a Roman Catholic. I will look at the other evidence presently. Then she goes on, " I hope that

"the dear little children are quite well;" and in the whole of this letter now comes one train of thought: "Oh Madgwick, do not let them hate me too! no, "speak kindly of me to them; sweet little Jessie, "how I should like to see her, but no! I shall "never see any one of my once kind friends again. "I shall never consent to return to England with "the world scoffing at me and my friends neglecting "me; no, such being the case I must submit, and "here I remain."

But it is said all this is to be attributed to a change of religion. I confess I cannot arrive at that conclusion; but I arrive at this conclusion, that she had determined at that period never more to return to her husband's house, nor to his bed; and that this is expressed, according to the evidence in the case, for the first time ; for not a single syllable is elicited from any one of the witnesses that there was any such intention on the part of Mrs. Davidson at the time she was residing in Regent's Park; and I must say, this letter is strong corroborative proof of the argument that was addressed to the Court by the counsel for Mr. Davidson, that the fact of leaving Regent's Park was part of a plan which was afterwards carried into effect, never to return to her husband, but to throw herself into the arms of Mr. Lalouette on arriving at Paris. "If I have ever "said anything in a hasty moment to offend you, "and for all my past conduct, I must humbly ask "your pardon and repent, every unkind word I "retract, and only remain firm to my faith. I "never shall change that now."

This is part of the evidence strongly relied upon by Mrs. Davidson's counsel, in order to show

1856.

May 17th.

DAVIDSON
*v.*
DAVIDSON.

that she was actuated by such strong religious motives to separate herself from her husband, to whom she had been married four months.

I cannot believe that if there had been any truth in this averment we should not have found some evidence leading to its probability at an earlier period, some preliminary circumstances rendering so great a change consistent with probability. But what are the circumstances relied upon? It appears that in Mr. W.'s letter reprimanding Mrs. Davidson for disobedience, he speaks of attendance at Wells Street chapel. This is the subsidiary evidence on which Mrs. Davidson relies in order to prove her a convert to the Roman Catholic faith. I know none of the merits or demerits of that chapel. I know it is a chapel where the service of the Church of England is performed, and that by episcopal authority, and I do not think I am entitled to assume that the attendance on any church of that description is demonstrative proof that its congregation either have become or are about to become Roman Catholics: I do not think I am entitled to go so far as that. I am told it is a place of notoriety; but surely it cannot be that the services are conducted in such a manner that any one who goes there is at once to be described as abandoning the faith they are worshipping under. This is proof the second. Now what is proof the third? It really does appear to what stress counsel are necessarily driven, for it is quite necessary in these cases that everything which the ingenuity or eloquence of counsel can urge in favour of their client should be brought forward. The last pretence is, that Mrs. Davidson was once heard to say she knew a lady who had been a convert to the Roman Catholic faith.

I am of opinion that this excuse, even if it stood alone and were not to be construed with all the circumstances proving the previous attachment to Mr. Lalouette, even if it were an isolated fact opposed to none, would utterly and entirely fail to prove the fact upon which so much has been assumed. Then, what are the consequences? That a false pretence has been put forward to justify Mrs. Davidson's refusal to accompany her husband, that I must seek for some other cause to account for that refusal, and what other cause has been assigned, or could be assigned, except her attachment to Mr. Lalouette? If there is an effect, there must be a cause; and if there be but two possible causes, and one wholly fails, you must necessarily resort to the other.

Here too, it must be remarked also—proved by this letter, proved also by Denman's evidence, that this lady was not only desirous of severing herself from her husband, but of being removed from all possible control, from any one known to the husband; for what does that letter state? She desired Denman might be dismissed, and a French maid of her own choosing might be substituted. This, too, is sworn by Denman—a French maid of her own selection.

Now, such is my view of the facts up to the 22d of May.

I now proceed, though not in minute detail, to examine the evidence of Ann Denman. It is, in my opinion, needless to go into a detail of all the evidence which has been given on this occasion, for

I do not found my judgment upon minute circumstances, but it will be founded upon and I trust
justified by the leading facts which have been deposed to by her, and which, as I conceive, have neither been controverted, nor can be controverted, in
this case. My judgment will be founded rather
upon the inferences I draw than from endeavouring
to show that the facts have been proved which have
been disputed by Mrs. Davidson's counsel.

Mr. Davidson departs by the train; no sooner is
he gone than Mr. Lalouette appears on the stage.
Now, was this a fortuitous event, was this a mere accident, that at the moment the husband departs the
lover appears—a lover with whom a correspondence
is proved to have been carried on till the very eve
of Mrs. Davidson's departure for Paris, as proved
by D'Alcorn. I can hardly suppose that counsel
seriously believed that the Court would come to the
conclusion that this was all purely accidental.

But be it so; strange and improbable as such a
solution is, what is the next step? Between 10
and 11 o'clock, this gentleman is received by Mrs.
Davidson in her lodgings, for what time it matters
not. Now, who is received? Stop and look at
these circumstances. The lover before marriage,
the beloved after marriage, the donor and the donee
of gifts and presents. Who receives him? The
wife who has just abandoned her husband without
reasonable pretext, who has clandestinely, as to her
own family, corresponded with him before marriage, clandestinely as to her husband afterwards.
These facts have not been grappled with.

Now, what stretch of credulity can induce any
one to believe that parties so circumstanced met for

1856.

May 17th.

DAVIDSON
v.
DAVIDSON.

an innocent purpose? All knowledge of human nature, all past experience, all experience in these courts, point to but one end. On what terms must the parties have been for such an interview to take place? Where was Mrs. Davidson's sense of her own honour, left in her own keeping, of which she ought to have been more particularly cautious when her husband was away? Where is her sense of fidelity to her husband when she so received the lover at the very time and very hour of her husband's departure? Can I believe that a woman so acting would be an exception from all ordinary frailty, an almost unexampled instance of female chastity?

I pursue the history. It verifies, and more than verifies, all I have said. In the evening—again I say, I care not at what hour, be it 9, 10, or 11 o'clock—and I care not whether Mrs. Davidson was dressed or half dressed, or redressed—Mr. Lalouette comes again, and is admitted by Mrs. Davidson. What signifies it how he got the key? He came, and was by her received. This is the substantive fact. No remonstrance of Ann Denman availed, and I will add that no remonstrance could have been made too strong.

They remained in the sitting-room till two o'clock in the morning—a fact which it will presently appear from the interrogatories is an admitted fact. Now I come to one which may be doubtful. "Mrs. Davidson was sitting on the young man's knee," says Ann Denman, "and kissing him in my presence." Now very little has been said or could be said as to this evidence—indeed none. Now suppose I omit this improper behaviour; suppose the Court should

1856.

May 17th.

DAVIDSON
*v.*
DAVIDSON.

be of opinion that Ann Denman was not to be credited in any particular except where she was corroborated. Why, what then? It leaves the case much where it was—much where it was—for I should not for one moment doubt the certainty of such familiarities from the circumstances I have detailed, whether a witness had deposed to them or not. The circumstances I have referred to perfectly convince my mind that the indulgence of such familiarities was a necessary and inevitable sequence to the familiarities and to all the facts to which I have before adverted, and the continuance of the parties in them.

Now what is the next step? Mr. Lalouette undresses and goes into Mrs. Davidson's bedroom. What matters it whether she asked him or not? What ought to have been her conduct had she not been carried away by her unlawful passion, and divested of all sense of duty to herself and to her husband? Why to have separated from him instantly—to have left the room and kept aloof from all such contact at any time, at any hour of the night, if she had had a sense of duty to herself. Assume what has been the excuse—that Mr. Lalouette was ill, though I do not credit one iota of that supposition. Her duty remained the same, and all that humanity in such a case, with due regard to decency and modesty, could have required, was to send for a doctor, and have left him in the care of Ann Denman.

Now let me see the version given at the end of the 11th interrogatory, where it is asked whether Ann Denman did not authoritatively interfere to induce Mrs. Davidson to send Lalouette away, admitting therefore the fact of such remonstrance, which is deposed to by Denman. Then the interrogatory goes on,—"Did not Mr. Lalouette say to you, you ought to know better, and if he were your mistress he would turn you out of doors? Did not Mrs. Davidson beg him to be quiet, and take no notice of what you had said?" This is the interrogatory addressed to the witness.

Now mark the effect of this interrogatory. In the first place the continuance of Mr. Lalouette in the apartments is admitted; secondly, that Ann Denman from a sense of its gross impropriety remonstrates in the strongest terms; that, thirdly, Mr. Lalouette, disappointed for the moment in his views, threatens Ann Denman. And what does Mrs. Davidson? Why so dead was she to all sense of her own honour and duty, so entirely forgetful of what she ought to have done, that instead of listening to that faithful voice which might by possibility have saved her, she takes part with her lover—repudiates that interference which might have saved her from destruction.

One more quotation from the interrogatories, and I might multiply them tenfold. Look at the 12th interrogatory, a very long one, I am not going through it, but a part I must read. Look at the 12th interrogatory, "Was not Mr. Lalouette asleep during the whole of the night, except at two or three short intervals? Is it not the fact that throughout the night the ministrant sat in a chair between the bed and the table reading a book? Did not you, Ann Denman, sit the greater part of the night at a little distance from the ministrant?

1856.

May 17th.

DAVIDSON
v.
DAVIDSON.

Is it not the fact that throughout the night you never left the room but for a few minutes?"

Now let me pause and survey the picture as drawn by Mrs. Davidson and her advisers, Lalouette fast asleep for hours in her bed. Where is the illness which has been conjured up for the occasion, and proved by no one? Where is Mr. Lalouette himself?—Undressed in Mrs. Davidson's bed. Where is Mrs. Davidson?—Sitting by the side of that bed for hours, watched if you please by her servant—for such is the picture—a married woman, a wife of four months' duration, the day she quitted her husband, that day and that very night receiving the object of her affection before and after marriage.

Can any one not fit to be an inmate of an asylum for idiots, doubt the feeling which subsisted between these parties. Give them the opportunity of the criminal indulgence of passions already so little restrained that all sense of duty and delicacy were gone, must not any one be satisfied what of necessity must be the case?

I have enough, and more than enough, to satisfy me of the criminal intention.

I will say a word or two more as to Denman's evidence. Much observation has been made upon her evidence, at the conclusion of the examination in chief, on the 22d article. Now I read this, and I continue this rather for the sake of showing that I have not spared my trouble in the consideration of this case, much more than from any necessity which the case itself requires.

Now this was her further deposition on the 22d article:—" There is one circumstance respecting one

"of the visits of the said Emile Lalouette to Mrs.
"Davidson which I have omitted to mention, and
"which I must confess did raise my suspicions as
"to something wrong having taking place between
"them.  It was the only occasion on which I can
"say that I had direct reason to suspect it.  I
"knew it was very wrong their being together as
"they used to be, but till this time I cannot say
"that it occurred to me to suspect that they had
"been criminal together.  It was I think on the
"occasion of the second morning visit.  While
"Mrs. Davidson and the said Emile Lalouette were
"together in the sitting-room, on that occasion I
"thought I heard the door of the room locked, and
"when the said Emile Lalouette was gone, I asked
"Mrs. Davidson why they had locked the door, and
"she said that Emile wished it, but that she found
"it would not lock, as I should find if I tried it,
"she said.  She came to me in my room on this
"occasion directly after the said Emile Lalouette
"was gone, and I noticed that her dress was"
so and so, and then she says she suspected adultery.

Now it is said this is an after thought, this is a
malicious feeling of Ann Denman—for some reason
never explained, and quite inconsistent with her
general conduct, and wholly inconsistent with the
letter produced—entertained towards Mrs. Davidson; that this is a malevolent exaggerated statement
for the purpose of destroying her case.

Now it does so happen that there is something
here like a corroboration of this statement, and in
a very extraordinary manner.  I refer now to the
evidence of Mr. Henderson :—" Mary Ann Denman

1856.

May 17th.

DAVIDSON
*v.*
DAVIDSON.

" has not, as suggested, more than once or indeed
" ever admitted or declared to me her conviction of
" the innocence of the ministrant of the crime im-
" puted to her in this cause. She stated when
" speaking of the night scene between the parties
" described in the libel that she did not see adul-
" tery committed, and that she could not say whether
" or no adultery had been committed on that occa-
" sion; but she stated her impression or belief to
" be, that on the occasion of one of the morning
" visits paid to the ministrant by the young man
" Emile, adultery had been committed by them;
" and she stated to me the ground of such her im-
" pression and belief, which, as she stated them,
" were, that while the ministrant and the young
" man were in the room together she heard the door
" locked; and that she observed, on the young man
" leaving, on that occasion, that ministrant's face
" looked flushed, and that her dress was extremely
" tumbled; and that on her Mary Ann Denman
" asking the ministrant why she had locked the
" door, the ministrant had said that Emile, the
" young man, had told her to do so."

Now this is a remarkable confirmation, to which
I am by all the rules of law entitled to resort to
show that Denman has spoken the truth. If, indeed, the credit of Denman had not been impeached,
it would not be consistent with the principles of
law to refer to any declaration she had previously
made for the purpose of showing that her evidence
was consistent with truth; but if you impeach
witnesses' credit, and charge them with wilfully inventing a story, it is then competent to refer to
other evidence to show that at an earlier period

they have made statements similar to and entirely in conformity with their evidence.

Now, this is a remarkable confirmation—a confirmation of what fact? why, a confirmation of this fact, that according to the evidence the statement of Mrs. Davidson herself was, Mr. Lalouette had proposed the locking. of the door. And for what possible purpose was the door to be locked when Mr. Lalouette and Mrs. Davidson were together alone, except for purposes which I need not further specify.

Now, then, I proceed to the conclusion of this judgment. I speak now as to the proof of opportunity, which I have incidentally glanced at as I went along. Presuming for the moment, though I am by no means satisfied rightly that the adultery was not actually committed on the night of the 22d of May, that is, up to six o'clock in the morning; yet I see no reason whatever to discredit Ann Denman, that at six o'clock she left the room for two hours; that the parties remained together; and she did not return till eight o'clock. Now, here was ample opportunity, and I doubt not Mrs. Davidson availed herself of it.

What was the attempt to get rid of this evidence? Why, reference was made to the answer to the 12th interrogatory, which was, whether she had not remained in the room all the night, and because the witness happened to answer, as she naturally would do, in the following terms—I had better read it to be accurate:—" It is the fact, that throughout the "night ministrant, whenever I went in, was sitting "in a chair which is between the bed and the table" —what is said, and what is the argument? That

1856.

May 17th.

DAVIDSON
v.
DAVIDSON.

the witness has said throughout the night, including the two hours in the morning, after six o'clock. I cannot say I think that is an argument which ought to overthrow the testimony of this witness.

Now, I entertain no doubt about the adultery being committed at that time; but there were other opportunities. I have noticed one, when the door was attempted to be locked, and there was ample opportunity on all subsequent visits. Denman states that Mr. Lalouette visited this lady every day, and sometimes twice a-day for the whole week. Why, to speak of want of opportunity, and compare this case with *Hamerton* v. *Hamerton*, where the parties were never brought together but on one occasion, and that in the house of a lady of irreproachable character, in her own drawing-room, in the middle of the day—to compare these cases together, and say the preponderance is in favour of Mrs. Davidson! There is as wide a difference as by possibility there can be in two cases. That case failed because the parties were not brought together; but this case will succeed, because they were brought together over and over again.

What is more—Mr. Lalouette accompanies this lady from the house—they are out for hours together, nobody knows where they go. Again, Mr. Smart traces them to a house where there was ample opportunity. In such a case as this, any practicable opportunity suffices where the ground is laid so clearly, so distinctly—where it is impossible for any man to doubt there was a criminal attachment which had entirely destroyed all Mrs. Davidson's just feelings of regard for her husband—extinguished her sense of propriety—for less stringent terms would not suffice. To suppose, when opportunity occurred, as it did, to suppose there was not a consummation of that which had been sought for for so long a time, would be to suppose that which never occurred in cases of which I have had cognizance in this court, nor I believe in the annals of human nature.

I entertain no doubt; I believe the adultery is most clearly established, and I pronounce for the separation.

---

The wife appealed from the sentence in the Consistory Court, but the husband having petitioned the House of Lords before the Court was inhibited, the process was transmitted to the House of Lords, and the husband obtained a divorce, the cause never having been brought up to the Court of Arches.

*Exceptive allegation—Pleading.**

1856.

March 6th.

DAVIDSON
*v.*
DAVIDSON.

Dr. Lushington.

I have read the whole of the papers and the evidence in this case, but it is right I should state that I have not read the whole of the evidence and the papers with any view of making up my mind on the matter in issue, because that can be done only at the ultimate hearing of the case, when the evidence is discussed, and I have also heard the arguments of counsel. But it has always been expedient in these cases, though it has not always been customary, that the Court should be in possession of the evidence before it hears and determines the admissibility of any exceptive allegation.

My experience in these matters undoubtedly is, that generally speaking exceptive allegations answer very little purpose. There are very few instances on the records of this Court, though there are some, in which the case has been in any degree affected by the admission of an exceptive allegation. But, however that may be, if an exceptive allegation is offered, and it be framed in conformity with the established rules which govern these matters, the Court has no option and no right on its own part to reject such allegation; and it is not necessary that the Court, in admitting an exceptive allegation to proof, should come to the conclusion that the witness shall be proved to be utterly unworthy of credit. That is not neces-

*Where a witness is asked in interrogatory whether he has not made admissions, if the admissions are pertinent to the issue, and he denies having made them, an exceptive allegation to prove the fact of his making such admissions is admissible.*

---

* See *antè*, p. 133.

sary to be determined beforehand, but in admitting the allegation to proof the Court must determine this question, whether the witness may not have his credit to a certain extent affected, if the allegation which is offered be admitted and proved.

It is impossible to doubt that this witness, against whom the exception is offered, is the most material witness in the whole case, for without her it would not be contended for a single moment that there would be any evidence as to the actual commission of adultery.

Let us see what are the rules which have been acted upon in this court and in other courts. I remember the time when, I regret to say, there was some doubt as to the rules which governed the admission of an exceptive allegation in this court. I think I can find instances where they were admitted where now upon principle they would be rejected. For that principle I cannot refer to a better authority than the authority of the judges in the *Queen's case*, 2 Br. & B. 285. . The result of that case on this point I conceive to be this, that if upon cross-examination, in chief it could hardly arise, a question be put to a witness touching a fact or a declaration, verbal or written, foreign to the issue to be tried, the party so putting the question must abide by the answer, and cannot be permitted to contradict it by other testimony for the purpose of discrediting the witness.

This was the judgment of the whole of the judges upon that occasion, and it was founded upon a series of cases at common law, of which there was one very memorable case, *Spenceley* v. *De Willott*, reported in 7 East. 110, where Lord Ellenborough said—the

1856.

March 6th.

Davidson
v.
Davidson.

case is not before me, but I remember it very well, when an attempt was made to move for a new trial on this account—" I have overruled it over and over again ; I hope the next time it arises a bill of exceptions will be tendered, for I am sick of overruling the point." That is the doctrine so laid down; but I apprehend the converse of the doctrine to be true: that upon cross-examination, if a question be put to a witness touching a declaration, verbal or written, pertinent to the issue, in that case, you are not forced to abide by the answer, but you are at liberty to contradict it.

Now, in this court we have generally expressed ourselves to the same effect, though rather in a different manner, because we have always said this, if you except to the evidence of a witness, the fact must be pertinent to the issue, and not pleadable before publication ; and we have said also, with respect to a declaration, if you except to a declaration, that this must be pertinent to the issue. The question, therefore, which the Court has to determine is, whether what is pleaded in this exceptive allegation was that which could have been pleaded before publication, whether it be pertinent to the issue or not, and whether, if pertinent to the issue, it is sufficiently stringent in any degree to affect the credit of the witness; because the Court never can say that the admission of the allegation if proved would utterly destroy the credit of a witness, and for many reasons this would be so. I take it that nothing would be more clear than this, that a witness may be produced in order to establish a case, and may swear falsely in one part altogether, and truly in another part, and that that witness may be believed when he or she swears truly, though it may be admitted he is actually perjured as to part; and if it were necessary to seek for an authority on that question I could at once give it, though my memory does not suggest the precise name;* but it will be found in a case, where the Common Pleas laid down, that you are not entitled to ask for a new trial though it is admitted that the witness may be perjured in part, because the other evidence the witness gives may be credible, the jury may have believed it, and the judge not thought fit to except to it. Therefore the Court is not to say in all these cases that the credit of the witness is to be destroyed, but to be affected ; and that being the case, it must see how far the evidence of the witness is strengthened and corroborated, or weakened, by all the rest of the testimony. There may be many facts and circumstances appearing from the evidence of other witnesses which may have an effect one way or the other, but on that it is not my business to enter.

I know of no case which militates against what I am saying in the slightest degree. The case of *Burgoyne* v. *Free*, 2 Hagg. 456, I could not altogether place much reliance on, and for an obvious reason, that the case of *Burgoyne* v. *Free* was a case in which there was a prosecution against a clergyman for immoral practices, and had reference to what we call in this court a criminal proceeding, which is governed by principles and rules somewhat varying from those to be considered in proceedings of a different nature ; and moreover,

---

* See *Bradley* v. *Ricardo*, 8 Bing. 59.

1856.

March 6th.

DAVIDSON
v.
DAVIDSON.

Sir John Nicholl stated in that judgment, he did not mean to go into the whole doctrine of exceptive allegations, but only so far as was pertinent to the admissibility of that plea.

With regard to the case of *Atkinson* v. *Atkinson*, 2 Add. 487, I confess I do not see its bearing on the present case. Now, if it was a mere question as to the belief of the witness or not, it has been truly argued on former occasions, and indeed decided, that the mere belief of a witness is not a necessary matter in the case at all one way or the other, because the Court founds its judgment upon facts deposed to, and not upon, as Lord Stowell expressed it, the logical deductions of the witness, and most rightly and most properly was it so decided. But there is another matter in *Atkinson* v. *Atkinson*, which is this, the examination in chief was on the 15th and 16th articles, and the facts in the exceptive allegation might have been pleaded before publication. I take it to be an indisputable principle that you shall not plead after publication that which might have been pleaded before; and that could not be done in this case. Again: in *Atkinson* v. *Atkinson*, the witness was not interrogated as to any admissions. "Suppose," says Sir J. Nicholl in that case, "that an interrogatory had been addressed to Hobbs to this effect: 'Have you never stated so and so, namely, your belief that the defendant never committed adultery with Mrs. Rolls either generally or *à fortiori* specifically; that is, have you never so stated to such and such persons, and so on?' Why the witness might then not improbably have admitted that she had so said, and might have accounted for her having deposed differently." It evidently was the opinion of the learned judge, who decided that case, that the matter ought to have been put in interrogatory. What would have been the effect of the contradiction on that interrogatory in the opinion of the learned judge is clear. In this case the question is put to the witness, who negatives the admission.

Then I examine this exceptive allegation for two purposes. I lay out of the question that it is impossible the contradiction could have been pleaded before, and I come first to see whether it is pertinent to the case; and secondly whether in itself it is a stringent contradiction. "When Mrs. W.," these are the words of the witness, "when Mrs. W., the ministrant's mother, arrived in Paris on the 29th May, and I opened the door to her, she did I think say, the very first thing, 'Oh, Denman, tell me, is it as bad as we think?—is she guilty?' or something to that effect." So far the witness admits the words of this interrogatory. Then the interrogatory goes on: "Did you not reply, Comfort yourself, madam, she is not guilty?" and the witness answers, "I did not reply, Comfort yourself, madam, she is not guilty; no, I am sure I did not." Now, that I apprehend to be a complete contradiction to the interrogatory which has been put; and I cannot help thinking that it is a very material interrogatory with respect to this case. It is pertinent to the issue, because it relates to the commission of adultery, which is the very issue in the case; and it is of importance for this reason, the witness can hardly be supposed to have forgotten so very material a declaration, if she did make it, as " she is not guilty."

1856.

March 6th.

DAVIDSON
v.
DAVIDSON.

It has been mixed up very ingeniously by the counsel for Mr. Davidson with a subsequent part of the interrogatory. " If nay, will you venture to swear that you never told the ministrant that those were your very words." That is a totally different and distinct inquiry altogether. The one inquiry is as to the fact, did you declare to Mrs. W. that in your opinion Mrs. Davidson was not guilty. The witness has answered; then the interrogatory goes on to a separate and distinct declaration of a different kind : " Will you venture to swear that you never told the ministrant that those were your very words?" Then she says, " I will venture to swear that I never told the ministrant that those were my very words."

It appears to me, with all my reluctance to admit exceptive allegations, that I have no power, looking at the rules and practice which have governed this court, to reject that article. The contradiction is complete; it propounds that she did reply in the words following: " Comfort yourself, madam, she is not guilty ;" and that such reply was made in the presence and hearing of the said B. W. It is a complete contradiction, and pertinent to the issue.

With regard to the other, the 18th interrogatory, the answer to the interrogatory is: " I have not expressed to Mr. and Mrs. W., the father and mother of the ministrant, my belief that the ministrant is innocent of the charge of adultery. I have never expressed that belief to them; I have only told them as near as I could everything as it occurred the same as near as possible as I have in my evidence, but never expressed to them the belief interrogate." The alleged contradiction is that "on several occasions since her return to England in attendance on the said Katherine Ann Davidson, party in this cause, as well as previously, she has expressed to the said Mr. and Mrs. W., the father and mother of the said Katherine Ann Davidson, party in this cause, her belief in the innocence of the said Katherine Ann Davidson."

Now, it is said this is immaterial; and it is said the question to the witness is in respect to immaterial matter. So it is as to the facts, but not at all immaterial with regard to the credibility of the witness, whether she has made a declaration to that effect; it is the most material fact of all. It does not require, in order to effect the declaration of a witness, that the declaration should be matter of great importance; it must be pertinent to the issue or it falls within the bann of Lord Tenterden; but if pertinent to the issue, it need not be of such materiality as to affect the whole case.

Looking to the whole of the allegation, I regret to say that I feel myself under the necessity of admitting this allegation.

FYLER *v.* FYLER.

*Husband and wife—Separate income—Costs.*

1856.

Aug. 8th.

Where the wife is plaintiff and fails in her suit, if her income is large in proportion to the income of the husband, the Court will not order her costs to be taxed as against the husband, but will leave her to pay those costs herself.

IN this case the wife instituted a suit for separation, on the ground of adultery, against the husband. The husband recriminated. The witnesses were examined *vivâ voce ;** and the adultery of the husband and wife having been proved, the Court dismissed both parties. Before sentence, but whether before the witnesses were examined was doubtful, the proctor for the wife applied for payment of costs in the usual manner; when the matter was directed to stand over. The question now was, whether the wife was entitled to have her costs paid. The facts were stated in act on petition and affidavit.

*Bayford* and *Twiss*, for the husband.—The wife's income is £157 10s., made up of £55 10s. received by her of her trustees, and £102 paid by the husband. His net income is £308; out of which he has to pay for policies of insurance to secure money advanced by the trustees of the marriage settlement £160, he allows his wife £102—this leaves him £46 a year. (They cited, upon the general principle, *Wilson* v. *Wilson*, 2 Cons. Reps. 203 ; *Davis* v. *Davis*, ib. n. [DR. LUSHINGTON.— There and in other cases the Court kept the power as to costs in its own hands till the end of the suit] ;

---

* This is the first instance in which the examination was throughout conducted *vivâ voce* in court.

1856.

Aug. 8th.

FYLER
v.
FYLER.

*Beevor* v. *Beevor*, 3 Phill. 261 ; *Belcher* v. *Belcher*, 1 Curt. 444 ; *Walker* v. *Walker*, ib. 564.)

*Phillimore* and *Spinks*, for the wife.—The whole of the husband's income may be said to be derived from the wife, for the husband contributed nothing to the settlement; and it has been by borrowing the wife's money from the trustees that he has attained his present rank.　He has paid the costs in the suit up to the time when the wife's proctor was changed, and thereby admitted his liability to pay the whole. There is nothing to take the case out of the regular course, according to which the wife would be entitled to her costs *de die in diem : Barrow* v. *Barrow*, 17 Jur. 240.

DR. LUSHINGTON.

I must decide this case according to the ordinary practice of the Court.　The general presumption is, that the wife has no means, and then the husband must bear the burden ; but to this there are exceptions, as where the wife has a large income in comparison with the husband. If in such a case the wife is plaintiff, the Court will hold its hand till the end of the proceedings ; and if the wife succeeds, the husband is condemned in the costs, as in ordinary cases between parties not husband and wife.　And when the wife has no income whatever, however great her demerits, whether she be plaintiff or defendant, the husband must pay the whole costs, even the costs of vexatious appeals.

This case I shall deal with exactly as I should have done, had the question been raised on a question of costs *de die in diem*, entirely irrespective of the merits of either party, and I shall look merely to the means of the husband and wife. So far as the facts are before me, the husband has scarcely any income at all. The insurance is a proper deduction and of essential value to the wife, as it is the security for advances made out of the settled funds. *Davis* v. *Davis* is the authority which I shall follow; and as the wife has not succeeded, I shall not allow her costs to be taxed now against the husband.

---

## PREROGATIVE COURT OF CANTERBURY.

---

*In the goods of* C. COCKAYNE.

*Revocation—Intention—New will unexecuted.*

---

*On Motion.*

THIS deceased made her will, dated the 21st of May, 1839, and also a codicil, dated the 7th of October, 1852. The will was written on seven sides of letter paper; the seventh side, upon which were the signature of the deceased, and subscription of the witnesses, and a memorandum as to the place

A. having a will and codicil, cut off the last page of the will, on which were the names of A. and the witnesses, and desired B. to burn the page so cut off. A. then made some altera-

tions in the remaining pages of the will, desired B. to write out a new will, and send for A.'s solicitor. B. wrote the new will, but did not burn the part cut off, as A. knew. A. died before executing the new will.—Held, on motion, that the former will was entitled to probate, there being no intention to revoke, except in connexion with the completion of a new will.

where the deceased desired to be buried, contained
no dispositive part of the will. On the day before
her death the deceased cut off this seventh sheet in
the presence of her servant, who deposed that on
that day the deceased took from a locked portfolio
the will and codicil, and that after having read the
will, the deceased with a pair of scissors cut off the
last sheet and gave it to the deponent, saying,
"Take and burn that, that's nothing." But that
the deponent, being the only person present, did
not like to take upon herself the responsibility of
destroying the paper, and accordingly left it on the
table near the deceased; that the deceased gave no
reason for so cutting off the last sheet, but deponent
believed, from previous recent conversations with
her, in which deceased expressed a desire to be buried
in Brislington Cemetery; that her reason for so
doing was, that the said half sheet contained a direction that she should be buried at Stapleton. The
deponent, after stating that the deceased then made
some alterations in the remaining six sides, deposed
that shortly after the alterations had been made,
she, by direction of the deceased, sent a letter to
Mr. Knapp, the deceased's solicitor, requesting his
attendance on the following day; that the deceased
then said to her, "I wish you would write this paper
for me, in case I may not be well enough to tell Mr.
Knapp when he comes to-morrow;" whereupon deponent proceeded to write, from her dictation, the
paper, which, when completed, the deceased endeavoured to sign, but from weakness was unable to
do so. The deponent folded up in an envelope the
will, including the half sheet cut off, the codicil, and
the paper or intended new will, and placed them in

a drawer, where they remained until after the death of the deceased, save on the occasion when they were on the following day produced to Mr. Knapp. This gentleman deposed, that in compliance with the letter sent to him, he came to the deceased; that the papers having been produced by the servant of the deceased, she, the deceased, pointed to the paper written by the said servant, but was unable further to express her intentions. And deponent, finding his assistance of no avail, shortly afterwards left the deceased, who died on the same day.

In some particulars the proposed new will was copied from the former will, but the instruments differed materially. The specific legacies were different; and the second paper appointed neither executor nor residuary legatee—the former will appointed both.

*Jenner* moved for probate of the former paper as originally executed.—The deceased had no intention to revoke that will unless she could execute another; and this she at once attempted, but was prevented by death. The codicil remained untouched; and the seventh sheet, though separated from the will, was preserved with the rest of the will, as the deceased well knew. The act of revocation was not completed; and the intention to revoke was dependent on being able to give effect to another will. The case came within the principle in *Winsor* v. *Pratt*, 5 Moore, 484 ; *Onions* v. *Tyrer*, 1 P. Wms. 445; *Brooke* v. *Kent*, 3 Moo. P. C. C. 348.

1856.

May 15th.

In the goods of
C.COCKAYNE.

SIR JOHN DODSON.

The circumstances of this case, looking to the preservation of the part cut off and the subsisting codicil, are singular; and I am strongly inclined to agree with you that the deceased had no intention to revoke this will, unless she could execute another. But I do not like to dispose of the case on an *ex parte* motion, and in the absence of parties who may be injured by the upholding this instrument, and who may call in the probate at any time hereafter.

The motion was granted subsequently, on the Court being satisfied that very great delay and inconvenience would be incurred if all the parties interested were cited.

*In the goods of* A. M. ASH.*

*Incorporation of Papers.*

---

*On Motion.*

---

1856.

May 26th.

THIS deceased left a will in her own handwriting, written on two sides of a sheet of paper, and dated 23d March, 1849, by which she " gave and bequeathed unto my sons Edward, John, William, and James .the articles of plate set down under their respective names in the annexed schedule." On the third and fourth sides of the same sheet of paper on which the will was written were lists of articles of plate, headed with the words " list of plate for ——," the name of each son being added; and at the end of each list was the deceased's signature, but without date or attestation. The subscribing witnesses were unable to depose whether these schedules were written at the time of execution or not.

*Robertson* moved for probate of the will with the schedules.

SIR JOHN DODSON.

These schedules are on the same sheet of paper with the will, which refers to them as in existence at the time when the will was written. They may, therefore, be considered as incorporated, and as such entitled to probate.

*Lists of plate signed by the testatrix, but not attested, and written on the same sheet of paper with the will which referred to them, as in existence, the will and schedules being in the handwriting of the testatrix, admitted to probate. No evidence could be obtained to show whether the lists were written at the time of execution.*

---

* See *In the goods of Hunt,* 17 Jurist, 720; *In the goods of Hakewell,* 4 W. R. 204.

*In the goods of* THE COUNTESS DOWAGER OF
PEMBROKE.

*Incorporation of Papers.*

---

1856.

*On Motion.*

---

May 26th.

---

A paper writ-
ten before the
will referring
to it, signed and
dated but not
attested, and
not found with
the will or pro-
duced at the
time of the
execution of
the will, not
admitted to
probate.

LADY PEMBROKE left a will dated 29th of July,
1853, and three codicils dated 29th of August,
1853, 21st of February, 1856, and 17th of March,
1856. By the first codicil she gave "to my
daughter Elizabeth, Countess of Clanwilliam, such
articles of plate as should be enumerated in any
list or catalogue found with my will or among my
papers, and marked or intended for her." No such
list or catalogue was produced at the execution of
any of the codicils, or found with the will; but in
a plate chest was found a sealed envelope indorsed
" July, 1851. List of plate to be divided off and
given to Lady Clanwilliam;" and inside the envelope was a list of articles of plate, headed "Lady
Clanwilliam," and signed and dated "Catherine
Pembroke, July, 1851."

*Addams* moved for probate of this list, as clearly
identified and in existence when the will and
codicils were executed.

SIR JOHN DODSON.

There is a case in 2 Curt. 831, *In the goods
of Sotheron,* which is an authority against this
motion; indeed, the facts in that case were much
stronger in favour of the incorporation of the

papers in question than the facts are here. In rejecting that motion, Sir H. Jenner said he was not aware of any case in which it had been held that a paper should form part of a will by merely being referred to. I must reject this motion.

1856.

May 26th.

In the goods of
THE
COUNTESS
DOWAGER OF
PEMBROKE.

---

## In the goods of JAMES SHILLING.

*Survivorship—1 Vic. c. 26, s. 33.*

---

### On Motion.

---

JAMES SHILLING died in July in the present year, having made and executed his will, and appointed his son Thomas Shilling sole executor and universal legatee. The deceased died a widower, and had no other issue. The deceased and his said son Thomas were driving home in a gig near the river Medway; the next morning the horse and gig were found in the river, and the bodies of both father and son drowned! No person saw the accident, and there was no proof as to which might have been the survivor.

Thomas Shilling left a widow and several children, and died intestate.

*Robertson* moved for letters of administration (with the will annexed) of the goods of James Shilling, deceased, to be granted to Charlotte Shilling, the administratrix of Thomas Shilling,

*A. and his son were found dead, and no evidence could be given as to which survived. A. by will had appointed his son executor and universal legatee. The son left a widow and children, but no will. Administration of the effects of the father, with will annexed, granted to the widow, as administratrix of her husband, whilst living the sole executor and universal legatee in the will.*

deceased, whilst living the sole executor and universal legatee named in the will of the deceased.
He relied upon the 1 Vic. c. 26, s. 33, which provides that if any person being a child or other issue
of the testator shall die in the lifetime of the testator
leaving issue, and any such issue shall be living at
the time of the death of the testator, the devise or
bequest shall not lapse; that this was a remedial
enactment, and there were no facts before the Court
to exclude its operation, so that it would govern
the present case.

SIR JOHN DODSON granted the motion.

---

## In the goods of JOHN POYER POYER.

### On Motion.

THIS was a question respecting the administration, with the will and codicils annexed, of the
unadministered goods of the deceased.

By his will, made in 1838, the deceased appointed
S., C., and K., executors and residuary legatees in
trust.

By the first codicil, dated December, 1844, after
reciting that by his will he had appointed such persons as executors and trustees, the testator revoked
the appointment of K. as an executor and trustee,
and every devise, bequest, interest, power, and

authority thereby given to or vested in him, and gave the real and personal estates comprised in his will to S., C., and N., upon the same trusts, and with the same powers as declared in the will, in all respects confirming the will except as to the substitution of N. instead of K. as executor and trustee. By the second codicil, dated March, 1847, he desired that C. and K., named in his will as his executors, be no longer regarded as such, and in their place he nominated D. and R. to succeed them; and after bequeathing an annuity and giving some legacies, he ratified and confirmed his will except as the same was thereby altered. On the 6th of July, 1850, the will and last codicil were proved by S. alone, D. and R. having renounced the probate. On the 13th of February, 1854, probate of the first codicil was taken by S., power being reserved to N., the executor and trustee therein substituted, to come in and prove. D. and R. renounced probate of this codicil also. S. and N. are since dead; and a grant of letters of administration of the unadministered goods of the deceased was required. The children of the testator, the residuary legatees named in the will on attaining the age of 21 years, were minors, and had elected their mother as their guardian to take administration of the unadministered goods of the deceased for their use and benefit. Upon this the question arose, whether the appointment of C. as residuary legatee in trust was revoked either expressly or by implication by the second codicil, and whether in that character he would not be entitled to the grant though his appointment as executor was revoked. It appeared by a decree of the Master of the Rolls, in a suit

1856.

Aug. 7th.

In the goods of
JOHN POYER
POYER.

respecting the trusts under the will, that the Master of the Rolls declared that the appointment of C. contained in the will of the testator, as one of the trustees thereof, and the devises and bequests to him as such trustee therein contained, were not revoked or affected by the codicils to the said testator's will, or either of them; that the appointment of K. contained in the will to be one of the trustees thereof, and the devises and bequests to him as such, were revoked by the codicil of December, 1844; and that such appointment was not set up or revived by the codicil of March, 1847.

*Swabey* moved the Court to grant the administration to C., as surviving residuary legatee in trust therein named. He cited *Hutchinson* v. *Lambert,* 3 Add. 427, and relied on the general practice of granting administration, with the will annexed, to the residuary legatee in trust where an executor fails to represent a testator.

*Deane,* on behalf of the guardian of the children, opposed the motion. (He cited *Coussmaker* v. *Chamberlayne,* 2 Lee, 243; *Boddicott* v. *Dalzeel,* ib. 294; and *Fawkener* v. *Jordan,* ib. 327.) The practice as to grants to residuary legatees in trust is correctly stated, but C. is a mere trustee; for the testator, by revoking his appointment as executor, has shown that he did not intend C. to take probate of, or interfere with the proving of his will. C. is not to get in the estate, though when got in it may vest in him. The testator evidently knew the distinction between the office of executor and that of mere trustee. He has revoked the appointment in one

character, and C. remains but a trustee, and to a
trustee, merely as such, this Court does not grant
administration.

1856.

Aug. 7th.

In the goods of
JOHN POYER
POYER.

SIR JOHN DODSON.

I am of opinion that the appointment and revocation as executor distinguishes this case from those
under the ordinary practice as to residuary legatees
in trust, and that I cannot grant the administration to a person who was clearly intended by the
testator not to be intrusted with it by this Court at
least. I shall decree the administration to the
guardian of the children.

---

### FARMER v. BROCK.

*Evidence—Corroborating facts—Witness discredited.*

1856.

June 9th.

PERREN MEHEW left a will dated July the 3d,
1854, in which he appointed R. A. Farmer sole
executor and residuary legatee, and by which he
gave several legacies to various persons, and an
annuity to F. W. Brock, who, as residuary legatee
in a former will dated January, 1853, now opposed
the will of 1854. There was also a codicil to the

The two sub-
scribing wit-
nesses were the
only witnesses
produced in
support of a
will. One of
them was dis-
credited.
There was no
evidence of in-
structions.
Will pro-
nounced for on
the evidence of the single witness, corroborated by the probabilities of the case.

will of 1853, made in June, 1854, by which Farmer was appointed executor of the will of 1853.

The will of 1854 was propounded in an allegation in common form, upon which the two subscribing witnesses were produced and examined. They deposed to the due execution of the will, but differed as to some not very material circumstances noticed in the judgment. There was no question as to the capacity of the deceased, nor was it contended that his signature was forged; and the attestation clause was complete. There was no evidence of instructions, and the evidence tended to show that the body of the will was in Farmer's handwriting. No counterplea was brought in before publication, but an allegation was brought in excepting to one of the witnesses, Ball, on the ground that he had admitted that the will was not signed by the deceased in the joint presence of himself and the other witness, and that on interrogatory he had denied having made such admission. Upon this exceptive allegation several witnesses were examined *vivâ voce;* the admission as pleaded was proved; and at the same time it was also proved that the witness Ball was 18 or 19 years old, and a potboy in the employ of a man named Wagener—had been tampered with by this Wagener, who had no interest in the result of the case, but expected he might make money out of one of the parties. At the time of execution both witnesses were in the employ of Farmer—Bird as nurse, and Ball as porter.

*Jenner* and *Deane*, for the will, submitted that the evidence of the unimpeached witness was sufficient to establish the will of a testator whose capacity was not disputed, and whose signature to the will was admitted to be genuine.

*Bayford* and *Phillimore, contrà.*—The evidence of a single witness, however credible, if unsupported by corroborating circumstances, was never admitted as sufficient proof of a testamentary act. Here there were no corroborating circumstances, but everything to raise a suspicion; no proof of instructions, yet the will written by the party propounding it, and who took the largest benefit under it, both witnesses being in his employ. (They cited *Theakston* v. *Marson*, 4 Hagg. 291.)

In reply, *Hatchwell* v. *Hatchwell*, 2 N. C. 513, and *Gove* v. *Gawen*, 3 Curt. 151, were cited.

JUDGMENT.

SIR JOHN DODSON.

After stating the facts. The discrepancy between the two witnesses is such that it cannot be explained away. They differ as to whether Farmer was present or not at the time of the execution of the will; whether they came once or twice into the room—the first time to sign their names, the second time to add their descriptions. Bird says Farmer was present all the time, and that they came up a second time at the request of the deceased himself, to "figure in their descriptions." Ball deposes that Farmer was not present, and that he, Ball, went but once into the room, and then wrote his name and address as they now appear. If these were matters of importance to the issue, and I were bound to decide between these two wit-

1856.

June 9th.

FARMER
*v.*
BROCK.

nesses, I should have little hesitation in trusting Mrs. Bird rather than the other, and for this reason, that her testimony throughout is consistent, whilst Ball contradicts himself. The material point, however, is whether the deceased signed the will in their presence, and they in his; and they both depose in the affirmative. But it is quite clear, from the evidence given upon the exceptive allegation, that Ball, in describing what took place at the execution of the will, has not kept to one story throughout; and one of the questions for my decision is, which of Ball's statements is true. I think the truth will be found where he is corroborated by Bird, and not in those accounts of the transaction which he gave whilst in the employ of a man who was clearly shown to have endeavoured to make money by inducing this young man to give a false history. Still Ball is discredited; and I am pressed with the argument that the Court cannot pronounce for this will on the testimony of a single witness; and in support of that argument, and to show the practice of this Court in this respect, cases were cited, as *Theakston* v. *Marson*, 4 Hagg. 291. The marginal note of that case is correctly drawn. It was the case of an unfinished pencil memorandum; very different, therefore, from the present case. There were no adminicular circumstances whatever; and the whole depended upon the bare testimony of one witness. In *Moore* v. *Payne*, 2 Lee, 595, it was held that one witness was sufficient if corroborated by circumstances. So in *Mackenzie* v. *Yeo*, 3 Curt. 125, the evidence of one witness was held not sufficient to sustain the paper, in the absence of any circumstance leading up to the probability of the transaction, there being, on the contrary, various facts adverse to the validity of the will; and in the very next case in the same volume, *Gove* v. *Gawen*, where the two witnesses differed, the will was pronounced for on the evidence of one, the probabilities of the case showing that testimony to contain the real account. In no case, then, has it been held that there must of necessity be more than one witness. "The solemnity of the civil law is not requisite with us," observes Sir G. Lee, in *Moore* v. *Payne*, "it is sufficient if there be adminicular proof to corroborate the one witness." What, then, are the circumstances in this case? There is the codicil to the first will, where Farmer is introduced as an executor, and that codicil was prepared by a solicitor, and is unimpeached. Brock takes under the will propounded, in the shape of an annuity, a very considerable benefit, and so do other friends of the testator. The signature is not disputed, the capacity is not denied; nor, in fact, can I altogether disregard the evidence of Ball himself, given on oath, in support of a proper execution, and agreeing with the testimony of Bird. I, therefore, pronounce for the will.

## BREMER *v.* FREEMAN AND BREMER.

1856.
———
March 31st.
February 1st,
5th, 19th.
August 16th.
———

*Will—Domicil by the law of nations—Domicil by the law of the country in which the testator resides—Costs.*

A., a British-born subject, left England many years before her death, resided in Paris for the last 15 years of her life, and died there; assumed for many years an Italian name, and described herself and was described in legal documents as widow of an Italian. There was no evidence of the fact of marriage; and the statements made by the deceased in respect to the marriage were contradictory. She had real property in India, the bulk of her personalty in England, and made her will in the English form, disposing of her property,

THE deceased died at Paris, in April, 1853. She left a will made according to English law, and executed in Paris on the 19th of September, 1842, in the following words: "I, Fanny Allegri *née* Calcraft, the only surviving child of the late H. F. Calcraft, a lieutenant-general in her Majesty's service in the East Indies, and who resided and was buried at Brighton, in England, at present residing in Paris, in the kingdom of France, widow, do make and declare this my last will and testament in manner following." She then devised certain real property in India to D. A. Freeman, gave 1000 francs each to the two persons who might be with her in her last illness, 500 francs to two charitable institutions in Paris, and the remainder of her property "unto and equally among the said D. A. Freeman and my cousins, E. A. Bremer, Susan Bremer, James Grignon Bremer, and H. Bremer, children of the late Captain Bremer, R.N., or such of them as shall be living at my decease." And she appointed D. A. Freeman and J. G. Bremer (one of such

with the exception of four small legacies, amongst English persons.—Held, that by the law of nations the deceased was domiciled in France; but that as she had not been naturalized, nor obtained an authorized domicil in and as required by the law of France, she might by the French law make a will in the English form, and that such will was entitled to probate in this country.

1856.

March 31st.
February 1st,
5th, 19th.
August 16 h.

BREMER
v.
FREEMAN
and
BREMER.

cousins) executors. This will was prepared by Mr. T. Freeman, the solicitor of the deceased, and the father of Mr. D. A. Freeman.

Mr. D. A Freeman and Mr. J. G. Bremer took probate of this will in the Prerogative Court on the 24th of June, 1853; but some doubt having subsequently arisen respecting the domicil of the deceased, and consequently the validity of her will, Susan Catherine Bremer, who was also one of the next of kin and entitled in distribution, on the 28th of October, 1853, called in the probate. This probate was brought in, and Mr. Freeman denied Miss Bremer's interest; an appearance was also given for Mr. Bremer, who was the brother of Miss Bremer, and he declared he did not propound the will.

The suit then went on as an interest cause, in which Mr. Freeman was ultimately condemned in the costs.

The interest cause being ended, the will was propounded in an allegation in common form, upon which the two subscribing witnesses only were examined, the drawer of the will, Mr. T. Freeman, not being produced. A responsive allegation on the part of Miss Bremer was, after opposition, admitted, which pleaded—

1. The death of the deceased, leaving property invested in her name as Fanny Allegri.

2. Her birth at Calcutta in 1795; her residence in England from an early age until the year 1825, when she left England and never afterwards returned.

3. Her residence in Italy, and her marriage to an Italian named Allegri; that she lived and cohabited with him; and that she and Allegri on all

1856.

March 31st.
February 1st,
5th, 19th.
August 16th.

BREMER
v.
FREEMAN
and
BREMER.

occasions, save as regards her family and friends in England, owned and acknowledged each other as husband and wife, until the death of Allegri, six months after the marriage; that by reason of the marriage having been clandestine and kept secret from the knowledge of her father, &c., neither the exact time or place of the marriage and cohabitation can be ascertained; and that the deceased throughout her subsequent life referred to her marriage, and the death of her husband.

4. Pleaded a letter from the deceased to J. G. Bremer, dated 1st of October, 1840, in which occurred the passage, " I had requested my dear Mrs. C. to write to inform you of my great calamity* which had befallen me, and to tell you also of my change of name, and that I have been a widow more than ten years; but my loved sister never would acknowledge my marriage, because I did not ask her father's consent. I very much regret not having done so, and I own I did wrong."

5. That the deceased, after the death of her father (which occurred in April, 1834), was known and passed by the name of Allegri, was described in legal documents, prepared by and in the possession of T. Freeman, as Fanny Allegri, widow, and was so described by the said T. Freeman in two letters written by him to J. G. Bremer and S. C. Bremer, respectively, on the 7th and 8th of March, 1848.

6. That on the death of General Calcraft, in 1834, the sister of the deceased left England and resided with the deceased at different places on the Continent, until the summer of 1838, when they,

---

* Referring to the recent death of her sister.

the two sisters, took up their final and permanent abode in Paris.

1856.

March 31st.
February 1st,
5th, 19th.
August 16th.

BREMER
v.
FREEMAN
and
BREMER.

7. Pleaded various letters.

8. Occupation of apartments in Paris under leases ; and the renewal of the last lease for three years, from the 1st of July, 1851.

9. Permanent residence at one house in Paris.

10. Declarations of intention to remain permanently in France, and never return to England ; purchase of a vault in perpetuity on her sister's death, and declarations of her own intention to be buried in that vault with her sister.

11, 12. Pleaded various letters.

13. Description of deceased as "Fanny Allegri, born Calcraft, widow," in an act of notoriety on her deceased, executed by T. Freeman and another, at the instance and with the concurrence of D. A. Freeman, in July, 1853, and forwarded for registration in Paris, by D. A. Freeman.

14, 15, 16. Exhibits.

17. That by reason of the premises the deceased was, at the dates of her will and death, domiciled in France ; and that no paper was valid as her will unless executed according to French law.

18. Set out the French law, and pleaded that such law applied equally to natural-born subjects of France as to foreigners who have become domiciled in France by fixing their residence with an intention of permanently remaining.

19. That the paper propounded was not executed according to French law.

The witnesses produced upon this allegation were cross-examined by Mr. Bremer; and application was made to the Court, on behalf of Mr. Freeman, to

1856.

March 31st.
February 1st,
5th, 19th.
August 16th.

BREMER
v.
FREEMAN
and
BREMER.

direct the evidence given upon such cross-examination to be struck out on the ground that the will was in reality opposed by Mr. Bremer, who was in fact the party in the cause though using his sister's name, and that to allow him to interrogate her witnesses was in fact allowing him to interrogate his own witnesses. This application was rejected by Sir John Dodson.

A further allegation was brought in on behalf of Mr. D. A. Freeman, pleading—

1. That the deceased left England in 1827 and not in 1825.

2. That the deceased was never married to Allegri.

3. Residence abroad.

4. That during her residence in Paris she constantly expressed her intention of leaving as soon as her health would allow her, and that she had very trifling property in Paris.

5. Her expressions of dislike to climate, habits, &c., of France.

6. Various particulars as to deceased's mode of dealing with her property during her life as tending to show that she considered England as her home.

7. Exhibits.

8. That the deceased was not by reason of the premises ever lawfully domiciled in France so as to have acquired a domicil of succession according to the laws of that country.

9. That by the laws of France the succession to the personalty of all deceased persons, whether testamentary, or *ab intestato*, is dependent upon, and is governed and regulated by, the law of the place of the domicil of the deceased.

1856.

March 31st.
February 1st,
5th, 19th.
August 16th.

BREMER
v.
FREEMAN
and
BREMER.

10. That the laws of France in force at the time of the death of the deceased with respect to the validity of testaments, do not apply equally to natural born subjects of France as to foreigners who have become domiciled there by fixing their residence with an intention of permanently remaining, but that the succession, whether testamentary, or *ab intestato*, of a foreigner, who was neither naturalized nor authorized to establish his domicil in France, is governed by the law of his own country.

11. That although S. C. Bremer and J. G. Bremer are appearing in this suit by separate proctors, yet that the suit, so far as concerns the said S. C. Bremer, has been and is in fact and in truth conducted by J. C. Bremer, who is acting on her behalf herein; that he has throughout communicated with her legal advisers, and has given them every assistance in his power, and that he is desirous of securing and has throughout so acted as to secure her success and to oppose and prevent the success of D. A. Freeman.

12, 13. Exhibits.

14. That the materials of the allegation given in on behalf of S. C. Bremer were chiefly furnished to her or her advisers by her brother, J. G. Bremer, or some one acting on his behalf; that he has supplied the money necessary for defraying her expenses, and is responsible to the proctor of S. C. Bremer for the same.

15. That the interrogatories administered by J. G. Bremer to the witnesses produced upon the allegation of S. C. Bremer, were prepared after conference and consultation with the legal advisers in

1856.

March 31st.
February 1st,
5th, 19th.
August 16th.

BREMER
v.
FREEMAN
and
BREMER.

this suit of S. C. Bremer; that the French advocate who acted on behalf of J. G. Bremer, in preparing the said interrogatories, had previously assisted S. C. Bremer in collecting evidence, and also by seeing, conversing with, and interpreting on behalf of the witnesses produced by S. C. Bremer, upon the allegation.

16. That J. G. Bremer has frequently declared and admitted that his interest in opposing the will propounded is identical with that of his sister, S. C. Bremer; and that he hoped she would succeed, and was doing all he could to help her.

The admission of this allegation, which was admitted as above after reformation, was opposed as originally brought in on behalf of Miss Bremer, and also Mr. Bremer.

SIR JOHN DODSON, however, after hearing Miss Bremer's counsel, refused to hear Mr. Bremer's counsel in opposition to the admission.

Upon these allegations, besides the several witnesses to facts, were examined eight members of the French bar, Messrs. Frignet, Senard, and Paillet, on the part of Miss Bremer; and Messrs. Marie, Blanchet, C. de Lisle, Hebert, and Vatismesnil, for Mr. Freeman.

*Sir J. D. Harding, Q.A.*, and *Phillimore*, for Mr. Freeman.—The domicil of origin is retained till a fresh domicil is acquired by fact and intention; the mere act of residence will not effect a change of domicil, without the intention of permanent residence: *Munroe* v. *Douglas*, 5 Madd. 279; *Somerville* v.

*Somerville*, 5 Ves. 759 ; *Munro* v. *Munro*, 7 Cl. &
Fin. 842 ; *De Bonneval* v. *De Bonneval*, 1 Curt.
856 ; *Attorney-General* v. *Dunn*, 6 M. & W. 527 ;
*Craigie* v. *Lewin*, 3 Curt. 435; *Stanley* v. *Bernes*,
3 Hagg. 373. In the present case the deceased had,
neither in fact nor by intention, abandoned her
original domicil, whether Anglo-Indian or English,
and acquired a French domicil when she made the
will.   The will was valid therefore when executed;
and even admitting that she subsequently acquired
a French domicil, that would not revoke the will.
If the marriage of the deceased was meant to be
relied on to show the change of domicil, the op-
posers of the will should have proved the marriage, which they have not done; for the bare
passing by the description of Madame Allegri,
widow, is no proof of the marriage.   Again: Supposing the deceased to have been domiciled in
France, then the case is met by *Collier* v. *Rivaz*,
2 Curt. 858, which is directly in point, and shows
that under the *Code Civil* the will of a British-
born subject domiciled where the code is in force,
is valid, if executed according to the law of England.

But this deceased was not, according to the evidence of the French lawyers in the case, domiciled
in France.   She had obtained no authorization from
the Government to establish her domicil there; and
that authorization, they depose, is an indispensable
condition, without which the foreigner is considered
by the French law as a mere resident.   Nor does
the case rest upon the bare evidence of these French
advocates, for their opinions are supported by several French cases; and the text writers also state
that under the *Code Civil* the foreigner has no

1856.

March 31st.
Februa y 1st,
5th, 19th.
August 16th.

BREMER
*v.*
FREEMAN
and
BREMER.

1856.

March 31st.
February 1st,
5th, 19th.
August 16th.

BREMER
v.
FREEMAN
and
BREMER.

means of acquiring a French domicil other than by the authority of the Government (*Demangeat. Hist. de la Condition Civile des Etrangers en France*, 369; *Demolombe Cours de Code Civil*, vol. I., b. 1, tit. 1, ch. 3). And as the deceased had not obtained the authorization of the Government, it follows that she was not domiciled in France, and consequently the will is valid, being executed according to the law of England, the domicil of the testatrix.

*Jenner* and *Spinks*, for Miss Bremer.—One contention in this case is, that a residence fixed and permanent for fifteen years in one country, and an absence from the country of original or subsequently-acquired domicil, coupled with expressed intentions of never returning to the latter, are not sufficient to constitute a domicil in the places of such continued residence. Every case cited on the other side from an English Court, on domicil, negatives that contention. Apart, then, from the question of marriage, and by the law of nations, the deceased was domiciled in France at the time of her death; and this reflects back upon the time when the will was executed, for she never moved from Paris in the interval. But how stands the case upon the marriage of the deceased? If this were a case in which a question of legitimacy or of inheritance depended on the proof of marriage, possibly the marriage could not be deemed established; but here the marriage is pleaded but as a circumstance in the case showing how completely the deceased had given up her English domicil when she assumed a foreign name. But is, in a question of marriage, reputation not to be considered? She was treated and described by all persons, including her solicitor, as a widow, in letters, in legal documents, as mortgages and conveyances—in the very will before the Court —in the jurat and affidavit of Mr. D. A. Freeman, when he proved the will.

Five French advocates have been examined on the part of Mr. Freeman; three on the part of Miss Bremer; and, upon the point whether a domicil can be acquired in France by a foreigner without authorization, they are totally opposed; it is clear, then, that from the opinion of these learned persons the Court can derive no great assistance, nor arrive at any satisfactory conclusion. But there were cases cited from the French Tribunals, and these, it is said, went to determine the question. These cases, however, are not easily reconciled with each other; and when the French advocates were pressed on interrogatory with the conflict between their own cases, they answer, "That there are many decisions of a contrary nature, but they do not place much reliance upon them;" or, "That they were cases in which French interests were concerned, in opposition to the interests of foreigners;" or, "That those decrees were made in special cases, and come under the practical adage, that decrees are good for those who obtain them." There is, however, one case upon which this Court can rely (*Lanenville* v *Anderson*, 17 Jur. 511), and since affirmed by the Judicial Committee. There the deceased had no authorization of the French Government; the point was directly raised in the case; and yet this Court and the Court of Appeal both pronounced for the French domicil, and the will was referred to the French tribunals to pronounce upon.

1856.

March 31st.
February 1st,
5th, 19th.
August 16th.

BREMER
*v.*
FREEMAN
and
BREMER.

1856.

March 31st.
February 1st,
5th, 19th.
August 16th.

BREMER
v.
FREEMAN
and
BREMER.

*Deane,* for Mr. J. G. Bremer, after submitting that for testamentary purposes domicil might be acquired by a foreigner in France without authorization, and that the deceased was so domiciled, referred to the general practice in cases of co-plaintiffs and co-defendants, and cited *Wood and others* v. *Goodlake and others,* 2 Curt. 82 ; *Dyce Sombre's case, antè,* p. 22 ; and *Hyde* v. *Cates and Hyde,* not reported, but decided in this court in June, 1853, in which last case the will of a single woman without a parent was opposed by a niece, and also by a brother, who had originally joined in taking out probate as one of the executors. The rule of practice, therefore, justified the course pursued by Mr. Bremer.

At the close of the argument, SIR JOHN DODSON directed that Mr. Freeman, the drawer of the will, should be produced and examined *vivâ voce.* This gentleman deposed to the deceased having stated to him that she was not married, but that she would not use her maiden name. He proved the instructions for the will.

The French cases cited throughout the argument were,—

LYNCH's CASE, reported in Sirey, 1851, of which the abstract is,

" *La loi qui régit la succession d'un étranger décédé en France, quant aux meubles qui sont situés dans ce pays, est la loi du pays du défunt, alors surtout que celui-ci n'avait pas un domicile légal en France, et qu'il n'a ancun héritier Français.* (*Cod. Civ.* 3, *L.* 14 *Juill.,* 1819.)

1856.

March 31st.
February 1st,
5th, 19th.
August 16th.

BREMER
*v.*
FREEMAN
and
BREMER.

" *En conséquence, les tribunaux Français sont incompétens pour connaître d'une demande en liquidation et partage d'une telle succession.*

" *Par suite encore, un acte émané du tribunal
étranger compétent, qui autorise l'un des héritiers à
administrer provisoirement la succession du défunt,
doit s'appliquer aux meubles situés en France, quand
même ils ne seraint pas spécialement désignés dans cet
acte ; pourvu, bien entendu que l'acte dont il s'agit ne
contienne rien de contraire aux principes du droit
Français.*

" *Ainsi, si cet acte attribue à l'héritier administrateur
le pouvoir de disposer des biens du défunt, les autres
héritiers ne peuvent demander aux tribunaux Français
l'autorisation de faire procéder eux-mêmes à la vente
des meubles situés en France.*

" *Et si le tribunal étranger a assujetti l'héritier administrateur à fournir caution pour sa gestion des
biens situés à l'étranger, il convient que les tribunaux
Français exigent aussi de lui une caution à l'égard des
meubles situés en France.*"

THORNTON *v.* CURLING, Dalloz' Reports, 1827 :—
" *Doit être réputée ouverte en France la succession
d'un étranger qui y est mort depuis la loi du 14
Juillet, 1819, après avoir obtenu du gouvernement la
jouissance des droits civils et y avoir transféré son
domicile, conformément à l'autorisation qu'il avait ob-
tenue, et cela, encore bien que cet étranger ne serait
pas naturalisé Français. En conséquence, c'est devant
le tribunal dans le ressort duquel il est mort que doivent
être portées les contestations qui s'élèvent entre le fils
du défunt et le légataire étranger qu'il a institué, au
sujet de sa succession, et, par exemple, sur la validité*

1856.

March 31st.
February 1st,
5th, 19th.
August 16th.

BREMER
*v.*
FREEMAN
and
BREMER.

*ou invalidité du testament qu'il a laissé; le legataire demanderait en vain le renvoi devant les juges du pays du testateur.* (C. C., 13, 110; C. pr., 59.)"

CARLIER D'ABAUNZA, Sirey's Reports, 1842 :—

"1° *Les consuls étrangers ne jouissent pas en France des prérogatives et immunités attachées à la qualité d'agens diplomatiques; en conséquence, ils ne sont pas affranchis de la contrainte par corps, ni de la saisie conservatoire de leurs meubles, à raison des dettes qu'ils ont contractées.*—Res seulement par le trib. de 1ʳᵉ instance.

" *Dans tous les cas, ils ne pourraient prétendre à ces prérogatives qu'autant qu'ils auraient obtenu l'exequatur du Gouvernement Français.*

" 2° *La résidence prolongée d'un étranger en France et l'établissement par mariage qu'il y a formé, n'équivalent pas pour lui à un domicile, susceptible de l'affranchir de la contrainte par corps, à raison des condamnations rendues contre lui.* (*Loi du 17 Avril, 1832, art. 14.*)

" *Ces circonstances ne suffisent pas davantage pour l'affranchir de la saisie conservatoire de ses meubles, à laquelle est soumis tout débiteur forain.* (*Cod. proc. 822.*)"

BREUL'S CASE, Gazette des Tribunaux, 21st July, 1852 :—

" *L'article 13 du Code Napoléon, qui dit que l'étranger admis par le Gouvernement Français à établir son domicile en France, y jouit de tous les droits civils, n'a pas eu pour objet de déterminer les conditions que devait remplir un étranger pour acquérir un domicile en France.*

" *L'étranger qui a fixé depuis près de trente ans*

*son habitation réelle en France, qui ne l'a pas quittée pendant cet intervalle de temps, reunit tous les conditions légales et constitutives du domicile. C'est donc aux tribunaux Français que doivent être soumises les questions relatives à la succession de cet étranger mort en France.*"

1856.

March 31st.
February 1st,
5th, 19th.
August 16th.

BREMER
*v.*
FREEMAN
and
BREMER.

LLOYD's CASE, Sirey's Reports, 1849 :—

" *Le mari, étranger de naissance, mais domicilié depuis longtemps en France, qui se marie sans contrat dans ce pays, avec une Française, doit être réputé avoir consenti à la communauté légale établie par la loi Française, et cela, encore que le fait de son domicile n'ait pas été accompagné de l'autorisation du gouvernement nécessaire à l'étranger pour établir son domicile en France; cette autorisation, requise pour que l'étranger jouisse de tous les droits civils Français, n'est point nécessaire pour l'établissement de la communauté, qui est purement du droit des gens. (Cod. Civ. 13 et 1393).*"

DE VEINE *v.* ROUTLEDGE, Sirey's Reports, 1852:—

" *1°. La possession d'état, à défaut d'acte de naissance, est un élément essentiel de la preuve de la filiation légitime.*

" *Spécialement :—Lorsqu'il n'a pas été tenu de registres de l'état civil dans le lieu et à l'époque de la naissance d'une personne (une fille) qui se dit enfant légitime d'un homme qui aurait été marié, il ne saurait être pleinement suppléé à son acte de naissance par des déclarations du prétendu père, consignées dans des actes authentiques dressés pour le mariage de l'enfant réclamant, et portant qu'il est né en légitime mariage du déclarant et de son épouse décédée . . . , alors que cette*

1856.

March 31st.
February 1st,
5th, 19th.
August 16th.

BREMER
v.
FREEMAN
and
BREMER.

*déclaration n'est pas corroborée par une possession d'état conforme, suffisamment caractérisée. (Cod. Nap. 319.)*

*" 2°. La déclaration faite dans un acte authentique par un individu, qu'il se reconnaît le père légitime de tel enfant dénommé, insuffisante à elle seule pour établir une telle filiation légitime, peut au moins valoir comme a·te de rcconnaissance d'enfant naturel. (Cod. Nap. 334.)*

*" Et, bien qu'une telle reconnaissance fût faite par un étranger au profit d'une autre personne pareillement étrangère, et qu'elle fût dans le principe inutile et sans effet légal à cause de la législation personnelle des deux parties, qui ne donnait aucun droit aux enfans naturels à l'égard de leurs parens, si ultérieurement l'enfant a acquis la qualité de Français, il peut invoquer cette reconnaissance et réclamer le bénéfice qu'y attache la loi Française.*

*" 3°. La succession d'un étranger, quant aux meubles situés en France, est régie par la loi Française, alors que le défunt avait son domicile légal en France, et que sa succession est réclamée par un héritier Français contre des légataires universels étrangers. (Cod. Nap. 3, L. 14 Juill., 1849.)*

*" 4°. Un testament olographe fait par un étranger en France, et dont l'exécution est demandée devant les tribunaux Français, ne peut être déclarée valable qu'autant qu'il réunit toutes les conditions de formes reconnues essentielles dans la législation Française, et quel que soit à cet égard l'état de la législation du pays auquel appartient le testateur ; en conséquence, un tel testament est nul s'il n'est pas écrit en entier de la main du testateur, ou s'il n'est pas daté. (Cod. Nap. 970, 999.)*

*" On ne peut voir un testament olographe valable*
*dans une lettre qui ne contient pas formellement les*
*dispositions du testateur, mais qui annonce seulement*
*d'une manière générale et sommaire ses volontés, en se*
*référant au surplus pour les détails à un autre acte*
*testamentaire.* (*Cod. Nap.* 970.)"

1856.

March 31st.
February 1st,
5th, 19th.
August 16th.

BREMER
v.
FREEMAN
and
BREMER.

ONSLOW v. ONSLOW, Dalloz' Reports, 1836:—

*" L'étranger qui se trouvait, lors de la promulgation*
*de la loi du 30 Avril, 1790, établi en France, y avait*
*un domicile continu depuis cinq ans, et y avait épousé*
*une Française, était naturalisé de plein droit, sans qu'il*
*fut tenu de prêter le serment civique. Ce serment*
*n'était exigé, par cette loi, de l'étranger qu'elle naturali-*
*sait, que pour être admis aux avantages de la qualité*
*de citoyen actif.*

*" Les lois postérieures à celle du 30 Avril, 1790, et*
*notamment la constitution de 1791, qui exigeaient des*
*étrangers la condition du serment, n'ont disposé que*
*pour l'avenir, et n'ont pu enlever la qualité de Français*
*à l'étranger qui, aux termes de la loi de 1790, avait*
*été naturalisé sans prêter serment.*

*" Un état peut, en vertu de son droit de souveraineté,*
*déférer à un étranger qui a fixé sa résidence dans son*
*territoire, la qualité de régnicole, sans le consentement*
*ou la volonté de celui à qui une pareille qualité est*
*attribuée.*

*" L'étranger qui ne veut pas accepter la qualité de*
*régnicole à lui déférée par l'état sur le territoire duquel*
*il est venu s'établir, doit quitter le territoire de cet état.*
*S'il continue d'y demeurer, il est censé s'être soumis à*
*la loi qui lui attribue de nouveaux droits en lui donnant*
*une novelle qualité.*

*" La simple mesure d'ordre public, par laquelle il a*

1856.

March 31st.
February 1st,
5th, 19th.
August 16th.

BREMER
*v.*
FREEMAN
and
BREMER.

été enjoint à un étranger naturalisé Français de sortir de France, n'a pu avoir pour effet d'enlever à cet étranger la qualité de Français que la loi lui avait conférée.

" *L'étranger qui, avant le Code Civil, a fixé sa résidence en France, et manifesté par plusieurs actes l'intention d'y rester à perpétuelle demeure, a acquis irrévocablement un domicile légal en France, et ce, nonobstant toutes lois postérieures qui auraient exigé d'autres conditions. Il en est de même depuis la promulgation du code civil, encore bien que l'étranger n'ait pas obtenu l'autorisation du gouvernement.* (C. Civ. 13.)

" *La succession d'un étranger naturalisé Français, qui s'est ouverte en France où il avait son domicile légal, est régie par la loi Française, tant à l'égard des biens meubles que des immeubles situés en France, dont la succession se compose.*

" *On doit considérer comme meuble faisant partie de la succession d'un étranger domicilié en France, et soumis, par conséquent, à la loi Française, le prix d'immeubles situés en pays étranger, et spécialement, en Angleterre, lorsqu'il a été payé par l'acquéreur transporté et placé en France. C'est en vain qu'un des héritiers prétendrait avoir le droit de réclamer ce prix comme propriétaire, par suite du privilège du statu réel de l'Angleterre.*"

THOMAS GIL DE OLIVAREZ'S CASE, Le Droit, 11th October, 1854 :—

" 1. *Toute succession est régie, quant aux immeubles, par la loi de la situation, et quant aux meubles, par celle du domicile.* (Art. 3 du Code Napoléon.)

" *Spécialement, la succession mobilière d'un étranger décédé en France doit être partagée entre les divers*

*cohéritiers selon les proportions établies par la loi Fran-
çaise, si le défunt avait son domicile en France.*

"2. *L'acquisition par un étranger d'un domicile en
France est indépendante de l'autorisation qui peut être
accordée aux étrangers par le gouvernement d'y fixer
leur résidence. Le domicile tient au droit des gens; il
est toujours déterminé par le lieu du principal établissement.*

"3. *Les droits et actions purement mobiliers, bien
que recueillis en France, doivent, comme tous les autres
meubles, être partagés d'après la loi du domicile de
l'étranger.*

"*Il n'y a lieu pour les cohéritiers Français d'invoquer
l'application de l'art. 2 de la loi du 14 Juillet, 1819, s'il
n'y a pas dans la succession d'immeubles situés en
France, surtout quand il s'agit de la succession d'un
Espagnol.*"

*Querieux* v. *Riencourt,* 1 Sirey, 109; *Duke of
D'Aremberg's case,* 1 Dalloz, 382; *De Laurencin* v.
*Liot,* 1 Sirey, 118; *The Harmony,* 2 Robins. 322;
*Dalrymple* v. *Dalrymple,* 2 Cons. Rep. 54; *Duchess
of Kingston's case,* 2 Add. 21; *Whicker* v. *Hume,*
15 Jur. 567.

After the argument the DUKE OF MECKLENBOURG'S
CASE was sent to the Court. The abstract of the
case, as determined by the Tribunal Civil de la
Seine, 1ʳᵉ ch., was, "*La succession de l'étranger doit
être considérée comme étant ouverte en France, lorsqu'il
est constant en fait que le décédé avait dans ce pays
son principal établissement, et ce alors même qu'il
n'aurait pas obtenu du Gouvernement Français la
jouissance des droits civils.*

VOL. I. P

*[margin]*
1856.

March 31st.
February 1st,
5th, 19th.
August 16th.

BREMER
v.
FREEMAN
and
BREMER.

1856.

March 31st.
February 1st,
5th, 19th.
August 16th.

———

BREMER
v.
FREEMAN
and
BREMER.

"*Par suite les tribunaux Français sont seuls compétens pour connaître des difficultés relatives à l'ouverture de cette succession.*"—Le Droit, 16 Mars, 1856.

From this decree there was an appeal to the Cour Impériale de Paris, 1ʳᵉ ch., and the abstract of the decree of that Court was, according to the report in the Gazette des Tribunaux, 27 Juillet, 1856, "*La succession de l'étranger, décédé en France, sans avoir été autorisé à y établir son domicile, et à y jouer des droits civils, est régie par la loi de son domicile d'origine, s'il a manifesté par des actes exprès l'intention de conserver sa nationalité et l'esprit de retour dans son pays natal, si ses héritiers sont étrangers et si les immeubles dépendant de la succession sont situés hors de l'empire Français.*

"*Le long séjour de cet étranger en France, et ses importantes spéculations dans des entreprises fondées en France n'entrainent pas sa renonciation au domicile d'origine.*"

And according to the report in Le Droit, of the same date, "*Les tribunaux Français sont incompétents pour statuer sur les difficultés relatives à l'ouverture de la succession d'un étranger décédé en France, lorsque les héritiers sont étrangers, que les immeubles sont situés hors de France, lorsqu'il est constant, en fait, que le défunt a conservé avec le gouvernement dont il était sujet les rapports qu'il jugeait les plus propres à maintenir sa nationalité.*

"*En vain opposerait-on que depuis longtemps il habitait la France et qu'il avait pris part à des spéculations de diverse nature.*

*" Ces circonstances ne sauraient entrainer la renonciation au domicile d'origine."*\*

1856.

March 31st.
February 1st,
5th, 19th.
August 16th.

BREMER
v.
FREEMAN
and
BREMER.

JUDGMENT.

SIR JOHN DODSON.

After stating the contents of the several allegations. From these averments by Miss Bremer on the one side, and on the other by Mr. Freeman, the executor, it is quite obvious that there are two principal questions for the decision of the Court. First, in what country was the deceased domiciled at the time of making the will and at the time of her death; and, secondly, what was the nature of that domicil, and the legal effect thereof, upon her testamentary acts.

The first point for consideration then is, in what country had this deceased lady her legal domicil? It is admitted on all sides that she was born in the East Indies in 1795, where her father was then serving as a military officer in the service of the East India Company. There can, therefore, be no doubt that her domicil of origin was Anglo-Indian. In 1805, she, together with her sister and mother, came to England, where her father afterwards came, and she resided with him and the family until some time in 1825. It is, therefore, I apprehend, equally clear, that, down to that period of time,

---

\* It would seem that the Court of Appeal reversed the sentence, upon the ground that the deceased duke had by express acts manifested his intention of returning to his native country, and had maintained such relations with the government of his own country as proved his intention to preserve his original domicil. The fact of his not being naturalized or authorized was a proof of his intention to adhere to his original domicil, rather than a legal defect in his French domicil.

P 2

1856.

March 31st.
February 1st,
5th, 19th.
August 16th.

———

BREMER
v.
FREEMAN
and
BREMER.

namely, 1825, her domicil was, to all intents and purposes, English.   Her father had sustained her; he had personal property as well as real property; and it was the sole abode of himself, his wife, and and two children down to 1825, when this lady quitted England, her mother having died, and went to the continent with Miss Pickar, who had been her governess.   She proceeds then to Rome and to other parts of Italy; and it is alleged, that there is not any evidence to show in what particular state of Italy she took up her abode; nothing to show that she fixed her domicil or continued her residence within the dominions of any particular state or government in that part of Europe.   She was a mere traveller, going wherever curiosity, or pleasure, or any other motive might induce her.   If the matter had rested here there would have been no pretence for asserting that the lady had cast off her English domicil, and acquired an Italian domicil.   There is, however, a circumstance of very grave importance averred by Miss Bremer in her allegation, namely, that this lady whilst in Italy intermarried with an Italian gentleman, named Allegri.   The fact thus averred, if supported by adequate proof, would, in the opinion of the Court, be sufficient effectually to change the domicil of the deceased, to destroy the English and establish the Italian; for the domicil of the wife would, by necessary implication, follow the domicil of her husband.   Having married with an Italian in Italy, she would immediately acquire the Italian domicil. But how stands the proof in respect of the alleged marriage?   Where was it celebrated?   Was it at Rome or Naples or Genoa, or in what other town or place of the Italian States? There is no evidence of it on either side. Was any entry made in the parish books of any place there or elsewhere? Who performed the ceremony, or was present on the occasion? Was there any acknowledgment or repute? Upon all these matters there is an entire absence of proof. It is true that the deceased has asserted it, both orally and in writing; but surely such assertions, unsupported by other testimony, can hardly be deemed satisfactory or conclusive. But how stands the matter upon the representation of the deceased herself? The marriage is said to have taken place in 1830, but it was not announced to her relations for many years afterwards, I think not till the year 1840 or 1841. It is said that she concealed it, because she had not her father's consent; but her father died in 1835, and the marriage, in point of fact, was never declared till after the death of the sister in the year 1840. It is true that in 1840, upon the death of her sister, she used the name of Allegri, but she did not do so till after the death of her sister. The sister always denied her belief in the truth of any such marriage; she never would admit it. In 1840 the deceased assumed that name in Paris.

The first avowal she makes of it to any of her friends or relations in England is to be found in a letter which is before the Court among other documents, and addressed to Mr. James G. Bremer in these terms, "Boulevard des Capucines, No. 17, Thursday, 1st October, 1840. My dear cousin, I had requested my dear good Mrs. Connell to write to inform you of the great calamity which had befallen me, and I cannot imagine why she neglected to do so, and to tell you

1856.

March 31st.
February 1st,
5th, 19th.
August 16th.

BREMER
v.
FREEMAN
and
BREMER.

1856.

March 31st.
February 1st,
5th, 19th.
August 16th.

BREMER
v.
FREEMAN
and
BREMER.

also of my change of name and state.  I have been a
widow more than ten years, but my loved sister
never would acknowledge my marriage because I did
not ask her father's consent.  I very much regret
not having done so, and I own I did wrong.  My
loved sister had been ill for several months," and so
forth.  Then she states—it is, perhaps, better to
read the whole, for there is some reference to a
return to England, the only reference I can find—
" No words can express how wretched I am, for I
loved her more as my child than my sister.  I have
not any intention of returning to England"—this
is a declaration which may, perhaps, have some
effect when we come to consider the question of
domicil, or the intention of returning to England
—" I shall leave France when I can."  Leaving
France when she could looks as if she had not
taken up her abode there.  There is in the testimony of some of the witnesses an explanation of
what she means by leaving France—that she did not
mean to leave it permanently, so as to give up her
abode in that country, but only for the temporary
purpose of travelling.  " But that does not depend
upon me, but upon the arrangement of the property
which she has left me, which is of course in the
hands of her executor.  Your letter, dated the
23d ult., I only received this morning.  I hope you
will not accuse me of negligence."  It concludes in
a formal way, nothing having any bearing at all on
the present question.  Therefore, it is clear from
this, though she says she was married as early as
the year 1830, that her sister never would believe
she was married, or at least never would admit the
marriage.

From that time, from the time of the death of the sister in Paris, she assumes the name of Allegri; and we find in the very commencement of the will itself she describes herself as Fanny Allegri *née* Calcraft, and at the termination of the will her signature is Fanny Allegri *née* Calcraft. From that time she appears to have passed by the name of Allegri in Paris, and to have been known almost entirely by that name.

1856.

March 31st.
February 1st,
5th, 19th.
August 10th.

BREMER
*v.*
FREEMAN
and
BREMER.

Upon this evidence, even so far as it goes, I think the Court could not come to the conclusion that this lady had been married to this gentleman, Signor Allegri, in Italy, or that there was any contract of marriage between them which would have changed her domicil. The sister does not seem to have given credit to it; and if she had any connexion with Signor Allegri, if she lived with him at all, it does not appear there is any evidence that she married him. *Prætexit nomine culpam.* She may have called him her husband, though there is no evidence of their living as husband and wife, or pretending so to be. But in point of fact there is evidence in this case to show that the deceased herself admitted she never had been married to Signor Allegri. After the case had been argued, I thought it right and convenient that Mr. Freeman, the solicitor, who drew the will, and who seems to have had an intimate knowledge of many of the proceedings of the family, should be examined, and the Court, availing itself of the power which it has under the Act of Parliament, thought proper to have Mr. Freeman called before it, and have him examined *vivâ voce* in this Court. In the course of that examination he was asked, amongst other things, with respect to the

1856.

March 31st.
February 1st,
5th, 19th.
August 16th.

BREWER
*v.*
FREEMAN
and
BREWER.

marriage of Madame Allegri, whether she was married, or whether she was not. His examination upon the point is this: He is asked, " You called the deceased Madame Allegri just this moment; was she a married woman or a spinster, or what was she?"—The answer to that is, " I should state to you, when I first acted for her, her property at Millbrook, near Southampton, had been sold in the lifetime of Miss Emily Calcraft, of whose will I was the sole executor." *Q.* " What was the date of that sale?"—*A.* " It was, I should say, somewhere about midsummer, or the latter part of the year 1840; and it remained incomplete. I was not acting at that sale Messrs Barney were the solicitors; but in consequence of the death of Miss Calcraft, I had to communicate that event to them, and it occasioned my being joined in the assignment as the executor, and upon that occasion the draft was sent to me. I altered it from Fanny Calcraft to Fanny Allegri, widow, it having been stated to me, on the occasion of the will being sent over, that she was a widow." *Q.* " It having been stated by whom?"—*A.* "By Mr. Connell, in a letter he wrote me on the occasion of the death, sending me a copy of Miss Calcraft's will." *Q.* " Is that all you know, the only reason for describing her as a widow?"—*A.* " That was all I knew at that time. I had never heard she had that name till I got that letter." *Q.* " In point of fact, that is all you know about it?"—*A.* " The purchaser here desired to have the deed executed before some witnesses resident in England, and that occasioned me to go to Paris with my son, and then I inquired of her where Signor Allegri was buried, as I thought that evidence might be wanted. She appeared very much agitated, and said it could not be necessary—it was quite unnecessary; she would not listen in fact to there being anything of that sort required; and the consequence was, that she executed the deed, and I left her that day." *Q.* "How did she execute it—in what name?"—*A.* "As Fanny Allegri; and the next day she sent for me, and she then said she had had no rest, that she was not married." *Q.* "Do you know at all where Signor Allegri died?" The answer is, "I was never able to learn. I wished her to take the name of Calcraft, but that she was not willing to do; and I never could learn where Signor Allegri was, whether he was living or dead, further than she represented, when her sister joined her, she heard he was dying in Russia. Whether that was the case or not I had never any means of ascertaining." But here it is, when he pressed her, when there was a necessity for executing these deeds he pressed her to make use of the name of Calcraft as a spinster and an unmarried person. He then pressed her to know where Signor Allegri was buried; he thought the evidence might be wanted; she was greatly agitated on the occasion, and she insisted on executing the deed in the name of Allegri; she did so. The next morning she calls on him and states she has had a sleepless night— that she had not been married. Therefore I think there is quite an end of the Italian domicil; for, in point of fact, upon her own confession—her own admission—she never was married to Allegri.

The next question is, whether any other foreign domicil has been established? I think it is quite clear there is no other foreign domicil, unless it be a domicil from residence in France, having quitted

1856.

March 31st.
February 1st,
5th, 19th.
August 16th.

BREMER
*v.*
FREEMAN
and
BREMER.

1856.

March 31st.
February 1st,
5th, 19th.
August 16th.

BREMER
v.
FREEMAN
and
BREMER.

Italy after the death of her father, and being joined by her sister, they went to reside at Paris, and at Paris she continued to reside down to the period of her death. It is not pretended that the deceased was naturalised in France, there is no averment of that kind; neither is it said that it was a domicil by the authorization of the French Government. It is a domicil *de facto* only, a domicil by the *jus gentium;* that is, she had taken up her abode meaning to remain there the rest of her life, and not to return to her former domicil in England. The question is, whether it was her fixed place of abode, and whether she had made up her mind to live there?

Perhaps it may be convenient here just to restate a few of the facts. It seems that in 1834 General Calcraft, the father, died, leaving his fortune in equal shares to his two daughters. Emily, who was appointed sole executrix, shortly after joined her sister on the continent, and they are said to have lived together at various places for short periods; and finally, in 1838, to have taken up their abode in Paris until the periods of their respective deaths, namely, Emily in 1840, and the deceased herself in April, 1853; that is, she lived at Paris for the last fifteen years of her life.

As to the length of time she lived there, it was justly observed by the Queen's advocate that time alone will not constitute a domicil, that a person may continue in one place for fifty or any greater number of years, and yet may always have an intention to return to his or her own country; that the original domicil is not .considered and proved to have been abandoned merely from the length of time the party has resided in a foreign country.

1856.

March 31st.
February 1st,
5th, 19th.
August 16th.

BREMER
v.
FREEMAN
and
BREMER.

Undoubtedly this is quite true. The long duration of residence in one place is a material ingredient, from which intention may be collected; but a person may live fifty years in a place and not acquire a domicil, for he may have had all the time an intention to return to his own country. But the question here is, whether the deceased had not taken up her abode in France, and had no intention to return to England. The letter to Mr. Bremer, which I have already read, from the deceased declares she did not mean to return to England, and I cannot find any declaration of a contrary tendency in any part of the evidence before the Court. There she was not detained by business for any particular time, no necessary avocations kept her in France, she might have quitted it at any time she thought proper, but there she continued for fifteen years according to the evidence. Her sister having died, and having been buried there, she having purchased a grave in Pere la Chaise, she determined to be buried in the same grave, the same spot with her sister, and she meant to live and die at Paris. The question is, whether that is borne out by the evidence in the case. She had no other home; it was the sole place of her abode. When she was at Paris she must be considered as at home; if she went away, had gone away from Paris, it must be considered that she had gone away from home; and when she returned, that she came back to home. She did not, however, leave France, and therefore there is no necessity to make inquiries as to that.

The evidence in this case is given by some of the persons who knew her about the year 1842; there is no witness who goes back further than that. She went to Paris in 1835; and the first witness who has

1856.

March 31st.
February 1st,
5th, 19th.
August 16th.

BREMER
v.
FREEMAN
and
BREMER.

been examined on this point is a witness of the name of Derville, who was acquainted with the deceased, and in fact waited and attended upon her, she being a nurse. This witness has been examined by Miss Bremer, the lady who opposes the will. She says, on the 8th article, "I do not know when Madame Allegri first came to Paris, or where she lived before she resided in the Boulevard des Capucines. The deceased hired her apartments there unfurnished, and furnished them with her own furniture." That is not taking merely temporary lodgings or ready-furnished lodgings; she hired apartments according to the evidence of this witness, and they were furnished by herself. In point of fact they were furnished by herself and her sister originally. "At the time I knew the deceased her sister was dead, but she had a lady's maid living with her whom she discharged about seven years before her death. I do not know on what terms the deceased held the apartments she occupied in the Boulevard des Capucines, but she told me she rented them on a lease of three, six, or nine years, and that it was renewed as the term expired." That is the declaration as coming from the deceased—not that she had hired apartments for a week or a month, but upon lease for three or six years, and so forth; and they were renewed. It is clear from other evidence in the case that at the time of the death one of the leases was still subsisting, one of them had not expired. "Madame also told me that the last term would "expire in July last, and that she should not then "renew it, as the noise of the Boulevards annoyed "her." That is something like leaving these apartments; but she goes on, however, to state, "but that

" she should remove to the Place Vendôme." The reason assigned by this witness for removing to the Place Vendôme would be, because it was more quiet, but there is no change whatever of domicil —it is only a change from one part of Paris to an adjacent part.

On the 10th article she says, " Madame Allegri " used to tell me latterly, that if she recovered her " health, she should travel, and go to Switzerland, " Italy, Savoy, or some other such place;" that is, if she recovered her health she would go to these places to travel, not that she would go to settle in any of these places.   " And that she should take an " apartment in the Place Vendôme in Paris, and " reside there six months out of the twelve.   I used " to say to her sometimes, 'But, if you were to die, " madame, whilst you are travelling?' 'Oh, then,' " she said, 'I should be brought back to Paris, and " buried near my sister, in the Cemetery of Pere la " Chaise.'   She often spoke to me of England and " of the Brazils, but she never spoke to me of her " going back to England."   What the meaning of speaking to her about Brazil is I cannot tell ; whether it is some mistake of the witness I do not know; but she declares she never spoke to her about going back to England.   " She never spoke " to me either for or against England, but she told " me, 'I am like you, I have become a Roman " Catholic.' "   So she had changed her religion after she left England, but she does not seem to have been a very strict Roman Catholic, for when she was dying, she declined to have a Roman Catholic priest to attend on her.   " She never said any- " thing to me against the climate or religion of

1856.

March 31st.
February 1st,
5th, 19th.
August 16th.

BREMER
v.
FREEMAN
and
BREMER.

1856.

March 31st.
February 1st,
5th, 19th.
August 16th.

BREMER
v.
FREEMAN
and
BREMER.

"England. The only thing she said about it was,
"that persons were cleaner in England than in
"France. She felt the loss of her sister very much,
"and could not speak of her without tears. Only
"four days before her death," she says, "the
"deceased, then referring to her lamentable state of
"health, said, 'I have one consolation, I shall be
"buried near my sister;' and the deceased frequently
"before that, and at long periods before that,
"spoke of being buried near her sister."

Again, as to quitting France, upon the 6th interrogatory she says, "She often, as I have before
"deposed, spoke of travelling in Italy. She fre-
"quently spoke of Italy as a country where she
"should like to travel, but she always spoke of
"spending six months of the year in France." She
repeats, on a later interrogatory, that the deceased
told her over and over again she should return to
France for six months.

Another witness of the name of Chappé deposes
very much to the same effect. "The deceased
"was living at No. 19, Boulevard des Capucines.
"I never knew her to reside any where else from
"the period of my first becoming acquainted with
"her. She has several times told me she wished
"to be buried near her sister, or alongside of her.
"She constantly spoke to me in that way during her
"last illness, and on the very last night of her life.
"She did not see Maillochon during her last illness."
Maillochon was a person who was employed to take
care of the grave of the sister. It appears that
she was in the habit of paying Maillochon a trifle
annually or periodically for taking care of the
sister's grave. Upon the 6th interrogatory, she

says, " I never heard the deceased express any
" intention of returning to England. I never
" heard her speak on subjects of that description.
" I never heard her say that she preferred France
" to England. She never spoke to me about Eng-
" land, or anything connected with that country."
There are one or two other witnesses who depose
very much to the same effect, but there is nothing
opposed to them, so it really would be a waste of
time to go through the testimony of those persons.

The case comes to this, that the deceased lodged
for the last fifteen years of her life—that she herself
furnished the apartments, in Paris, that she never
quitted them, that she declared she should never
return to England. She writes to her relation,
Mr. Bremer, that she should never return to England. Though she spoke of leaving Paris, yet it
was only for six months of the year; and that she
should keep a house at Paris, namely, at the Place
Vendôme, a short distance from the Boulevard des
Capucines, where she had been residing, and where
she continued to reside down to the period of her
death. Then, I think, upon this evidence I am
bound to hold that the deceased was domiciled at
Paris both at the time she made the will and also
at the time of her death. She was there for the last
fifteen years, which includes the date of the will.

Accordingly, the Court having arrived at that
conclusion with respect to the fact of domicil, then
the next point for consideration is, as to the making
of her will, by what law that was to be made,
being domiciled in France *de facto*, according to the
*jus gentium*. In France she was not naturalized,
and was not domiciled by authorization; and the

1856.

March 31st.
February 1st,
5th, 19th.
August 16th.

BREMER
v.
FREEMAN
and
BREMER.

1856.

March 31st.
February 1st,
5th, 19th.
August 16th.

BREMER
v.
FREEMAN
and
BREMER.

question is, what is the effect of that upon the will of the deceased, and whether the will ought to be in the English form or according to the French form, in order to be a valid testamentary paper. Now it may be as well to see the contents of the will itself before I enter upon this question, for I find in many of the cases decided in the French courts that the contents of the wills of persons making their wills in France, in the circumstances stated, have been considered of importance, to see whether there were French executors, whether there were French heirs, the amount of the property, and so forth.

The will of the deceased commences by describing her as "Fanny Allegri *née* Calcraft, at present residing at the Boulevard des Capucines in Paris, in the kingdom of France"—so that it was the place of actual residence according to that— "the only surviving daughter of the late Henry Fox Calcraft, lieutenant-general in his late Majesty's service in the East India Company, who resided and was buried at Brighton in England." Then she proceeds to devise to Daniel Alexander Freeman a house at Calcutta and all other property in the East Indies. So that in the first place here is a property of considerable value, £300 per annum, in the East Indies—that is, in the British dominions, and not within the territory of France. She then goes on to give one thousand francs each to the two persons who shall be with her in her last illness. They might very possibly, probably would, be French. There is a legacy of £40, that being one thousand francs, to each of the two persons that might be with her—not describing them by name

or national character, but who might accidentally
be in attendance at the time. Then it goes on to
give 500 francs each to the bureaux of the first and
second arrondissements at Paris. These were for
charitable purposes, for the poor belonging to the
first and second arrondissements ; and she gives
500 francs to the English Charitable Fund.

The residue of the property, whether in England,
France, or elsewhere, she gives equally between
Daniel Alexander Freeman and her cousins Eliza
Ann Bremer, Susan Bremer, James Grignon Bremer,
and Henry Bremer. Of the last four, I apprehend,
only two are living, according to the testimony of
Miss Bremer, for she describes herself and her brother
as the only two next of kin of the deceased. Then
she appoints Mr. Daniel Alexander Freeman and
Mr. James Grignon Bremer the executors of her
will. So that the executors are English; the property
is all in the British dominions, with the exception of
£38; and the whole property is left to English
people, except the trifle left to the two persons who
might be in attendance upon her at the time of her
death; and these little charities of 500 francs each to
the bureaux of the arrondissements, and the charity
for poor English persons. The property in India is
considerable. There was also very considerable
property in England. In short, the whole is in
England, and is left to English persons, and English
persons are appointed the executors.

By what law is the validity or the invalidity of this
will to be decided, so made by a person so circumstanced as to domicil as she was ?

The law of England, I apprehend, as applicable
to a case of this kind, is clear. That the will must

185 6.

March 31st.
February 1st,
5th, 19th.
August 16th.

BREMER
v.
FREEMAN
and
BREMER.

1856.

March 31st.
February 1st,
5th, 19th.
August 16th.

BREMER
v.
FREEMAN
and
BREMER.

be deemed good or bad according to the law of the country where the deceased was domiciled, that is to say, in this instance in the view which the Court takes of it according to the law of France. What that law may be, it is certainly a matter of some difficulty to ascertain; for notwithstanding the great industry and research of the counsel, and the very able and erudite arguments addressed to the Court on this occasion—and for which the Court feels greatly indebted to them—and the authorities cited both from English law, and also the cases decided in the French courts, the matter may well occasion some hesitation to a person not conversant with French law, and make him extremely anxious to ascertain what is the real state of that law; since MANY of the CASES that have been cited are so irreconcilable on some points that it is difficult to ascertain what the real law is, and the opinions of the very eminent and learned French advocates examined are directly opposed to each other.

The 13th article of the *Code Napoleon* is the foundation of the French law, or rather constitutes the French law, on this matter—that is, in these words, "*L'étranger qui aura été admis par le gouverne-*
"*ment à établir son domicile en France y jouira de*
"*tous les droits civils tant qu'il continuera d'y*
"*résider.*" So that a stranger who has received the authorization of the government, and established his domicil in France, is to enjoy all civil rights there. I apprehend among those civil rights is the testamentary right, and this right he will enjoy, provided he has received the authorization of the government to establish his domicil there. It seems to follow, as a necessary consequence, that those

1856.

March 31st.
February 1st,
5th, 19th.
August 16th.

BREMER
v.
FREEMAN
and
BREMER.

who have not that authorization, or have not been naturalized, will not enjoy the same rights. Upon this law Dr. Phillimore cited some eminent authors who have written upon it, and he has favoured me with their works. The first of these is Mr. Demolombe. In his work called " *Cours de Code Civil,*" "in the First Book, relating to persons, the title is, " *De la jouissance et de la privation des droits civils.*" He divides this title into three chapters : first, what persons enjoy these civil rights; secondly, how those persons who enjoy them can be deprived of them; thirdly, what is the legal condition of strangers in France. At page 143, section 140, are these words, " *Nous avons vu que la législation de chaque pays se compose de deux éléments, savoir, du droit public et du droit privé. Le droit privé, ou le droit civil, suivant l'acception moderne de ce mot, est celui qui règle les intérêts des particuliers, la propriété, la famille, les conventions, etc.: il est la source des droits civils, c'est à dire, des facultés, des avantages, dont la jouissance appartient à tous les Français.*" I have cited this partly to show the law, and partly to show that the *droit civil* applies not only to political rights, as was contended by the counsel for Mr. Bremer, but embraces other civil rights — that it is not confined. Certainly the words are used by some authors with no small degree of ambiguity. Sometimes *droit civil* is put in opposition to political rights, and sometimes it includes them; but, according to this author, the *droit civil* is what I have mentioned. It goes on as to the quality of Frenchmen, p 144, " *La qualité de Français ne suffit donc pas pour avoir les droits politiques; il faut de plus être citoyen.*" There must be something more; it is not domicil

Q 2

1856.

March 31st.
February 1st,
5th, 19th.
August 16th.

BREMER
v.
FREEMAN
and
BREMER.

that will give political rights, but in order to enjoy
political rights he must be a citizen. *"Et ce titre,*
*"dans ce cas, n'est plus, comme très souvent, le*
*"synonyme de Français, de regnicole; il indique*
*"spécialement l'aptitude à exercer les droits politiques.*
*"Ainsi, tous les Français jouissent des droits civils,*
*"mais les Français citoyens seuls des droits poli-*
*"tiques."* There are other passages which were
cited by the learned counsel having a bearing on the
same question, but it is quite unnecessary to go
through them. What I have read is quite sufficient
for the purpose.

There is another author, M. Demangeat. He goes
through the whole of the matter, and comes to his
*résumé.* The *résumé* is in these words, p. 369 : *"En
résumé, je crois donc qu'il faut dire que, sous l'empire
du code civil, l'étranger n'a d'autre moyen d'acquérir
un domicile en France que d'obtenir la permission du
gouvernement; et c'est à ce principe que je rattache
comme conséquences les règles que nous allons par-
courir."* So that it is quite clear, from the writings
of these gentlemen, that the mere fact of the domicil,
according to the law of nations, is not sufficient—
that there must be the authorization of the government in order to confer the civil rights.

Various witnesses have been examined, both on
the one side and on the other ; and perhaps it may
be convenient to refer to some of their testimony,
in order to see the view which they take. In the
first place there are the witnesses who have been
examined on behalf of Miss Bremer. The first of
these witnesses is M. Frignet. Upon the 17th
article he says he is an advocate at the bar
of the Council of State, and of the Court of

Cassation—the highest court—and successor to Monsieur Bonjean, formerly minister and president at the Council of State. He is, therefore, a person very high in office, a person of great eminence; and of course anything coming from him is well worthy of attention. He says, "I am also a docteur en droit, the highest legal title known in this country. I knew nothing whatever of Madame Allegri, the party in this cause, deceased. The will of a person domiciled in France, to be considered valid there, must be in conformity with the laws of France, in virtue of the principle *locus regit actum*, and more particularly so when the will is brought under the cognizance of French tribunals." Then he says, "this was so ruled in the Court of Cassation last year in the case of *Browning* against *De Veine;*"* in which the will of an Englishman domiciled there was held by that Court to be invalid, in consequence of its not having been made conformably to the laws of France.

It will be necessary that the Court should examine that case with some degree of particularity afterwards. I may here state that this gentleman refers to a decision of the Court of Cassation in 1853. I have not been able to see a copy of the decision of that Court in 1853; but there is the decision of the Court immediately below the Court of Cassation—the Appeal Court of Paris. The highest court to which you can appeal on a point of law is the Court of Cassation. As I understand the matter, they affirmed the decree of the Court below. So, in fact, the report of 1852 is in con-

1856.

March 31st.
February 1st,
5th, 19th.
August 16th.

BREMER
*v.*
FREEMAN
and
BREMER.

---

* *De Veine* v. *Routledge, antè* p. 205.

1856.

March 31st.
February 1st,
5th, 19th.
August 16th.

BREMER
v.
FREEMAN
and
BREMER.

formity with this decision, to which he refers in 1853—the decision of the Court of Cassation. I observe that every one of the witnesses examined in this case on the one side and on the other, when they refer to the case of *Browning* v. *De Veine*,[*] speak of it as in 1852 before the inferior court. I apprehend, as far as I can make out the statements of these gentlemen, the decision really is to the same effect.

Then he goes on to depose, " There is no differ-" ence in the law of France as to the execution " of wills in or since the year 1842 and the present " time. We are always ruled by the *Code Napo-" leon* in reference thereto. It is necessary to " distinguish the various forms by which wills may " be made in France." Then he proceeds to describe that there are three forms of making a will in France, namely, the authentic, the mystic, and the holograph form. It is unnecessary to go through his evidence on that point, for that is an admitted fact. It is well known as being the law of France. He goes on again, " The laws of France as to the execution of wills, as I have just stated them, apply as well to foreigners domiciled in France as to French subjects." That is put generally to those domiciled in France, whether domiciled by naturalization or not. He goes on, " In as far as the law of the country to which they belong requires them to conform to the law of the country in which they are domiciled. It is necessary to attend to the distinction between the law as to property and the law as to persons." So

---

[*] *De Veine* v. *Routledge*, *ante*, p. 205.

that *locus regit actum* is the principle. Then there is to be domicil; and it is the law of France which is to govern that as far as the law of other countries allows. Then he states the distinction between the law as to property and the law as to persons. "The law attaching to property is always the *lex loci rei sitæ*." So that is always the case. *Locus regit actum*, whether a party is domiciled or not, is to apply. So that to any stranger being in France and making his will there, unless this is to be qualified by what has been said as to domicil, the rule *locus regit actum* would apply—even to the testament of any person dying in France, if he had only been there twenty-four hours. That certainly is not the law followed with regard to British subjects. Then if the rule is what it is stated to be, that it is valid or invalid according to the law of France, according to the place where the party is domiciled, and the law attaching to property is always the *lex loci rei sitæ*, that would be a qualification. Supposing it to be always the law of the country where the property is situated, then, according to M. Frignet, this will made in France would not operate on property in England—not at all, because that is always according to the law of the country where the property is situated; and *locus regit actum* applies to all personal property whatever. Then he is examined on interrogatory, and inquiries are made of him as to the *Code Napoleon*. Upon interrogatory (the 17th) he goes back to the case he before mentioned, *Browning* v. *De Veine*, and he speaks of it in this way: "First, when the foreigner makes his will in France, it must, according to the case I have before cited, *Browning*

1856.

March 31st.
February 1st,
5th, 19th.
August 16th.

BREMER
*v.*
FREEMAN
and
BREMER.

1856.

March 31st.
February 1st,
5th, 19th.
August 16th.

BREMER
v.
FREEMAN
and
BREMER.

v. *De Veine*, be made conformably to the law of France, because *locus regit actum;* and in that case the Courts of France are competent to adjudicate on the validity or invalidity of the will," and so forth. Upon the next interrogatory he says, "The law of France, on the principle that the personal law follows the person, and that moveable property is dependent on the personal law, would, in the case of a foreigner dying intestate in France without a French domicil, distribute his moveable property according to the law of his own country. Conformably to the principle *locus regit actum*, a Frenchman in a foreign country must make his will according to the law of the country in which he is residing, though this rule of law is doubted among jurists of eminence in French law." So that a Frenchman must always, whether domiciled or not in a foreign country, make his will in that form. "The rule is laid down upon the principle *locus regit actum*, and not upon any hypothesis of convenience to the testator."

He goes on, in answer to the interrogatories, to cite other cases, to which the Court will presently refer; the case of D'Aubanza, which is an exhibit annexed to the interrogatories; and also to the decision of the Superior Court upon the same case; but I do not think that that case of D'Aubanza has any strict application to the present. He then goes into the case of Lynch, which must be examined by the Court.

Such is the evidence, then, of M. Frignet; and the evidence of the next witness, M. Senard, an advocate of the Court of Appeal, is, I think, very much to the same effect. He goes on the principle

*locus regit actum.* "When a foreigner has fixed his
" principal establishment in France, and has resided
" there for a long time, he will naturally, as it seems
" to me, come to adopt the forms of instruments as
" used in that country, as he has adopted the habits
" and customs of the place itself; but this is of
" course optional, not obligatory upon him. It is
" not the fact of domicil that creates the necessity
" for his conforming himself, in the execution of
" instruments, to the forms of French law. That
" necessity is derived from the maxim, *locus regit*
" *actum.*" So that he puts it quite as strongly as the
first witness.

1856.

March 31st.
February 1st,
5th, 19th.
August 16th.

BREMER
*v.*
FREEMAN
and
BREMER.

The third and the last witness who has been examined on that side is M. Paillet, who is an
advocate of the Cour Impériale. He gives his
evidence very much in conformity with the two
witnesses whose evidence I have adverted to, and
he puts the law on the same principle. Now, on the
other side, five eminent jurists have been examined;
and I must briefly advert to the result of their testimony, and then consider the cases referred to by
them, and which have an important bearing on the
case. The first of those who has been examined is
M. Marie. He is an advocate of the Imperial
Court at Paris, and a Minster of Justice of the
Order of Barristers of the Imperial Court. He
expresses his opinion thus: "According to my
" opinion, the party deceased referred to was not,
" by reason of the premises just read and translated
" to me" (that is the statement as to her having
been resident in France for the time I have stated,
and not being domiciled by authorization and not
naturalized), " ever lawfully domiciled in France,

1856.

March 31st.
February 1st,
5th, 19th.
August 16th.

BREMER
*v.*
FREEMAN
and
BREMER.

"so as to have acquired a domicil of succession "according to the laws of that country. I say, that "she had not a legal domicil. A distinction, a "great distinction, must be made between a domi- "cil in the ordinary meaning of the word—which "is the place where a person generally resides—and "his domicil in the legal sense." He, therefore, takes the distinction, and he seems to come exactly to what one would naturally suppose is the meaning of the *Code Napoleon*, article 13, that it applies to those who are domiciled there by the authorization of the government. "This latter domicil," he says, "consists—as very properly stated by M. De- "mante, professor of the School of Laws—in the "connection established by law between the person "and the place where he resides. Thus, for ex- "ample, when the law of France declares, in the "article 10 of the *Code Napoleon*, the place where "the succession shall be opened shall be determined "by the domicil, the law refers to the legal domi- "cil we have defined above, which is constituted, "not by the caprice of the residing party, but by "the observation of certain legal dispositions which "the *Code Napoleon* has clearly defined in articles "102 and the following, and not to the actual "or *de facto* domicil above described, constituted by "mere residence. As an instance, suppose a per- "son having his legal domicil at Bordeaux, came "to reside at Paris, and died at Paris, that would "not be a domicil at Paris, but it must be con- "sidered according to the real domicil at Bor- "deaux." Then he says, "There are in France "foreigners who are established without the above "authorizations, but who have resided for a long

" time past in a permanent manner, without any
" intention of quitting." That seems to describe the
state in which this lady was. She had resided in
France for a long time without any intention of
quitting it. " It has been asked, whether an excep-
" tion should not be made with regard to the above
" foreigners. My opinion is, that even in such cases
" the article 13 must still receive its application.
" M. Proudhon has given a qualification to this class
" of foreigners; he has called them 'Incolats;' and he
" says, 'It is just that their persons and their acts
" should be subjected to the legislation of the
" country where they have come to reside in a
" permanent manner.' This idea may be very
" liberal, but in presence of the law as it stands it is
" arbitrary and false." So that he does not at all
yield to that. Then, as to the case and the decrees,
which are referred to by M. Proudhon and M. Merlin,
speaking of these, he says, "There are to be found
" objections raised to the above doctrine, supported
" by some decrees of the Courts of Justice; but
" these decrees are, in my opinion, to be considered
" more as having been made in view of special
" cases, than as containing the general principle of
" law on the subject. These decrees, thus made, in
" special cases have given rise, to the practical
" adage, that decrees are good for those who ob-
" tain them. Therefore, in applying the above
" principles to the present case, I maintain that
" Madame Calcraft, the deceased, had obtained no
" legal domicil in France, because she did not obtain
" an authorization from government to establish
" one, which I consider an indispensable condition to
" a legal domicil in France." His opinion, therefore,

1856.

March 31st.
February 1st,
5th, 19th.
August 16th.

BREMER
v.
FREEMAN
and
BREMER.

1856.

March 31st.
February 1st,
5th, 19th.
August 16th.

Bremer
v.
Freeman
and
Bremer.

is strong; and in reference to these cases, he says they form exceptions, and there were reasons why they varied; and, I think, when the cases come to be examined, it does appear that the general rule is, that the party must be domiciled by authorization; that, under particular circumstances, where there are French interests concerned, and especially if the property is immoveable property in France, then the French law would consider the matter in a different point of view.

Upon the interrogatories the witness says, " I " have, from having had read to me the first eight " articles of the allegation upon which I have been " examined, expressed an opinion to the effect that " the deceased in this cause was not, by reason of " the premises contained in these articles, ever law- " fully domiciled in France so as to have acquired " a domicil of succession according to the laws of " France. I mean to express thereby, that as the " deceased had not obtained an express authority to " establish a legal domicil in France, no act of her's ' could supply the deficiency of that authority. I " do mean to give it as my opinion of the laws of " France, that no foreigner can obtain a lawful " domicil in France, so that the succession to his " property shall be regulated by the law of that " country, unless he shall have received the express " authorization of the government of France, al- " though a contrary opinion has been expressed by " Proudhon and other writers." So that he adheres to that opinion, notwithstanding these cases which are referred to, and notwithstanding the opinion entertained by M. Proudhon. He then refers to the case of *Onslow*, to *Lloyd's case*, and *Thornton's*

· *case*, which was very much discussed in the course
of the argument, and to which the Court will
shortly advert ; and also to *Breul's case.* He
speaks of *Routledge* v. *De Veine,* as the other witnesses do, as having been decided in 1852.

The Court does not think it necessary to go
through the other witnesses examined. There are
five witnesses, and they all take the same view of
the case, opposed to that taken by M. Frignet,
M. Senard, and M. Paillet. · There are five of them
express their opinion one way, and three the other.
With such differences the Court must have some
difficulty in deciding the points of course. But it
may be as well now to refer to the cases upon which
the advocates have been examined—the French
jurists—and which were also discussed before the
Court in the argument in this case.

The first of these cases was one from *Sirey's Reports* in 1851, *Brown Lynch* v. *Martin Lynch.* The
summary of the case, which is put at the commencement of it, and I take that summary to be
what we should put in our reports as the marginal
note, is this: " Foreigner—Succession—Moveables—
Competency — Provisional administrator—Bail.—
The law which regulates the succession of a foreigner
deceased in France, as to moveables which are
situated in that country, is the law of the country
of the deceased, especially if such person had not a
a legal domicil in France, and had not any French
heir." So that there are two distinctions; and this
will account for some of the distinctions in the
other cases, since the having a French heir seems
to make some difference. " Consequently, the
French tribunals are incompetent to take cogni-

1856.

March 31st.
February 1st,
5th, 19th.
August 16th.

BREMER
v.
FREEMAN
and
BREMER.

1856.

March 31st.
February 1st,
5th, 19th.
August 16th.

BREMER
v.
FREEMAN
and
BREMER.

zance of a demand in liquidation and division in such a succession. Consequently, an instrument emanating from the foreign competent tribunal, which authorizes one of the heirs to administer provisionally the succession of the deceased, ought to be applied to the moveables situate in France, although even they should not be specially named in that instrument; provided, however, that the instrument in question does not contain anything contrary to the principles of French law. Thus, if that instrument attributes to the administrative heir the power to dispose of the goods of the deceased, the other heirs cannot demand from the French tribunals the authority to proceed themselves to the sale of the moveables situate in France."

Now, the tribunal of the Seine, from which this was an appeal, had decided as follows:—"As to the demand for an account, liquidation, and division—Whereas Francis Lynch was born in Ireland, and had his domicil there during a long time; whereas he had never been naturalized a Frenchman, and did not even obtain from the king the right to establish his domicil in France; that thus, therefore, he died an Englishman." That seems a direct decision in point. This man was born an Irishman; though he was resident in France he was not naturalized by any law, and he was not domiciled by any authority of the government; the consequence was, he died an Englishman, therefore he might make his will in the English form. "Whereas his fortune is all per-"sonalty, and therefore regulated by the personal "statute, that is to say, by the English law, which "followed him on to the soil of France, as the "French law follows the Frenchman into a foreign "country, and continues to regulate there his capa- "city and his status;" so that it is not only a consequence, but it is here stated as a necessary consequence, that he may make his will according to the law of England, just as a Frenchman may make his according to the law of France. "Whereas the law of the 14th of July, 1819, is "without application in this case; because, on the "one hand, his succession is all personalty; and on "the other hand, Francis Lynch leaves no French "heir." Neither is there in this case any French heir, neither is there immoveable property. All the property the deceased has in France is personal property, and that of small amount, the bulk of the property being in England.

Now it is, I think, hardly necessary to go further into this case, it cannot be clearer; but look at the decree of the Appeal Court, "The Court, adopting "the reasons of the first judges, confirms, and "nevertheless orders, that Martin Lynch should be "called on to give security for 20,000 francs in "respect to the valuables found in France;" that is, he was the executor appointed, and he had taken probate in England, he had given security for the amount of property in this country, and the French adopted the English will; they only said he must give security for the due administration of the property in France, but they pronounced for and held the English will to be good.

The next case that was adverted to by the jurists was that of *Thornton* v. *Curling.* The summary of that case is, "Civil rights—Foreigner—Competency

1856.

March 31st.
February 1st,
5th, 19th.
August 16th.

BREMER
v..
FREEMAN
and
BREMER.

1856.

March 31st.
February 1st,
5th, 19th.
August 16th.

BREMER
v.
FREEMAN
and
BREMER.

" —Succession.—Ought to be held opened in France,
" the succession of a foreigner who died there since
" the law of the 14th of July, 1819, after having
" obtained from the government the enjoyment of
" civil rights, and having transferred to that country
" his domicil conformably to the authorization which
" he had obtained, and that, although the foreigner
" was not a naturalized Frenchman." So that is
the point in that case; he had been domiciled in
France; he was not naturalized but domiciled by
authorization; and being so domiciled he must be
considered a Frenchman, and must adopt the French
form. That is exactly the converse of the other
case. In *Lynch's case* the deceased had obtained a
domicil but not authorization, therefore the English
law prevailed; but here, in *Thornton's case*, was an
Englishman who had obtained a domicil by authorization, and it was held that he was to be
considered a Frenchman, and was to make use of
the French form.

The decree of the Court of Paris in this case was :
" Considering that Thornton was not naturalized a
" Frenchman, and was only admitted to establish
" his domicil in France, he died a stranger; that in
" all cases the disposition of the moveables of a
" stranger existing in the place where he dwelt is
" submitted to the legislation of his country, de-
" clares the judgment incompetently rendered, and
" sends the parties to proceed before their natural
" judges."

The Court of Paris reversed in this judgment
the decree of the Court of the Seine, which had
held that Thornton was domiciled in France, that
moveables are regulated by the law of the domicil,

and that it was for the French tribunals to take cognizance of the question. But the Court of Cassation, the last court of appeal, reversed the judgment of the Court of Paris, and made this decree: " The Court having looked at the articles 13 and " 110 of the *Code Civil*, and 59 *Code de Procédure*, " considering, first, that the judgment of the first " instance, not contradicted on this point by the " decree appealed from, recognises in fact that " Thornton had been authorized by a royal decree " to establish his domicil in France; that he had " effectively established and preserved it there; " also, that he died in Paris; and that thus, under " the terms of the article 110 of the *Code Civil*, " it was at Paris that his succession opened; se-" condly, that the actual proceedings are between " the son of Thornton, his natural and legitimate " heir, and Curling, in his quality of testamentary " heir; and that the question is, to pronounce on " the validity or invalidity of the testament of the " deceased; and that, under the terms of the article " 59 of the *Code de Procédure*, this question ought " to be carried before the tribunal of the place " where Thornton had acquired his domicil, and " consequently before the tribunal of the Seine. " Thirdly, that these principles are so much the " more applicable to the case, although Thornton " had not been naturalized a Frenchman, in that " the royal decree which admitted him to establish " his domicil in France, conferred on him, con-" formably to article 13 of the *Code Civil*, the " enjoyment of civil rights; and that having been " in consequence of that disposition subject during " his life to the jurisdiction of the French tribunals,

1856.

March 31st.
February 1st,
5th, 19th.
August 16th.

BREMER
*v.*
FREEMAN
and
BREMER.

1856.

March 31st.
February 1st,
5th, 19th.
August 16th.

BREMER
v.
FREEMAN
and
BREMER.

" as well in reference to his person as to the goods
" which he had in France, the difficulties relative
" to the succession to these goods are necessarily
" subject to the same jurisdiction; whence it fol-
" lows, that in sending the parties before other
" judges, the decree appealed from has violated the
" laws above cited, which makes it unnecessary to
" examine the first point, which remains reserved
" to the parties; pronounces the judgment erro-
" neous, and reverses it."   So here is a clear decision
on that point in *Thornton's case;* he having been
domiciled by authorization, the law applies to him
in the manner stated.

Now, these two cases so far are perfectly clear.

The next case is that of D'Abaunza, which has
been referred to, but which has very little application
and very little bearing on the present case, and which
the Court will not think it necessary to go through.

The same may be said as to another case, that of
*Verity* v. *Mackenzie.*

Another case is *Breul's case,* and which is referred
to by several of the witnesses examined both on the
one side and on the other.   That came on for
hearing in July, 1852, and was a question as to
domicil, and the competency of the French tribunals.   The summary of it is this: " The article 13
" of the *Code Napoléon,* which says that the foreigner
" admitted by the French Government to establish
" his domicil in France enjoys there all civil rights,
" had not for its object to determine the conditions
" which a foreigner ought to fulfil in order to ac-
" quire a domicil in France.   The foreigner who
" has fixed his residence for more than 30 years in
" France, and who has not quitted it during that

"interval of time, unites all the legal conditions
"constituting domicil. It is, therefore, to the
"French tribunals that ought to be submitted ques-
"tions relative to the succession of that foreigner
"who has died in France." This is apparently in
direct contradiction to the two former cases which
I have commented upon; but it is necessary to see
the whole of the facts of it. The following are the
circumstances in which the question presents itself:
M. Justin Breul, born in 1799, a Hanoverian
subject, came to establish himself in Paris; there
he established a manufactory of bronzes and porce-
lains. On the 10th of April, 1847, he married
at Paris a Frenchwoman. No contract was entered
into for regulating the pecuniary conditions of the
marriage. This is the important circumstance, this
is what gives the colour to the case—the marriage
in France to a Frenchwoman, and with regard to
the effect of a marriage so contracted in France as
to a community of goods. On the 8th of September,
1851, Breul died in Paris. He left a will, made in
the holograph form, deposited with a notary—that
is, according to the French law. The natural heirs
of Breul were strangers. Some were domiciled in
Hanover, another at Frankfort-on-the-Maine, another
at Brunswick. A suit was brought by the widow
against the natural heirs. The question of incompetency was there raised. The decision of the Civil
Tribunal of the Seine was as follows:—"Considering
"that according to the article 110 of the *Code*
"*Napoléon*, the place where the succession is opened
"is determined by the domicil; that according to the
"article 102 the domicil is the place of the principal
"establishment—considering that in fact Breul had

1856.

March 31st.
February 1st,
5th, 19th.
August 16th.

BREMER
*v.*
FREEMAN
and
BREMER.

R 2

1856.

March 31st.
February 1st,
5th, 19th.
August 16th.

BREMER
v.
FREEMAN
and
BREMER.

"inhabited Paris more than thirty years; that at a
"very early period he established there an important
"house of commerce; that he never ceased directing
"it up to his death, and in it he realized important
"profits; that it has been articulate, and not con-
"tested, that in this long interval Breul never
"quitted Paris, not even in order to make a journey
"to Hanover, where he was born; that he married
"at Paris a Frenchwoman; that he therefore united
"'all the conditions constituting a domicil; that
"it is in vain to oppose the dispositions of the 13th
"article of the *Code Napoléon;* that in effect this
"article, which says that the stranger who has been
"admitted by the French Government to establish
"his domicil in France, enjoys there all rights which
"are found under the rubric of civil rights, has not
"for its object to determine the conditions which a
"stranger must fulfil in order to acquire a domicil
"in France; that it has always been recognised by
"jurisprudence, that the stranger who had fixed
"his real habitation in France, and who had had
"the intention of fixing it there, even without the
"authority of the government, did not the less re-
"quire a domicil in France." Certainly that seems
to go directly the reverse of the former cases, and
the considerations there stated. But the decree goes
on: "Considering, on the other side, that according
"to the article 19 of the same code, the widow
"Breul, who had lost her nationality by the fact of
"her marriage with a stranger, had, by her widow-
"hood, recovered her quality of a Frenchwoman."
So that was one of the considerations, that he had
married her without any agreement or any stipulation as to community of goods, and that upon his

death she recovered her condition of a natural subject of France; therefore there were the interests of
a French subject concerned. " That on these two
" grounds the tribunal has been rightly resorted to.
" For these reasons, without delay nor having re-
" gard to the exception taken of its incompetency,
" it retains the cause for decision." That is all the
Court does. Then it is upon these two grounds,
not upon a consideration of a domicil without authorization, but upon these two grounds, that there
was a marriage between the parties without any
agreement or stipulation as to a community of
goods, and that the wife was a Frenchwoman, and
the moment the husband died her natural character
of a French subject returned to her, that the Court
retained the cause for decision. It is not an absolute decision on the facts or law at that time, but
the Court retained the cause for decision.

But at a later period a decree is made by the
Imperial Court of Paris. This decree that I have
alluded to was upon the 11th of July, 1852, and
the decree on appeal on the 17th of December, 1853,
and what fell from the latter Court is this: "Con-
" sidering that the husband and wife Breul were
" married at Paris on the 10th of April, 1847,
" without having regulated by deed their matrimo-
" nial conventions; that thus under the terms of
" articles 1393 and 1400 of the *Code Napoléon*, their
" marriage is submitted to the rule of community—
" considering that the quality of a foreigner which
" belonged to Breul could not prevent the applica-
" tion of these articles; that, in effect, the law, in
" disposing as it has done, supposes that the parties
" voluntarily abstained from establishing by writing

1856.

March 31st.
February 1st,
5 h, 19th.
August 16th.

BREMER
*v.*
FREEMAN
and
BREMER.

1856.

March 31st.
February 1st,
5th, 19th.
August 16th.

BREMER
v.
FREEMAN
and
BREMER.

" their conventions, and that there has been formed
" between them a tacit contract which the law alone
" consecrates, and of which it regulates the conse-
" quences ; that foreigners, capable of stipulating
" in all contracts dependent on the law of nations,
" as that which is in question, can, on marrying in
" France, accept tacitly the rule of community esta-
" blished by the law in the same manner as they
" might have stipulated it expressly in a deed—
" considering, however, that in order to apply these
" principles to foreigners it does not suffice that the
" marriage should have been contracted in France;
" that it is necessary also that the will of the con-
" tracting parties should be manifested by certain
" acts—considering that the establishment of a
" domicil in France has always been considered as
" the most positive manifestation of that will ; that,
" without doubt, this domicil ought to have an im-
" portance which distinguishes it from a simple re-
" sidence, but that it is not necessary that it should
" have been authorized by the government in the
" terms of article 13 of the *Code Napoleon,* since that
" authorization has for its object to confer on the
" foreigner all the civil rights belonging to national
" persons, and that these rights are not necessary for
" the regulation of matrimonial conventions purely
" of the law of nations—considering that, in the
" case for decision, Breul, at the time at which he
" was married, inhabited Paris, where he had
" founded, more than twenty years since, an im-
" portant commercial establishment; that this esta-
" blishment was the only one which he carried on;
" that he had never preserved either domicil or re-
" sidence in the country of his birth; that having
" collected in this country before his marriage an

1856.

March 31st.
February 1st,
5th, 19th.
August 16th.

BREMER
v.
FREEMAN
and
BREMER.

"important succession, he had realized all the value " of it, and had placed the products in France, where " already was placed the remainder of his fortune; " that these facts show, in an incontestable manner, " that Breul had in France, at the time of his mar- " riage, a settled domicil," not naturalization, but " *un domicile sérieux*"*—" considering also that " Breul preserved that position up to his death; that " in his will he declared it in express terms, and at " several times that he was married under the rule " of Community; that thus wishing to maintain, as " far as he could, even after him, the seat of his " fortune in France, he ordered, by this act of his " last will, that the capital of which he disposed in " usufruct should be placed either in French rentes " or on mortgage on goods situate in France; that " there cannot, therefore, exist any uncertainty as " to the wish of Breul to submit to the French law " the regulation of the civil conditions of his mar- " riage; that therefore there was community of " goods between the husband and wife Breul." That is the conclusion to which they came after these considerations, simply that there was com- munity of goods between husband and wife, and in consequence of that " the Court pronounces that " there is community of goods between the husband " and wife Breul conformably to the articles 1393 " and 1400 of the *Code Napoléon*." That is the sum total.

There is no absolute decision there, though they state the consideration of his being domiciled, the great number of years which he had lived in France, and likewise that the marriage was without an agree-

---

* *Sérieux: Terme de Jurisprudence. Qui n'est pas simulé.—Dict. de L'Académie.*

1856.

March 31st.
February 1st,
5th, 19th.
August 16th.

BREMER
v.
FREEMAN
and
BREMER.

mentas to community of goods, his desire that his property should remain in France, and the fact that the widow was a natural born Frenchwoman, and on that ground they pronounce there was a community of goods. Certainly there are facts in that case that do not appear to be in accordance with the cases I before cited, but the judges do not seem to rely upon them; and the decree that was made, and the only decree that was made, respects this community of goods.

*Lloyd's case* comes next, and the summary is this: " The husband, a foreigner by birth, but domiciled " from a long time in France, who marries without "contract in that country with a Frenchwoman, " ought to be considered to have consented to the "legal community established by the French law; " and that, although the fact of his domicil was not " accompanied by the authorization of the govern- " ment necessary to enable a foreigner to establish " his domicil in France, this authorization, required " in order that the foreigner may enjoy all French ".civil rights, is not necessary for the establishment " of the community," that is, the community of goods, " which is purely of the law of nations." Therefore that seems to be a case very much to the same effect as the Breuls' case. As to Mr. Lloyd himself, it really seems to be hardly known to what country he did belong, though I think he turns out from one part of the case to have been an English-man, but where he was born or came from no one knows. He married in France without any stipu-lation, and the French tribunal came to this decision upon the community of goods; and beyond that the case of Lloyd does not go.

The next case, which is the first mentioned by M. Frignet, is *De Veine* v. *Routledge*. That came before the Court of Appeal, and is reported by Sirey, and is stated to have been decided in the Court of Cassation in 1853. I have no doubt it was so, but it seems, according to the statement of M. Frignet, that the decision was the same as that which took place in 1852 in the first Court of Appeal, and subsequently in the Court of Cassation, the next highest court, and the decision seems to have been sustained by the Court of Cassation according to the evidence before me.

There are various points in that case which it is not necessary to go through, but the third is this: " The succession of a foreigner, as to moveables " situate in France, is regulated by the French " law, when the deceased had his legal domicil in " France, and his succession is claimed by a French " heir against foreigners as universal legatees." This is one of those cases referred to by the counsel where they speak of the variations in these decisions, some of them in consequence of there being French heirs, and in other cases because there are moveables in France. In this case, though there was no domicil by authorization, yet in point of fact the deceased was domiciled there according to the law of nations; but there was a French heir in the case, and the Court held that the French heir should not be injured by a disposition leaving the property in the way in which it was disposed of in the will.

" Fourthly, a holograph will, made by a foreigner " in France, of which execution is demanded before " the French tribunals, cannot be declared valid

1856.

March 31st.
February 1st,
5th, 19th.
August 16th.

BREMER
*v.*
FREEMAN
and
BREMER.

1853.

March 31st.
February 1st,
5th, 19th.
August 16th.

BREMER
v.
FREEMAN
and
BREMER.

"unless it unites all the conditions of form recog-
"nized as essential in French law, and whatever
"may be in that respect the state of the law of the
"country to which the testator belongs; conse-
"quently, such a will is null, if it is not written
"entirely in the hand of the testator, or if it is not
"dated." They adhered to the French law on that
point.

Now, another case which was cited was, I think,
from the journal *Le Droit;* that was *Olivarez's case.*
I do not know that it carries the case at all further,
or puts it in any different point of view at all.

But the case of *Onslow* was very much discussed,
and perhaps it may be as well to advert to that; it
was a case of naturalization. The summary of it
is this: "The foreigner, who was at the time of the
"promulgation of the law of the 30th of April,
"1790, established in France, had had there a con-
"tinuous domicil for five years, and had married
"there a Frenchwoman, was naturalized of full
"right, without being bound to take the civic
"oath." The sum and substance of this case of
*Onslow's* was, that he was domiciled in France, but
never domiciled according to the requirements of
the *Code Napoléon*—never domiciled there by authorization of the government. But it turns out
he had acquired a domicil, and he was domiciled
there before the *Code Napoléon* was in force; in
fact, before there was any *Code Napoléon* at all, he
had become a naturalized Frenchman; therefore,
the law applied to him as it would to a French
citizen or French subject. *Onslow's case* is given
at great length. It seems to have been taken
before the Court of Cassation; it goes to the

highest court; and it is upon the ground I have stated that he was to be considered a Frenchman, to be domiciled there as if he had been domiciled there by authorization, because he had been domiciled at the time when this act of authorization was not necessary, being domiciled in another form, and he did not lose that domicil.

Then, other cases have been cited, very especially the case of *Laneuville* v. *Anderson*, but I think it is hardly necessary for the Court to enter into that discussion. Mr. Anderson, who went to France and made his will there, left property in France to a lady to whom he had been long attached, with whom he had resided. He obtained immoveable goods in France, real property, and he left them to that lady; therefore, the French Court declared itself competent as to the property which was in France, and pronounced the property to be the property of Madame Laneuville.

There was also a case, which I think was not mentioned in argument, but which Dr. Deane, one of the counsel in this case, was kind enough to give to the Court; a case which seemed to be very much in point, and directly contrary to the conclusion which the Court has rather intimated its intention of arriving at. It is contained in the *Journal des Tribunaux.* This is a decision of the Civil Tribunal of the Seine upon the 14th of March in the present year. The case is this: "*Tribunal Civil de la Seine. Etranger—Domicile—* "*Succession—Ouverte en France—Compétence.—La* " *succession de l'étranger doit être considérée comme* " *étant ouverte en France, lorsqu'il est constant en fait* " *que le décédé avait dans ce pays son principal*

1856.

March 31st.
February 1st,
5th, 19th.
August 16th.

BREMER
*v.*
FREEMAN
and
BREMER.

1856.

March 31st.
February 1st,
5th, 19th.
August 16th.

BREMER
v.
FREEMAN
and
BREMER.

" *établissement, et ce alors même qu'il n'aurait pas* " *obtenu du Gouvernement Français la jouissance des* " *droits civils.*"    That is the first part of the summary, and it is quite clear that it is in direct opposition to several of the cases I have mentioned, because there is an express declaration that a domicil without authorization of the government will have the same effect as, in point of fact, the authorization has.    Then, "*Par suite les tribunaux Français sont seuls compétens pour connaître des difficultés relatives à l'ouverture de cette succession.*"

Then the report proceeds to state the case; it is very short.    On the 21st of June, 1854, died at Paris the Baron de Mecklenbourg.    He left neither ascendants nor descendants; his heirs according to the French law were four.    "*Ses héritiers,* " *d'après la loi Française, étaient quatre, pour un quart,* " *1°. Mme. la Baronne veuve de Mecklenbourg; 2°. M.* " *le Baron Christian de Mecklenbourg; 3°. Mme. la Ba-* " *ronne Elisabeth de Mecklenbourg; 4°. Conjointement* " *Mme. la Baronne de Reischach née de Rœder, et Mlle.* " *de Rœder; ces deux dernières par représentation de* " *Julie Anne, Baronne de Mecklenbourg, décédée, épouse* " *du Baron de Rœder.    Mais, aux termes du statut* " *Mecklenbourgeois, Mlle. de Rœder se trouvait exclue* " *de la succession, cette loi n'admettant la représenta-* " *tion en ligne collatérale que jusqu'au premier dégré;*" so that according to the French law they were divisible into four.    The Mecklenbourg law did not quite agree with the French law, because that does not admit a representation so far off as the French law does.

" *Lorsqu'il il fut procédé à l'inventaire, Mlle. de* " *Rœder n'était pas présente, et le notaire, sur la*

"*réquisition des héritiers, crut devoir appliquer aux*
"*parties les qualités que leur attribuait la loi du pays*
"*auquel appartenait M. le Baron de Mecklenbourg;*"
so that she not being present, the notary thought
proper to apply the Mecklenburg law, not the
French law, and therefore excluded Mlle. de Rœder.

"*Mlle. de Rœder a vu là une atteinte portée à ses*
"*droits, et avec l'assistance de Maier, son tuteur, elle*
"*a assigné ces cohéritiers pour voir dire que l'inventaire*
"*serait continué en sa présence, comme habile à se*
"*porter héritière pour un huitième du Baron de Meck-*
"*lenbourg.   Les autres héritiers ont conclu à l'incom-*
"*pétence du tribunal en se fondant sur ce que toutes*
"*les parties étaient étrangères, et que les biens que le*
"*défunt possédait en France ne se composaient que*
"*de meubles.   Le tribunal, sur les conclusions de*
"*M. le substitut Pivard, après avoir entendu M.*
"*Dufaur pour Mlle. de Rœder, et M. Bethmont pour*
"*les défendeurs, a rendu le jugement suivant.*"

Then we have the judgment: "*Attendu qu'il*
"*résulte, soit de toutes les circonstances de la cause,*
"*soit des documens produits, que le Baron de Mecklen-*
"*bourg avait à Paris son principal et même son unique*
"*établissement; que, depuis 1828, il n'en avait con-*
"*servé aucun à l'étranger.   Attendu qu'il résulte de*
"*ce fait la conséquence légale que le dit Baron de*
"*Mecklenbourg avait son domicile à Paris, et que sa*
"*succession s'y est ouverte.*"   So that, considering that
he lived there—that he was under the French law and
was domiciled there, though there was no authorization—considering that—"*Attendu qu'il importe peu*
"*que le Baron de Mecklenbourg n'ait pas perdu la*
"*qualité d'étranger, et n'ait pas été autorisé par le*
"*Gouvernement Français à jouir en France des droits*

1856.

March 31st.
February 1st,
5th, 19th.
August 16th.

BREMER
*v.*
FREEMAN
and
BREMER

1856.

March 31st.
February 1st,
5th, 19th.
August 16th.

BREMER
v.
FREEMAN
and
BREMER.

" *civils ; que, en effet, la jouissance légale de ces droits*
" *est indépendante de la question de domicile, qui ne*
" *repose que sur celle de savoir où est en France le*
" *principal établissement de l'étranger qui y réside—*
" *par ces motifs, le tribunal rejette le déclinatoire,*
" *se déclare compétent, dit qu'il sera plaidé au fond,*
" *renvoie la cause à quinzaine pour les plaidoiries ;*
" *condamne les parties de Laperche aux dépens de*
" *l'incident.*" So that this Court clearly decided in
this case that a domicil was sufficient without any
authorization ; and though it was opposed, and
though it was argued by counsel on the one side
and on the other, the Court was quite clear in the
decision, and condemned the other party in the
costs of the proceedings.

Certainly I was rather surprised, for I could not
by possibility at all reconcile this case with any of
the cases which have been referred to, some of
which went a very considerable length. There
was a discrepancy on some points between this case
and those which I have been referred to; but I was
very much surprised, and did not know how this
matter could be sustained. However, it does so
happen that there has been an appeal from this
decision, and that the superior court has reversed
the judgment ; they came to a different conclusion
there. The heading of the case is this, and it was
under the presidency of M. Delangle, the first president of the Imperial Court of Paris—" *Audiences*
" *des 15, 22, et 26 Juillet,* 1856. *Succession ouverte*
" *en France—Etranger—Domicile—Compétence—*
" *Succession du Baron Frédéric de Mecklenbourg.—*
" *Les tribunaux Français sont incompétens pour*
" *statuer sur les difficultés relatives à l'ouverture de la*

*" succession d'un étranger décédé en France, lorsque*
*" les héritiers sont étrangers, que les immeubles sont*
*" situés hors de France, lesqu'il est constant, en fait,*
*" que le défunt a conservé avec le gouvernement dont*
*" il était sujet, les rapports qu'ils jugeait les plus*
*" propres à maintenir sa nationalité. En vain oppo-*
*" serait on que depuis longtemps il habitait la France*
*" et qu'il avoit pris part à des spéculations de diverse*
*" nature. Ces circonstances ne sauraient entraîner la*
*" renonciation au·domicile d'origine."*

1856.

March 31st.
February 1st,
5th, 19th.
August 16th.

BREMER
*v.*
FREEMAN
and
BREMER.

The superior tribunal comes therefore to the decision of reversing the sentence that was so pronounced by the inferior court.

Well, then, this comes to be a case directly in point, and shows that this domicil by authorization is necessary by the French law; and therefore the conclusion to which the Court would arrive upon the evidence which has been given upon the testimony supplied by the French witnesses, by these eminent jurists, five on the one side and three on the other, considering the nature of the several cases which have been adverted to, and especially considering the last case that was decided, is, that it seems to me to be quite clear that it is necessary in order to establish such a domicil in France as to affect the succession of the testator and the mode of making wills, that that domicil should be by authorization.*

---

* In the course of his judgment, in *Wright's Trusts*, 25 L. J. Ch. 631, Vice-Chancellor Wood observes: " I have been but very little assisted by the " French opinions. M. Cremieux has assumed throughout the domicil to be " English. M. Dutilleul has not assumed that, but has argued upon it in " this way, in which he appears to be clearly wrong: he says that without a " licence from the government the rights of domicil cannot be acquired. " Now, three authorities have been cited which contradict that ; and there- " fore I have not been able to derive any assistance from the opinion founded " upon that hypothesis."

1856.

March 31st.
February 1st,
5th, 19th.
August 16th.

BREMER
v.
FREEMAN
and
BREMER.

In this case it appears to me that the deceased was domiciled in France according to the *jus gentium*, but no further; that there was no domicil by authorization, and consequently she was entitled to the privilege of making an English will, more especially when all the relations and all the parties who were benefited under the will, with some trifling exception, were English people, and domiciled in England; and considering that all the property was not in France, but, with the small exception of the goods in the apartments, was in England, I think the fact of making the will in accordance with the English form was perfectly right and proper, and it will be the duty of the Court to grant probate of the paper propounded.

I should have mentioned, in addition, the case of *Collier* v. *Rivaz*. In that case my learned predecessor came to a similar decision. It is quite true that did not relate to a domicil in France, it was in Belgium; but it appears that in Belgium the *Code Civil* of France is adopted, it was therefore under the same law. There were two eminent jurists examined in that case, and they came to the same opinion as the five gentlemen in the present case. Therefore the Court pronounced for the will in the English form, made by an English subject domiciled according to the law of nations in Belgium, but not domiciled there by the authority of the government of that country. It is the duty of the Court to follow in the same course, and accordingly I give my sentence for the will which was executed by the deceased, for there is no doubt whatever of the due execution of the will and the capacity of the deceased. The gentleman has been examined who

1856.

March 31st.
February 1st,
5th, 19th.
August 16th.

BREMER
v.
FREEMAN
and
BREMER.

got the instructions from the deceased, who drew up the will, and was present at the execution, and he deposes in such a way as to leave no doubt on this subject. I therefore shall pronounce for it.

There is only one matter more to be considered, that is with respect to the question of costs. I think it was quite right on the part of Miss Bremer to contest this will. There was so much doubt in the opinion of the French jurists and some of the French decisions as to the validity of an English will in the English form, that I think she was justified in calling in the probate of the will, and therefore I shall not condemn her in the costs of the proceedings.

But there is another part of the case, and that is with regard to Mr. James Bremer, who was one of the executors of the will. He took probate of it, and he was acting under it while it was an outstanding probate. I do not say there was anything improper after he brought in the probate in obedience to the monition that was served upon him. I do not say he was bound to defend the will, if he took a different view of the law. He had been advised that it was not a good will, that it could not be sustained, therefore I do not know that he was called upon to join Mr. Freeman, his co-executor, in supporting this will. I think he might have been justified in joining Miss Bremer, who was also a legatee. I think he might have been justified in joining her in opposition to the will, but I think that the course which he has taken is hardly that which can receive the sanction of the Court. It is left to Miss Bremer to carry on this suit; Mr. Bremer did not join her, but he conducted the cause on her behalf; and then when her plea is given in,

1856.

March 31st.
February 1st,
5th, 19th.
August 16th.

BREMER
v.
FREEMAN
and
BREMER.

and witnesses are produced and examined, he takes it upon himself to cross-examine them as if he was an adverse party.

Now, an application was made to the Court in the course of the proceedings to prohibit Mr. Bremer from addressing interrogatories to the witnesses, who were in point of fact his own witnesses. The Court, however, thought it was not at liberty to take that step, and to prohibit him from the course which he thought proper to take. The interrogatories which he might address to them might have been very proper. I thought it better that he should be allowed, if he chose, to pursue that course, but I confess at the same time the Court did not see with perfect satisfaction the course pursued, it did not quite become him, not that anything essentially wrong was intended, but I think the Court must do something to mark its sense of that proceeding. I shall not visit him with a serious penalty, but I think I must condemn him in something *nomine expensarum*. I think I shall not do injustice if I condemn him in £50 *nomine expensarum*.

I pronounce for the will. Of course Mr. Daniel Alexander Freeman, the executor, is entitled to the probate; whether Mr. Bremer will join him I do not know; the Court has not the power of excluding him.

NORTON *v.* BAZETT.[*]

*7 Wm. 4, and 1 Vic. c. 26, s. 9—Subscription in the presence of the testator.*

1856.

July 19th.
August 4th.

THE deceased left a will in his own handwriting, executed according to the evidence of the subscribing witnesses, under the following circumstances:—

During the morning he was engaged in writing in the private or inner room of the office, in which room the deceased and his partners usually sat. The outer room was the clerk's office, where the witnesses sat; the private room was entered from the outer room by a door which was habitually kept wide open, that is, the door was habitually rather more open than it would be if standing at right angles with the wall. The deceased was a particular man with reference to his clerks, and the door was kept thus open to enable him to look after them. It stood open in this way on the morning in question, and during the morning the witnesses passed into the deceased's room several times, and observed that he was engaged writing on his private affairs. This was apparent to them from the nature of the paper on which he was writing. Between two and three o'clock in the afternoon the deceased, being still in his room, called to the witnesses to come to him, and on entering they saw him sitting at his

*Where the subscription of the witnesses takes place in a different room from that in which the testator is, he must be proved to have been in a position whence he could have seen the witnesses as they subscribed their names.*

---

[*] This case has been accidentally misplaced.

table with two sheets of the said paper before him, both written upon. His table was in the centre of his room, and he was sitting at it, with his back towards the partition wall between his room and theirs. As they passed through the doorway his chair was a little on their left hand. Immediately as they entered, the deceased said, "This is my last will and testament which I have made, and I request you to witness my signature." The two sheets of letter paper before mentioned lay before him at the time, and he at once signed his name "William Norton" at the end of the will on the second of the two sheets of paper, in their presence. They were both standing by his side at the time, and he remained sitting in his chair. He then handed to them the last sheet of the will, and requested them to sign their names to it, and to add the words "Witnesses to the signature of William Norton." The table in the deceased's room was full of papers, and so, for convenience in signing, they took the said last sheet to their desk in the outer office; the other sheet of the will remained on the deceased's table. They went into the outer office and there signed their names respectively to the said last sheet in each other's presence, standing whilst they did so at that corner of the desk which was nearest to the said doorway. They so signed their names as witnesses, and added the words "Witnesses to the signature of William Norton." The desk could be seen from some parts of the said private room, but not from all parts of it, and not from that part at which the deceased was sitting when they left the room to sign their names. He was then sitting with his back to the door; his chair was not two

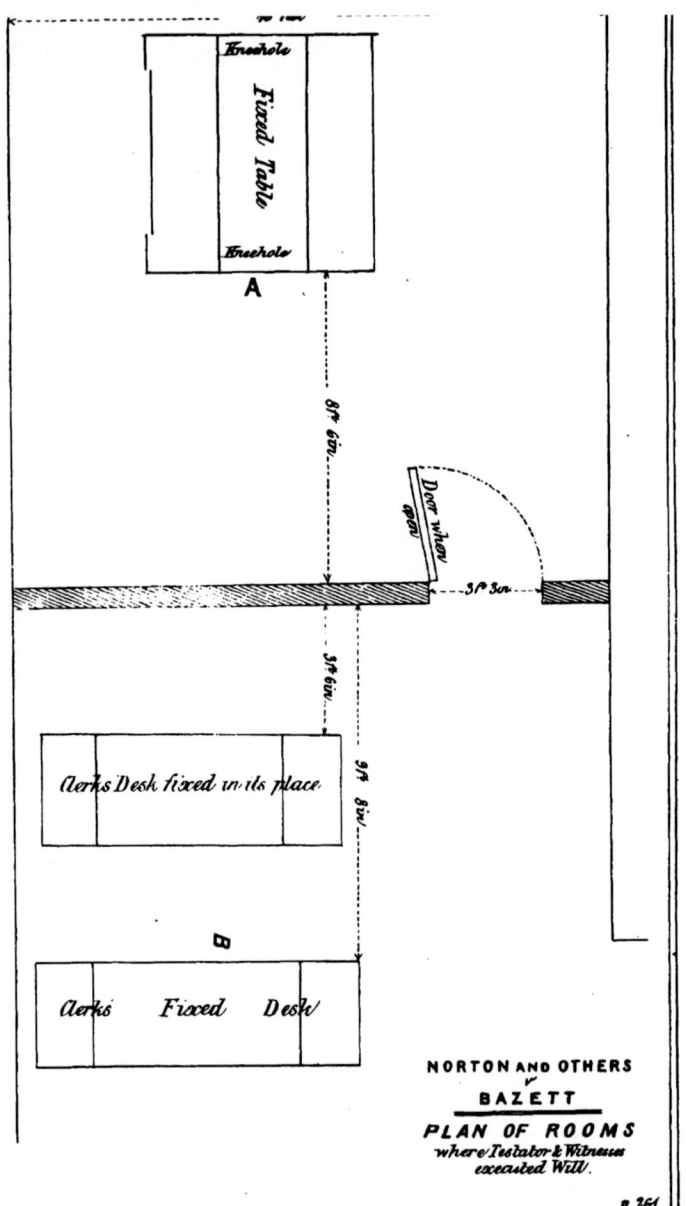

Kneehole

Fixed Table

Kneehole

A

8ft 6in.

Door when open

3ft 3in.

3ft 6in.

3ft 8in.

Clerks Desk fixed in its place

B

Clerks Fixed Desk

NORTON AND OTHERS
v
BAZETT

PLAN OF ROOMS
where Testator & Witness
executed Will.

p. 261

yards from the partition wall; and if he had moved a yard to his right hand from his chair, he could have seen the desk and witnesses as they signed their names; whether he did so move, the witnesses had no means of saying. As soon as they had signed their names, one of them returned alone into the inner room with the second sheet of the will, and gave it to the deceased, who then read over the signatures. When the will was brought back the deceased was standing up at that side of his table which was parallel with the said partition wall, with his back to the wall, and exactly in front of the chair on which he had been sitting when they left the room. He was apparently arranging his papers before leaving the office. How long he had left his chair they could not judge. They neither saw nor heard him between their leaving and returning to his room. The door between the two rooms remained open during all the transaction. They were absent from the deceased's room about two minutes whilst so signing their names.

Annexed to the interrogatories was the plan of the two rooms, on which the witnesses were requested to mark the places where the deceased sat and stood in the inner room, and they subscribed the will in the outer room.

A. was the place where the deceased was.

B. was the place where the witnesses wrote their names.

*Sir J. D. Harding,* Q.A., and *Twiss,* in support of the will.—Every presumption is in favour of a due execution of the will; the presence, if not actual, was constructive, and there was nothing to

1856.

July 19th.
August 4th.

NORTON
v.
BAZETT.

show that the testator did not move to some part of the room from which he might have seen the witnesses subscribe the will. The cases in which the question of presence has been considered may be divided into two classes, those in which the deceased was bedridden, or prevented from seeing by some physical impediment, in which the will has been pronounced against; and those in which, there being no physical impediment, the will was pronounced for, on the ground that as the deceased might have seen the witnesses, if he pleased, the presumption was that he did see them; and the present case is of this latter class. (They cited *Shires* v. *Glascock,* 2 Salk. 688; *Casson* v. *Dade,* 1 Br. Ch. Ca. 98; *Newton* v. *Clarke,* 2 Curt. 320; *Tribe* v. *Tribe,* 1 Rob. 775; *Hudson* v. *Parker,* ib. 14; *Tod* v. *Winchelsea,* 2 C. & P. 488; *Winchelsea* v. *Wauchope,* 3 Russ. 441.)

*Jenner* and *Deane, contrà.*—The distinction taken on the other side is unsound. The true principle to be extracted from the cases is this, that if all the persons concerned are in the same room, the act shall be presumed to have been done in their presence; and that presumption requires to be rebutted by proof that they could not, from some cause or other, see each other. But if the testator and the witnesses are in different rooms at the time of their respectively signing the instrument, then the presumption changes, and you must show that they could, as they were placed, see each other. Thus, in *Casson* v. *Dade,* had the carriage not been put back, the proof would have failed. The true and only safe test is, whether the witnesses and the testator were within the line of sight; unless this be proved, the execution is bad. (After commenting on the cases already referred to, they cited *Davy* v. *Smith,* 3 Salk. 395; *Doe* v. *Manifold,* 1 M. & S. 294; *In the goods of Ellis,* 2 Curt. 395; *In the goods of Colman,* 3 Curt. 118.)

1856.

July 19th.
August 4th.

NORTON
v.
BAZETT.

JUDGMENT.
SIR JOHN DODSON.

The question in the present case is, whether the witnesses subscribed their names to the paper propounded in the presence of the testator within the meaning of the word "presence" used in the 9th section of the Wills Act. The will is in the deceased's handwriting, on two sheets of paper, dated at the beginning the 13th, and at the end the 14th of July, as if he had been occupied two days in writing it out. The witnesses state that on the 14th he was busy in the inner room of his office writing on private affairs during the morning; that in the afternoon he called them into that inner room, from the outer room in which they sat, signed his name in their presence, and desired them to attest his signature, whereupon they returned to the outer office, wrote their names, and one of them brought back the paper. The door between the two rooms was open; but it appears from the evidence, and the plan which was brought in, that the place where the deceased sat in the inner room, with his back to the wall between the two rooms, was not visible to the clerks standing at the desk where they wrote their names. They could not see the deceased, nor could he see them, unless he had got up from the chair, and moved some two or three steps towards the open

1856.

July 19th.
August 4th.

Norton
v.
Bazett.

door. The evidence is, further, that when the clerk
who brought the will came into the room, the deceased had risen from his chair, but was standing in
front of that chair—had in fact merely got up to
sort his papers, or for some such purpose; and there
is no evidence whatever to show that he moved from
the table to any part of the room from which he
could see the witnesses.

In the course of the argument many, if not all,
the cases which could assist the Court in forming its
judgment were cited. In *Newton* v. *Clarke*, 2 Curt.
320, the whole transaction took place in one small
room, with only the curtain at the foot of the bed to
interrupt the view; and Sir H. Jenner held the will
to be well executed, observing that it would be
somewhat strange to say that what was done by a
person in the same room, and in the hearing of
another person, was not done in his presence. *Hudson* v. *Parker*, 1 Rob. 14, has not, I think, any very
great bearing upon the present case. *Tribe* v. *Tribe*,
however, in the same volume, p. 775, seems, until
closely examined, at variance with *Newton* v. *Clarke ;*
but it is clear that in *Tribe* v. *Tribe* it was proved
that the deceased could not by possibility have seen
the witnesses, and on that ground it was held that
although the witnesses subscribed in the same room,
still they did not so subscribe in the presence of the
deceased. I should observe that most of the cases
cited by counsel were also cited in *Newton* v. *Clarke*.
In 3 Curt. 118, there is the case *In the goods of Colman*, which very closely resembles the present; and
I can find no more sure or certain guide for my
instruction than that case. The only distinction is,
that there the deceased could not have moved—

here he was in a situation where he could not see without moving; and upon this distinction it has been suggested that he might have moved, and then he would have seen; but there is no proof in support of the fact suggested; there is no proof whatever that he did move; and I think it is too much for the Court to presume, that in the short space of time occupied by the witnesses in signing their names he did move. The conclusion to which I must come is, that where the witnesses subscribe in a different room from that in which the testator is, they must be shown to have subscribed in a position visible to the testator; that is not proved here, and I must pronounce against this will. I do so with much regret, but I have no discretion; and judging for myself, and in my own conscience, I cannot hold that there was a constructive presence such as would justify this Court, whatever the Court of Appeal may do, in pronouncing for this will.

*In the goods of* W. GREATA.

15 & 16 *Vic. c.* 24—*Operative signature—Words below signature.*

1856.

Nov. 14th.

*On Motion.*

THE deceased left a will, in which there was no appointment of executors. There was no attestation clause; and in the place where this clause is generally written were the words, "John Greata, executor," these words being written on the left of and a little lower than the signature of the testator. One of the subscribing witnesses deposed that the words were so written before the will was executed.

On the 6th of November *Deane* moved for probate to John Greata as executor. He cited *In the goods of Powell*, 1 Rob. 421, and submitted that since the words were not underneath, and did not follow the signature, they came within 15 & 16 Vic. c. 24, s. 1, and were entitled to probate.

SIR JOHN DODSON directed the motion to stand over, and on the 14th rejected the motion, observing that the words were not strictly speaking underneath the signature, but they were below; and though they did not follow, they certainly did not precede the signature, therefore they could not be included in the probate. The case was so far fortunate, that John Greata was one of the residuary legatees, so that he might take the administration with the will annexed.

. *In the goods of* JOHN TONAR.

*Executor—Revocation of appointment.*

*On Motion.*

1856.

Nov. 6th.

JOHN TONAR made his will with a codicil. By his will the deceased gave the residue of his property of every description to A. B. C. and D., upon the trusts in his will declared concerning the same; and of his said will he appointed the said A. B. C. and D. executors. By his codicil he revoked the gift of the residue of his property so given to A. B. C. and D. and in lieu thereof gave the same to A. B. C. and E., upon the trusts in his will and the codicil expressed and declared. And he appointed the said A. B. C. and E. executors of his will, and confirmed the same in all other respects.

*Spinks* submitted that as by the will A. B. C. and D., the residuary legatees in trust, were alone appointed executors, the revocation by the codicil of the bequest of the residue to them, and the bequest of such residue to the said A. B. C. and E., and the appointment of the said A. B. C. and E. as executors, was a revocation of the appointment of D. as an executor by the will.

SIR JOHN DODSON.

I perfectly agree with your interpretation, and decree the probate in accordance with the prayer.

## CONSISTORY COURT OF LONDON.

### JENKYN v. JENKYN.

*Adultery—Verdict for goods supplied to the wife after she had left her husband's house—Pleading.*

1856.

Nov. 18th.

THIS was a cause of divorce, by reason of adultery, brought by the husband against the wife. Several pleas had been given in, and an allegation was now before the Court on behalf of the wife, pleading that "W. brought an action against the husband, for the board and lodging of and for money lent to the wife; that the husband defended the action on the ground of the wife's adultery; that the wife was examined as a witness for the plaintiff and cross-examined by the defendant's counsel, and several witnesses examined on the defendant's part to prove the adultery, and notwithstanding their evidence the jury found for the whole amount claimed."

*Bayford* opposed the admission of this allegation.

*Addams* and *Spinks*, in support. — *Fraser* v. *Fraser*, 5 N. C. 20, was cited, where the wife had been allowed to plead a verdict for the defendant in a *crim. con.* action.

JUDGMENT.
DR. LUSHINGTON.

The present allegation is offered as responsive to

1856.

Nov. 18th.

JENKYN
v.
JENKYN.

certain additional articles brought in on behalf of the husband: and if the matter of this allegation be legal evidence, I am bound to admit it; if it be not, I am bound to reject it. There can be no doubt that verdicts against the alleged adulterer have been frequently admitted in pleading here— not however as proof of the adultery, but to show that the husband has not shrunk from exposing his witnesses to a *vivâ voce* examination in another court. But I repeat, the verdict is no evidence of adultery; and I well recollect a case before Sir H. Jenner Fust, in which he pronounced the husband to have failed on the ground that he had but a single witness; and though the husband had obtained a verdict and damages, yet he would not admit the verdict as adminicular evidence: *Evans* v. *Evans*, 1 Rob. 165. In *Fraser* v. *Fraser* the Court admitted the fact, that the husband had brought his action and failed—to be pleaded, not to show that no adultery had been committed, but to show that perhaps the verdict against the husband was founded on his neglect or connivance. But here is a verdict in an action between different parties, and for a totally different purpose. The very fact that the wife was examined shows that the jury gave their verdict from other facts which were brought before them, since she would not be a witness to prove her own innocence. All the usual objections to verdicts being pleaded apply to this case; and it would indeed be a grievous error to admit such an allegation. I therefore reject it

*Bayford* applied for the costs of the allegation, but the application was refused.

## PREROGATIVE COURT OF CANTERBURY.

*In the goods of* ELLEN STEINORTH.

**1856.**

**Nov. 22d.**

*On Motion.*

Administration to the Crown's nominee decreed, but not extracted, revoked at the instance of a creditor, without a fresh warrant; and an administration granted to the creditor, with the consent of the Queen's proctor, and upon the original decree and advertisements on behalf of the Crown.

THIS deceased died intestate and without any known relation, and on the 26th of April administration was decreed to Her Majesty's nominee after the usual decree and advertisements. It was afterwards ascertained that the deceased had died almost insolvent, and the Queen's proctor declined to take out the administration. A creditor then applied for administration; and on his behalf, and with the consent of the Queen's proctor, the Court was moved to revoke the administration decreed to the Queen's proctor, and to decree the administration to the creditor, without compelling him to take out a fresh decree or advertise. But the motion was directed to stand over, on a suggestion that the administration granted to the Queen's nominee could not be revoked without a warrant under the sign manual.

*Deane* renewed the motion, and referred to the case of *John George Stockwell*, in which case administration was, on the 6th of November, 1847, decreed to Her Majesty's nominee. The Queen's proctor did not take out the administration; and a

creditor then took out a decree with the usual
intimation against the Queen's proctor; and on the
28th of April, 1848, no appearance being given to
that decree, the administration was decreed to the
creditor. Again, *In the goods of Goldham* administration was, on the 14th of June, 1849, decreed to
Her Majesty's nominee; the Queen's proctor did
not take out the administration; and on the 17th of
January, 1850, the administration was revoked, and
administration granted to a creditor. In neither
case was a fresh warrant required.

Sir John Dodson.

If it had not been for the precedents referred to
I should have hesitated a long time before granting
this motion, which may now go as prayed.

1856.

Nov. 22d.

In the goods of
ELCEN
STEINORTH.

---

## Ernest *v*. Eustace.

*Administration—Practice—Judgment—Simple con-
tract creditor.*

### On Motion.

Sir W. C. Eustace died in February, 1855,
leaving a will and codicil. One of the executors
applying for administration, the Court will decree the administration to the simple contract
creditor if his debt be the largest, and the majority of interests be in his favour.

1856.

Nov. 22d.

Where a judg-
ment creditor
and a simple
contract cre-
ditor are both

and the residuary legatee was abroad, and gave no appearance to a decree served in the Royal Exchange on his agent; the other executor renounces. The deceased died possessed of shares in the Universal Salvage Company, which, in the year 1848, was ordered to be wound up by a decree of the Court of Chancery, under 11 & 12 Vic. c. 45; and in November, 1848, Mr. Ernest was duly appointed official manager. The deceased was made a contributory; and in June, 1855, an order was made on him for payment of the sum of £23 15s., as a contributory, to the official manager. This order was alleged to have been since registered as a judgment. The death of the deceased having been notified to the Master charged with the winding-up of the company, he, in November, 1855, made a further order, directing the proper steps to be taken for obtaining letters of administration, with the will and codicil annexed; and the usual decree, with intimation, was thereupon taken out by Mr. Ernest as a creditor.

*Bayford* moved the Court to decree the administration to Ernest, as a judgment creditor. (He referred to the *Affidavit of Debt; The Orders of the Master in Chancery;* 11 & 12 *Vic. c.* 45, *ss.* 93, 95; and 1 & 2 *Vic. c.* 110, *ss.* 18, 19.)

*Addams,* for Robert Fitch, opposed the motion, and asked for the administration to be decreed to Fitch, as a simple contract creditor to the amount of £115 0s. 6d. The will and codicil were brought in in obedience to a monition against the solicitors of the deceased, extracted by Fitch before any steps were taken on behalf of the official manager.

SIR JOHN DODSON.

The question is, whether the administration shall be granted to a simple contract creditor for £105, or to a judgment creditor, assuming Mr. Ernest to be so, for £23—the simple contract creditor being also the person in this case preferred by other creditors. I am not aware that there is any rule in this matter binding upon the Court. The registrar stated that the usual practice of the Court was to prefer the judgment creditor; but that I do not hold to be imperative upon the Court when the body of the creditors prefer the simple contract creditor, and the judgment debt is small. There are two cases in 2 Lee: *Kearney* v. *Whitaker*, 324; and *Carpenter* v. *Shelford*, 502, which, so far as the marginal note goes, seemed decisive as to the right of the judgment creditor; but when examined, they fail entirely, and leave the point untouched. In this case I shall not grant the administration to the judgment creditor, but to the simple contract creditor; and I take this course because the latter is the largest creditor, and is supported by a majority of interests.

## In the goods of H. P. Collett.

*Practice—Executrix during widowhood—Executors according to the tenor.*

1856-7.

Dec. 9th.
Jan. 23d.

A. appointed his wife executrix during widowhood; C. and D. residuary legatees in trust "to pay debts, funeral and testamentary expenses," &c. The widow alone proved, and died without having married again, leaving B. executor of her will.—Held, that C. and D. were executors according to the tenor, and entitled to probate of A.'s will.

The deceased died in March, 1855, leaving a will in his own handwriting, of which he appointed his wife executrix "during her widowhood, and so long as she shall continue unmarried." After legacies to his wife, he left his real and personal property to residuary legatees, upon trust, among other things, to pay debts and funeral and testamentary expenses. The consent of the widow in writing was made necessary in case the trustees thought fit to dispose of or convert any of the property, or in case another trustee was to be appointed. The widow proved the will in May, 1855, and died in September, 1856, without having remarried. She left a will of which she appointed an executor.

*Phillimore*, for the residuary legatees in trust.— The residuary legatees in trust, by the direction in the will to pay debts and funeral and testamentary expenses, were constituted executors according to the tenor; they would therefore have been entitled to have been joined in the probate with the widow in her lifetime, and after the death of the executor who proved would be entitled to come in to take probate: *Grant* v. *Leslie*, 3 Phil. 116; *Lynch* v. *Bellew*, 3 Phill. 424 ; *In the goods of Fry*,

1 Hagg. Eccl. 80; *Wms. Exors.* 250; *Harrison* v. *Harrison*, 10 Jur. 273, 1 Rob. 406. Again, the widow had no transmissible interest; the limitation of her executorship during widowhood, and so long as she continued unmarried, would prevent her executor from keeping up the chain of representation: *Bond* v. *Faikney*, 2 Lee, 371.

*Bayford,* for the executor of the widow.—The widow was executrix in the fullest sense of the word during widowhood. The contingency which might have determined her character as such not having occurred, she remained in the full enjoyment of that power up to the last moment of her life. Admitting that an appointment to pay debts and funeral and testamentary expenses would, standing alone, constitute an executor according to the tenor—still, in this case the limitations on the power of the trustees on those matters, where the widow's consent in writing was necessary, entirely altered their character.

JUDGMENT.

SIR JOHN DODSON.

On looking through the cases cited by counsel, I am of opinion that the residuary legatees in trust are, by the direction in the will to pay debts and funeral and testamentary expenses, constituted executors according to the tenor, and as such entitled to take probate of the will of the deceased. That the consent of the wife was necessary to enable them to do certain acts does not seem to me sufficient distinction from the decided cases.

*Bayford* asked for the costs of his party, on the

1856.

Dec. 9th.
Jan. 23d.

In the goods of
H.P.COLLETT.

ground that it was a question that could not be decided in the registry, and arose out of the ambiguous wording of the will itself.

SIR JOHN DODSON decreed costs out of the
estate.

---

# CONSISTORY COURT OF LONDON.

## SPRATT *v.* SPRATT.

*Pauper—Surgeon.*

1857.

Jan. 27.

A surgeon was
admitted a
pauper, and
swore that he
had no patients
or income.
The Court re-
fused to dis-
pauper him on
the allegation
of the adverse
party, that he
was capable of
earning an in-
come.

THIS was a cause of divorce by reason of adultery,
promoted by the husband against the wife. The
husband had been admitted a pauper; and the
wife prayed that he might be dispaupered. An
Act on petition was brought in, from which it appeared that the husband was a surgeon, and had
been recently discharged under the Insolvent
Debtors' Act. The wife however alleged that he
was again in practice, and receiving or earning or
at least capable of earning an income. The husband
denied that he had any income whatever, and
swore in affidavit that he had no patients since his
discharge.

*Deane*, for the wife, cited *Walker* v. *Walker*, 1 Curt. 560.

*Tristram*, for the husband.—The distinction between the present case and *Walker* v. *Walker* is, that here the husband cannot go into the market and sell his labour; he must wait till patients come to him. In *Walker* v. *Walker* the man was a skilled artisan, and if he chose to work and earn an income, had nothing to do but to offer his labour and be employed.

JUDGMENT.
DR. LUSHINGTON.

I think the counsel for the husband has taken the true distinction between this case and that referred to. I entirely disbelieved the husband's statement in that case, that no one would employ him; but in the absence of all proof to the contrary, how can I disbelieve the statement that the husband here has no patients, and consequently no income. The difference lies in the occupation of the two men. If proof can hereafter be given that Mr. Spratt is earning an income, the case may be brought before me again, but at present I cannot dispauper him.

## PREROGATIVE COURT OF CANTERBURY.

PAGE *v.* DONOVAN AND HANKEY.

1857.

Feb. 9th.

*Will—Execution—15 Vic. c. 24.*

The deceased made her will in France, and signed her name in the presence of a sufficient number of witnesses, not at the end of the will, but at the end of a notarial minute which followed in the same sheet with the will, and which minute was also subscribed by the witnesses.—Held, a good execution.

THE question before the Court, and raised on the admission of an allegation propounding the will, was, whether the signature of the deceased was in any position with respect to the end of the will so as to give effect to that will under the 15 & 16 Vic. c. 24, s. 1. The will was prepared by a French notary at Bordeaux; and after writing the will, he added, on the same sheet of paper and immediately following the end of the will, a notarial minute in these words: The present will has been dictated by Madame Lovelace, born Vanneck, to Mr. Verrière Chaisy, the undersigned notary, who has written it with his own hand such as she dictated it to him; and who, after having finished writing it, read it over to the testatrix in the presence of the witnesses, who declared that she well understood it, and persisted in the dispositions which she had just made. All that is above expressed and mentioned took place in the presence of Mr. Pièrre Cirode, tinman, of Mr. Matthieu Henri Hughes, stationer, of Mr. Jerome Latapie, furniture dealer, and of Mr. Pièrre Mignel, sworn interpreter—all

1857.

Feb. 9th.

PAGE
*v.*
DONOVAN
and
HANKEY.

dwelling and living at Bordeaux, Rue Huguerie, the first at No. 9, the second at No. 4, the third at No. 6, and the last named at No. 61—witnesses hereunto required, called by the testatrix, previously informed by the notary of the conditions prescribed for their capacity, of which an Act done and passed at Bordeaux, at the residence already mentioned of the testatrix, the said day, the 14th of April, 1852, about three o'clock in the afternoon; and the testatrix has signed, with the four witnesses and the notary, the minute of these presents, which remains with the latter, after reading over the whole will already mentioned by the notary to the testatrix in the presence of the witnesses. The minute is thus signed: Maria Lovelace, Pièrre Cirode, H. M. Hughes, Latapie Jerome, P. Mignel, and Verrière Choisy, the latter a notary.

*Addams,* in opposition to the admission of the allegation.—Under 1 Vic. c. 26, s. 9, and especially with reference to the construction put upon that section of the Act by the late judge of the Prerogative Court, probate would have been refused of this will as not duly executed; but the Wills Act Amendment Act subjects the case to different considerations. Section 1 of that Act enumerates various circumstances, under none of which shall the position of the signature of the testator be held to affect the due execution of the will. But the position of the signature of the testatrix in this case falls within none of the enumerated circumstances, unless indeed it is the following: that the due execution of the will shall not be affected by the circumstance of the signature of the testator

1857.

Feb. 9th.

PAGE
v.
DONOVAN
and
HANKEY.

being placed among the words of the "testimonium clause, or of the clause of attestation." It may possibly be contended that the signature of the testatrix is among the words of the testimonium or attestation clause in this case. But such is not the fact. After the enumeration of circumstances, the Act proceeds: "And the enumeration of the above circumstances shall not restrict the generality of the above enactment." What is the "generality" of the enactment which is so not to be restricted by this enumeration of circumstances? If it had been this: "Every will shall, so far only as regards the position of the signature of the testator, be valid if the signature shall be so placed that it shall be apparent on the face of the will that the testator intended to give effect by such his signature to the writing signed as his will"—then perhaps this will would have been well executed. But the enactment is this: "If the signature shall be so placed at, or after, or following, or under, or beside, or opposite to, the end of the will as to make it apparent"—and so on. To let in the generality of the enactment, the signature must be in one of those positions. But the signature in this case is in neither of those positions. It is neither at, nor after, nor following, nor under, nor beside, nor opposite to, the end of the will. It is, and purports to be, not under the will, but under a notarial minute of the will having been written from the dictation of the testatrix, and of its having, when written, been read over to and approved by her in the presence of certain witnesses; and it is this minute, and not the will itself, that the signature of the testatrix and the signatures of the witnesses both are and purport to be appended to.

*Jenner, contrà.*—Even if the Act were not a remedial Act, and entitled to a liberal construction, this case would fall within the very words of the first section. The signature is at the end of the minute, and the minute immediately follows the will. The minute is but a publication of, and an attestation clause to, the will. Why was the minute written? To give effect to the will. Why was the minute signed? To complete and give effect to the whole. Then it is apparent on the face of the will that the testatrix intended to give effect by such signature to the writing signed as a will. But supposing there was no minute at all, but a blank space left where the minute now appears, still the signature would have effect under this Act.

1857.

Feb 9th.

PAGE
*v.*
DONOVAN
and
HANKEY.

### JUDGMENT.
SIR JOHN DODSON.

The argument against you was, that this signature was written to give effect to the minute only, apart from the will. However, taking this as a remedial Act, I have no doubt that the signature is in a position to give effect to the will; and I admit the allegation.

## CONSISTORY COURT OF LONDON.

### HARMAR *v.* HARMAR.

1857.

Feb. 14th.

*Deduction from alimony—Practice.*

The husband cannot deduct from permanent alimony sums paid by him on account of debts incurred by the wife before the allotment of alimony *pendente lite*.

THIS was an application on the part of the husband to be allowed to deduct from permanent alimony certain sums which he had paid for debts incurred by his wife before either the allotment or the payment of alimony *pendente lite*.

*Addams* and *Twiss* for the husband.

*Bayford* and *Spinks* for the wife.

JUDGMENT.

DR. LUSHINGTON.

The parties to this suit were divorced at the instance of the wife, on the 2d day of July, 1856; and on the 8th day of August following permanent alimony was allotted, at the rate of £160 per annum. The citation was returned on the 10th day of November, 1855, and alimony *pendente lite* was allotted on the 10th day of February, 1856. It is alleged that the alimony (not specifying whether alimony *pendente lite* or permanent alimony) has been paid as it became due. The first inquiry is, whether this fact so pleaded is true. As to

alimony *pendente lite*, this averment is clearly contrary to the truth, and so appears to be from the
records of the court. I will not repeat at length
the averments contained in the answer to the act
on the part of the wife, and which are not controverted. The result is, that so far from the alimony
being paid when due, it was only obtained after
much delay and frequent application to the Court.
I am somewhat surprised that under such circumstances so erroneous a statement, if it refers to
alimony *pendente lite*, should have found its way
into these pleadings. With respect to permanent
alimony, nothing whatever has been paid; and
therefore the allegation is, to use an expression
scarcely sufficiently strong, wholly erroneous. It
is under these circumstances, not certainly the
most auspicious, that the Court is asked to stop the
payment of permanent alimony, by deducting from
it certain debts incurred before alimony *pendente
lite* was decreed. I believe this application to be
entirely novel; I am not aware of any case in
which an application in any degree similar has
been made to any Ecclesiastical Court. In *Brisco* v.
*Brisco*, 2 Hagg. Cons. 199, Lady Brisco had incurred
very large debts, for which her husband was made
responsible, and that for the purpose of putting her
husband to expense. There the application was
made before alimony was allotted, and the Court
very properly took the misconduct of the wife into
consideration in allotting the amount of alimony
*pendente lite*. This, however, is a very different
case. Here I am asked to deduct from permanent
alimony expenses incurred by the wife, principally
on account of her maintenance from the period of

1857.

Feb. 14th.

HARMAR
*v.*
HARMAR.

separation up to the allotment of alimony, which if duly paid would exempt the husband from responsibility. It is not alleged that during that period the husband furnished the wife with any means of subsistence whatever; and it is now established by the decree of this Court, that by reason of his cruelty, the wife was justified in separating herself from him. Under such circumstances, I will not enter into a consideration whether the expenses were extravagant or not; the whole fault is at the door of the husband; he compelled her to leave his home, and left her without the means of subsistence, and so situated it might be difficult for her to get credit and live economically. But be this as it may, the application is altogether too late, and such a deduction from permanent alimony would be without precedent; and as many such causes must *de faco* have occurred, and no such application made, it is unwarranted by the practice of the Court.

## CAMPBELL *v.* CAMPBELL.

1856.

March 16th, 17th. Apr. 22d.

*17 & 18 Vic. c. 47—Practice—Condonation—Delay.*

THIS was a cause of divorce by reason of adultery, brought by the husband against the wife. She pleaded condonation; and an application was made on her behalf, for a requisition to examine witnesses in Italy and Australia. The libel was brought in on the 31st of November; the wife's responsive allegation was brought in on the 13th of March; and a further allegation, on the part of the husband, containing fresh charges of adultery, on the 14th of March.

*Addams* and *Twiss* for the husband.

*Jenner* and *Deane* for the wife.

### JUDGMENT.

DR. LUSHINGTON.

Before I address myself to the particular circumstances of this case, I think it right to make a few observations upon the 17 & 18 Vic. c. 47, which directs a particular mode of taking evidence in ecclesiastical courts which did not exist before. I am not surprised that there has not been a clear understanding as to this statute, because it gives no directions whatever as to the manner in which its provisions shall be carried into execution. It is manifest that it embraces the whole cause from the

As a general rule, the Court will always accede to an application to examine witnesses *vivâ voce;* and where such application is intended for the whole cause, the pleadings must be concluded before any of the witnesses are examined. Condonation, or the renewal of conjugal intercourse, requires strict proof. In matrimonial causes there are few reasons for delay.

beginning to the end, in part or altogether, and at any time. The case may be heard entirely *vivâ voce*, or in part by deposition or affidavit ; and the Court is at liberty, even after there have been depositions or affidavits to examine the persons who made them *vivâ voce*. It appears advisable, when the application to take the evidence *vivâ voce* is intended for the whole of the cause, that all the pleadings should be concluded before any evidence is received. A different course may be followed where the application is made in the course of the cause. With respect to applications of this kind, it is *primâ facie* the duty of the Court to apply the Act, and direct the evidence to be given *vivâ voce* whenever the application is made. This must be the general rule, for it is clear that the inconvenience of stating special reasons would be very great ; much delay and expense would be incurred ; and indeed such a course would in many cases be very prejudicial, as it might disclose the nature of the case. With regard to the proof of adultery in the present case, it appears to me wholly unnecessary to enter into any detail of the evidence ; indeed it is not and cannot be contended, that the proof of criminal intercourse is not clear and decisive. The parties were originally resident in Australia. In 1856 Mrs. Campbell with six children left Australia, and arrived in this country in April. Mr. Smith, who had been in partnership with Mr. Campbell, received her, and took her to lodgings at 17, Bloomfield Road. Mr. Garstin immediately made his appearance, and became an inmate of that house. There is no direct evidence how that acquaintance commenced ; but from the declaration of Mrs. Campbell, she and her children received much attention from him during the voyage from Australia. Mr. Garstin remained in that house with Mrs. Campbell about a fortnight ; and in the beginning of May she with her children removed to No. 41 in the same street, and at No. 41 Mr. Garstin is again. On the 27th of May Mr. Campbell arrived from Australia, and joined his wife in Craven Street. About the 6th of June, having taken a house in Porchester Terrace, he removed his children, but Mrs. Campbell refused to accompany him. A few days afterwards a sister of Mrs. Campbell arrived in London, and by the joint persuasion of that sister and Mr. Smith Mrs. Campbell was induced to join her husband in Porchester Terrace. According to the evidence of Mr. Smith, some time after Mrs. Campbell had gone to Porchester Terrace circumstances came to Mr. Campbell's knowledge which induced him to prosecute further inquiries ; the result was, that Mrs. Campbell left Porchester Terrace and went to the Colonnade Hotel, whence she was removed by Mr. Campbell to Hampstead, and there, so far as relates to the intercourse between Mr. and Mrs. Campbell, the history ends rather abruptly. That was in July. There is evidence of Mrs. Campbell living in various lodgings up to November, and Mr. Garstin constantly being with her. I am not about to recapitulate the acts of indecent familiarity, or the circumstances which lead to the conclusion that an adulterous intercourse was carried on between the parties ; the proof of guilt is undeniable. Then what are the circumstances in this case which should induce the Court to delay pronouncing a

1857.

March 16th, 17th. Apr. 22d.

CAMPBELL
v.
CAMPBELL.

1857.

March 16th,
17th. Apr. 22d.

CAMPBELL
v.
CAMPBELL.

decree of separation? The evidence already produced on the part of Mrs. Campbell clearly will not suffice to establish condonation. Does justice require that I shall delay the decision of this cause until witnesses are examined in Australia and in Italy? Upon what are they to be examined? Not to prove Mrs. Campbell's innocence; if that were the object, no expense, no delay, no inconvenience, would justly be a reason for refusing the present application; but her guilt is admitted. The question is, whether there has been condonation of that guilt. Condonation is connubial intercourse with full knowledge of all the facts. Innocency and condonation are inconsistent pleas, but they may be pleaded. But the case then resolves itself into this: You cannot prove my guilt, but if you can you have pardoned me. It is pleaded on behalf of Mrs. Campbell, that from the 26th of June, and for several days afterwards, Mr. Campbell visited his wife at the Colonnade Hotel; was seen to approach her for the purpose of kissing her; spoke of having a bed made up for him in his wife's bedroom; that he remained in her bedroom for several hours, and renewed his conjugal intercourse with her. These averments are contradicted in plea by Mr. Campbell, on whose behalf it is pleaded that he never saw Mrs. Campbell at that hotel except in the presence of witnesses. Looking at the evidence, the Court is left somewhat in the dark as to what took place at that hotel; and certainly, so far as appears, Mr. Campbell did not act under the circumstances with great discretion in having those interviews with his wife. Possibly that apparent indiscretion may be explained by the fact that this

lady was at this time attended by a physician
eminent for his treatment of diseases of the mind,
and that the husband was seriously apprehensive on
that account.    But looking at the case as it stands,
has the Court good reason to believe that if the
delay asked were granted, the plea of condonation
would be established?    I have not from the pleadings or the evidence the least reason to conclude
that the witnesses now vouched will give any
evidence material to the only issue remaining. What
has the Court a right to expect, and what is offered?
The most undoubted proof of conjugal intercourse;
and a statement, perhaps an affidavit, from the wife,
upon which however I could not place much
reliance, that the witnesses would depose to
particular facts, which would leave no doubt of
renewed intercourse; but this is wholly wanting.
Nor does the case stand favourably in other respects.
The citation was returned on the 18th of November;
from the service of the citation she knew a defence
must be prepared.   On the 31st the libel was
brought in; she then knew the specific charges.
Her proctor then applied that the witnesses might
be examined *vivâ voce*, and so posponed the examination of the witnesses on the libel.   But her
defensive allegation was not brought in till the 13th
of March, and that after repeated notices to her
proctor, and though every fact was necessarily well
known to Mrs. Campbell herself.   For there is a
wide difference in the matter of dealing between
testamentary and matrimonial causes: in the first
the facts and the evidence may be unknown to the
party who has to set them up and procure it; but in
matrimonial causes every fact and circumstance is

1857.

March 16th,
17th. Apr.22d.

CAMPBELL
v.
CAMPBELL.

known. The proctor has used all diligence; his party has not. It is the duty of the Court to discourage these delays, and, unless justice most clearly demands it, to prevent a wife putting her husband to expenses, which might in some cases be ruinous. I am satisfied that justice requires me to reject the prayer of Mrs. Campbell, which I do not think is well founded, and which, if granted to a wife admitted guilty, will impose a most onerous expense on her husband, and procrastinate this case to an indefinite period. I must conclude this cause and pronounce for the separation.

# PREROGATIVE COURT OF CANTERBURY.

*In the goods of* ANN DADDS (*widow, deceased*).

*Will—Revocation under 20th section of Wills Act.*

1857.

April 18th.

Probate de-
creed of draft
copy of codicil,
which had been
burnt by testa-
trix's order,
with intent to
revoke, but not
in her pre-
sence.

THIS deceased died on 7th December, 1856, having made a will and codicil thereto, and thereof appointed Thomas Davis and George Sanders executors. The codicil, executed in 1852, was attached with sealing-wax to the first sheet of the will, and deceased, within a week of her death, ex-

pressed to a niece, Miss Osborn, who resided with
her, a wish and intention to revoke the same; but
being under an impression that some form was
necessary to be observed on the occasion, delayed
the revocation until she had an opportunity of
consulting Mr. George Sanders, one of the executors, about it.   On the day of deceased's death Mr.
Sanders and his wife, also a niece of the deceased,
were at her house, when she in their presence repeated her wish to revoke the codicil, and directed
Miss Osborn, who had her keys, to fetch it from
the drawer of a secretary in which it was locked
up, and which was in a room below stairs.  The
will, with the codicil attached to it, was there found
by Miss Osborn in an unsealed envelope, and
handed to Mr. Sanders, who, on opening them, observed that the codicil was written on one side of
half a sheet of foolscap paper, and in the handwriting of Mr. Davis, the sole executor.  Mr. Sanders then, in the same room below stairs, the deceased being in her bed in a room above, detached
the codicil from the will and read the same, which
bore the signatures of the deceased and of William
Hewson and Francis Hewson as attesting witnesses;
and on Mr. Sanders' suggestion that a disinterested
witness should be present at the revocation,
Catherine Harvey, a neighbour, was sent for, and
attended at the deceased's house.   Miss Osborn,
accompanied by Catherine Harvey, then went up
stairs to the deceased, who, in the presence of both
of them, desired that the codicil should be burnt
and destroyed; but as there was no fire in the bedroom at the time, she directed that it should be
taken back to the room below stairs for the purpose.

1857.
___
April 18th.
___
In the goods of
ANN DADDS
(widow,
deceased).

1857.
_____
April 18th.
____
In the goods of
ANN DADDS
(widow,
deceased).

Mr. Sanders being still in the room below stairs, the codicil was again handed to him; and he being again informed of the deceased's wish that it should be burnt, threw the codicil into the fire, whereby it was burnt and wholly destroyed, in the presence of his wife, Miss Osborn, and Catherine Harvey, but not in the presence of the deceased: so that the requirements of the 20th section of the Wills Act as to revocation were not observed, "or by the burning, tearing, or otherwise destroying the same by the testator, or by some person in his presence and by his direction, with the intention of revoking the same," and the codicil not legally revoked. The only existing copy of the codicil was the original draft of it written by Mr. Davis, at the deceased's request and by her instructions, when she was on a visit at his house in the latter part of February, 1852, and which draft had been in Mr. Davis's possession ever since. Shortly after the deceased left Mr. Davis's residence at the period mentioned, he copied this draft out fairly for execution on half a sheet of foolscap paper, and read it over, and as he did so compared the fair copy with the original draft; but having varied the language in and made some additions to the copy, Mr. Davis made corresponding alterations in and additions to the original draft; and the interlineations, obliterations, and additions appearing in the draft before the Court were the alterations and additions then made by Mr. Davis, except the word "lives," obliterated in the 14th line of the first page of the draft, which was inserted in the copy and by mistake obliterated in the draft: there were some words appearing in pencil in the draft, inserted in contemplation of further alterations in the copy, but which were not made therein. The codicil so prepared for execution was inclosed in an envelope and forwarded by post to the deceased with a letter from Mr. Davis, wherein he brought to the deceased's notice and directed her to fill in the blank spaces left in the codicil for the recital of the date of the will, and also for the date of the execution of the codicil; and Mr. Davis afterwards received information from the deceased, either by letter or otherwise, that the codicil had been executed by her. Some time in March, 1852, the deceased took a paper writing which was on half a sheet of foolscap paper, and which she described as a codicil, to the house of Francis Hewson, and there duly executed such paper in the presence of Francis and William Hewson, and then took the paper away with her. The deceased frequently mentioned, in the spring of 1852, to Mr. Sanders and Miss Osborn, that she had made a codicil, but they did not then see to it. Mr. George Sanders, who read the codicil before it was burnt, believed the draft as altered to be a true and correct copy of it. On the above statement, verified by affidavit,

*Middleton* moved the Court to decree probate of the will and copy of the codicil without the obliteration of the word " lives," and the interlineation in pencil of the words " trust aforesaid" in the said copy, limited until a more authentic copy of the said codicil should be brought into and left in the registry of this court, to be granted to Mr. Thomas Davis and Mr. George Sanders the executors.

SIR JOHN DODSON decreed probate as prayed.

1857.

April 18th.

In the goods of
ANN DADDS
(widow,
deceased).

*In the goods of* SARAH LEACH (*widow, deceased*).

*Practice.*

---

1857.

*On Motion.*

---

May 5th, 14th.

---

L. appointed R. sole executrix and residuary legatee. R. died without proving, and appointed A. and B. executors. A. alone proved R.'s will, power being reserved to B.—Held, that B. must be cited as well as A. before administration with will annexed of L. could be granted to a legatee.

SARAH LEACH died on the 20th of October, 1856, having made her will, dated 20th of December, 1844, and therein appointed her daughter, Mary Jeffs Read (wife of George Read) sole executrix and residuary legatee. Mrs. Read died in the lifetime of the testatrix, leaving issue living at the time of the death of the testatrix ; and the residuary bequests thereby became vested in her under the 33d section of the Wills Act. Her husband, Mr. Read, survived her and is since dead, having made his will and appointed Charles Poulton and Edmund Pullein executors, but Poulton alone proved the will in August, 1856, power being reserved to Pullein, the other executor. Under these circumstances H. A. Deane, a legatee, applied for and obtained on the 19th of February a decree with intimation against Poulton (as the sole legal personal representative of Mr. Read, who was the husband of Mrs. Read, the daughter and residuary legatee of Sarah Leach) to accept or refuse letters of administration (with the will annexed) of the goods of the said testatrix. The question raised was, whether Pullein, who had not proved, should not be cited as well as Poulton, who had disappeared.

*Bayford* moved the Court for a decree against Poulton only, as the acting executor and sole legal personal representative of the testatrix.

1857.

May 5th, 14th.

In the goods of
SARAH LEACH
(widow, de-
ceased).

SIR JOHN DODSON.

I am clearly of opinion that the administration should not be decreed without citing the executor to whom power has been reserved. The citation must, therefore, be taken out against him, as well as against the acting executor.

---

# CONSISTORY COURT OF LONDON.

---

## ANONYMOUS.

1857.

May 16th.

*Impotency—Responsive allegation—Pleading.*

THIS case came on for hearing on admission of the wife's responsive allegation in the circumstances fully set out in the judgment.

*Addams* and *Twiss* for the husband, in opposition to the allegation.

*Jenner* and *Phillimore*, for the wife, *contrà.*

The husband brought a suit of nullity of marriage, by reason of impotency, against the wife, who pleaded in answer matters in contradiction to the husband's case, and also the adultery of the husband.—Held, that it was not competent to the wife to plead the husband's adultery at that stage of the cause.

JUDGMENT.

DR. LUSHINGTON.

The only question which I have now to decide is, whether the responsive allegation given in on the part of the defendant is or is not admissible in whole or in part; but it appears to me that I cannot properly decide that question without looking to the whole proceedings in this case, and briefly referring to the principles and authorities applicable to cases of this description. This is a suit brought by the plaintiff for the purpose of having his marriage with the defendant declared null and void, by reason of her incurable malformation and consequent inability for sexual intercourse. An appearance having been given to the citation, a libel was brought in on January 17th. I now propose to state what I apprehend to be the contents of and objects sought to be ascertained by the libel and allegation. The libel stated the marriage to have taken place in July, 1840, plaintiff being at that time 27 years of age, and the lady past 21. It pleads cohabitation save as to sexual intercourse at various places in England, Ireland, the Continent, and Canada; that they so cohabited, save with occasional separations, until January 19th, 1855; and then, in the usual form, the inability of the lady for sexual intercourse from unnatural contraction. The 7th article pleads special facts to account for the delay in bringing this suit: it pleads that the plaintiff was aware of this defect, but believed it to be capable of remedy; that plaintiff consulted divers medical persons, who so assured him that he remained in that belief until he was informed to the contrary by medical persons who had been consulted by defendant; that this information was received shortly before the month of January, 1855; that he thereupon separated himself from her, and gave instructions for the suit before he went on service to the East; that he returned in June, 1856; and the citation issued in August following. The 8th article pleads, in supply of proof, a letter alleged to have been written by the defendant in March, 1851, after consultation with Dr. R. The Court admitted this libel after consideration; and it is not necessary now to repeat the reasons which induced the Court so to do. It appears, however, that no witness has been examined upon it, nothing done; why or wherefore the Court is not informed. In this Easter Term an allegation was given in on behalf of the defendant, the admissibility of which was debated on May 7th. The objects sought to be attained by this allegation were twofold: it pleads facts which, it has been contended, ought to bar the husband from prosecuting and succeeding in this suit; and, further, certain facts which will entitle the defendant to a decree of separation, on account of cruelty and adultery. These are two distinct and separate objects. It cannot be denied that defendant is entitled to plead all facts which could bar the suit of the husband: whether she is entitled to proceed for a divorce by reason of adultery and cruelty, is a question subject to different considerations. I have said that defendant is entitled to plead all facts which can legally bar the husband from succeeding in his suit. That some facts would have this effect no one can doubt, as, for instance, denial of malformation, averment of sexual intercourse. But there are other facts which, in this as in all other cases of a similar kind, when offered as a bar to the suit, give rise to questions of great difficulty. Such a case may be generally described to be of this kind. True it is that the wife may be incapable of sexual intercourse, but the husband is barred by his delay or other conduct. This is the doctrine laid down, as I apprehend, in *B.* v. *B.*, 1 Eccl. & Adm. Rep. 248. So far is clear. But when the inquiry is pushed further, and it is asked what is the delay and what is the conduct which shall bar the suit, I feel that all is involved in doubt and obscurity. If I consider the question of time, I do not find that any period has been fixed. If I look to other circumstances I am still more in the dark, for I am not aware of any authority which has attempted to define them. I know nothing more painful than to have to exercise a judicial discretion without landmarks to guide the judgment. If I look to the principle by which the institution of these suits is governed, it affords me little light to discover my way in such a combination of facts as now presents itself. What is the principle, the foundation, of the right to claim a decree pronouncing a marriage void where one of the parties is incapable of consummation? It is partly stated in the case already referred to; and to that judgment I am justified in referring, for it is the judgment of all the Judicial Committee who heard the case: first, because the great chief purpose of marriage cannot be fulfilled; secondly, because by such a marriage the temptation to evil courses is not removed; thirdly, because in some cases, especially where the defect is on the husband's side, continued cohabitation would be destructive to the health and comfort of one of the parties. There was one such case a few years since of a very distressing

1857.

May 16th.

ANONYMOUS.

character. There are many other reasons which I
need not recapitulate. If either party cognizant
of disability married, the Courts have considered
the so doing such a wrongful act, that they have
condemned the party in costs. The Judicial Committee in *B. v. B.* laid down a general proposition,
that such a suit may be barred; and it is equally
my wish as it is my duty to carry out that judgment,
to which I was not only a party but in which I
was the organ of the Court. But there are in-
herent difficulties in the subject matter which render the application of the principles so laid down
a very anxious task. Time is one. What combination of circumstances constitutes insincerity,
another. Assuming all the facts in this allegation
proved, do they together form such a state of facts
as the Judicial Committee intended to be comprised
within the general principles laid down? Except
in case of extreme old age, it is obvious that the refusal to allow a remedy on account of the remissness
of the husband, though he personally may not be entitled to complain, leaves untouched one reason for
entertaining the suit, the prevention of illicit intercourse. Then, with regard to what is called in
some preceding cases, and in *B. v. B.* the insincerity of the suit, I have great difficulty in saying
what would constitute insincerity and what sin-
cerity. Suppose a man anxious for issue, that
motive would not constitute insincerity. Suppose
a man anxious to marry another woman, I could
not hold that to be insincerity. Suppose a man to
indulge in illicit connections, could that be proof
that he was insensible to the incapacity of his wife
for conjugal intercourse? I do not think that pro-

x 2

position maintainable; it might rather bear the other way. Could such criminal connection alone bar the suit? No such argument has ever been advanced, and there is no precedent for so holding. Insincerity is therefore something different. I cannot attempt to define it; it must be a combination of circumstances which show that the alleged grievance was not the motive which led to the commencement of the suit, but what would constitute such a case cannot be defined beforehand. Governing myself so far as I can by the judgment of the Judicial Committee, and being of opinion that after the lapse of so many years the wife is entitled to a large indulgence for her defence, I think it right to admit—first, so much of this allegation as contradicts the malformation; secondly, so much as may possibly form a bar to the suit, on the ground of the conduct of the husband showing it to be insincere. I will presently point out the articles which I think ought to be admitted, some with reformation. I will now address my attention to the important question, which has been raised in this suit for the first time, namely, whether the wife proceeded against can allege adultery committed by the husband, and pray a separation from bed and board on that account, and that too at the same time when the other question which necessarily arises in such a suit as this is under investigation and not decided, the validity of the marriage. The absence of all precedent, where similar cases must have occurred, calls upon the Court to be careful that it does not establish one without great consideration; for the presumption is, that there would have been a precedent if, in the opinion of the profession, such a course of proceeding could have been maintained. We all know that in suits for separation by reason of cruelty or adultery, the first thing to be proved is the marriage; it is called the foundation of the suit. If the marriage be denied, it must be proved before the proceedings can go further ; publication of the evidence as to the marriage is decreed, and the question of marriage decided before the suit goes further. The usual and appropriate issues in a cause of this description are : Is the malformation proved ? and is the party proceeding barred *personali exceptione ?* Suppose this allegation admitted as it stands, two things must be proved to justify the Court in pronouncing for a separation: first, that there has been a valid marriage ; secondly, that the husband has committed adultery. But suppose that it should be proved, as is pleaded in this case, that the husband is barred *personali exceptione,* such a decision would prevent, whatever be the merits of the case and truth of the charge, the husband from obtaining a decree of nullity; but would such circumstances authorize the Court to pronounce the marriage valid ? I exceedingly doubt if the Court could do so, and such a decree I apprehend to be indispensable to a decree for divorce. But suppose another state of things, that the malformation should be proved as well as the bar, could the Court pronounce for the validity of the marriage under such circumstances ? That I do doubt exceedingly. Take the third case, that the malformation was disproved, and the bar proved also, there would then be less difficulty, but still in effect the proceeding would be the commencement

1857.

May 16th.

ANONYMOUS.

of a new suit.   It may, however, be asked, In what
position is a woman left when the husband from
any cause has failed in a suit of this description? Is
she without remedy?   I think not where the malformation is disproved.   I think that in such case
the wife would be clearly entitled to bring a fresh
suit for divorce, and that the husband would be
barred from setting up the malformation by the
decree in the former suit.   What would be the case
if the wife brought the suit after a decree that the
husband was barred *personali exceptione*, but the
malformation proved, I will not venture to speculate
upon : it is a very different thing to pronounce affir-
matively, and to dismiss a suit by reason of a bar.
I will now examine the cases cited.   *Best* v. *Best*,
1 Add. 411, determines only that where a suit is
brought, the basis of which is a valid marriage, as
for cruelty, the husband may plead the wife's adultery, not only as a defence, but also for the purpose
of obtaining a decree for separation against her.   In
*Robins* v. *Wolseley*, 2 Lee, 149, Sir W. Wolseley
sued his wife for a divorce for adultery ; she denied
the marriage, and pleaded that it was void by
reason of a prior marriage.   Sir G. Lee was of opinion that Sir W. Wolseley should not be permitted
to prove the adultery till the question of marriage
should be disposed of.   This is a strong case ; for
Sir W. Wolseley was *prior petens*, and moreover he
asked to examine witnesses *de bene esse*, whose evidence he might have lost.   Sir G. Lee said it would
force the wife into a suit, whilst it was still *sub
judice*, whether she was subject to such suit or not.
I think this case has some bearing on the present,
because here the validity of the marriage is denied

by the husband; and he commences this suit to prove its validity, and until that question is decided it cannot be known whether he is, to use Sir G. Lee's words, subject to such a suit or not; that is, a suit for separation by reason of adultery. I am unable to perceive any distinction as relates to this question between a void and what is called a voidable marriage ; a voidable marriage is equally void *ab initio*, but for civil consequences there must be a decree pronouncing it so to be. In *Guest* v. *Guest*, 2 Hagg. Cons. 322, the validity of the marriage had been already pronounced for in a cause of divorce, and Lord Stowell held that it was a bar to a suit of nullity by reason of malformation. But the decision would have little bearing upon this case were it not for the expressions of Lord Stowell ; speaking of divorce by reason of adultery, he says: " The validity of the marriage is the foundation of the whole proceedings ; there can be no adultery if there was no marriage." It has always been held, both here and at common law, that the first point to be proved is the marriage ; to which I will add, that if in a suit for adultery the marriage be denied, it must be proved before the party can go into evidence of adultery. *Mayhew* v. *Mayhew*, 2 Phill. 11, is to the same effect. *Clowes* v. *Clowes*, 2 N. C. 77, is to the effect, that in a suit of nullity, if the libel be rejected, the wife may give in an allegation praying restitution ; and if the libel here had been rejected I should not have doubted that the wife, without further citation, might have prayed for restitution, or proceeded for a divorce for adultery. In *Catterall* v. *Catterall*, 5 N. C. 468, 1 Rob. 304, 9 Jur.

951, I rejected the libel pleading the nullity of the marriage, but allowed the husband to proceed with a suit for divorce by reason of adultery. But the distinction between this and other cases is, that in this case the validity of the marriage is a question pending before the Court, and undecided. In *Catterall* v. *Catterall* the question of marriage was disposed of. The results of these cases were twofold : first, if the marriage be denied, that question must be disposed of before evidence can be taken as to adultery or cruelty ; second, that without fresh citation the Court may, in any matrimonial suit where the validity of the marriage has been disposed of, receive an allegation pleading adultery or cruelty, and separate the parties if it be proved. Therefore, I am of opinion, both upon principle and authority, that I ought not now, at this stage of the cause, to admit the article pleading adultery to proof; but I am equally clear, for the same reason, that the Court might possibly come to a decision in this case which would justify the Court in receiving this, or an allegation to the same effect. This allegation must therefore be reformed by omitting the article pleading adultery. Were I to admit them *hoc statu* (I mention this not as a reason guiding my judgment, for that is governed by the reasons already stated), the husband could not defend himself by pleading condonation of the wife's adultery, which matters would require consideration. Dr. Phillimore pressed the Court not to order an inspection. I am very sensible how painful this must be to any lady, and certainly would make no such order save *ex debito justitiæ*. If the allegation had pleaded merely matters in bar,

not putting in issue the malformation, I might
have deliberated whether I would not have delayed
ordering the inspection until publication had passed
as to the plea in bar, for if that plea were good
and proved there would have been an end of the
suit; but this allegation puts in issue the malformation, and all the facts to prove the contrary:
how is it possible I could receive evidence on one
side, and not legal evidence on the other? It was
said in the course of the argument that Professor S.
had seen the defendant since the suit commenced;
that may be so, but still that is *ex parte* evidence
only as to the evidence between the parties. There
is still an additional reason the defendant has
brought with reference to this very question of
malformation, a most serious charge against the
plaintiff. She has charged him with having caused
an appearance of malformation, by giving her the
venereal disease. Surely it would be against all
justice to allow that article to go to proof, and not
permit the plaintiff by the only possible process to
rebut that charge, and prove his original case. I
shall admit all exhibits which are in the handwriting of plaintiff; they are legal evidence, and
their applicability to this case will be best discussed
when publication on the whole case passes: one
article will be sufficient for the purpose of intro-
ducing these exhibits.

1857.

May 16th.

ANONYMOUS.

## PREROGATIVE COURT OF CANTERBURY.

RUDALL *v.* WARREN (*by his Guardian*).

**1857.**

May 26th.
June 4th.

*Will—Void devise and bequest attending it—Gift over—Administration.*

Where a devise of realty for a charitable foundation is void under Mortmain Act, a bequest to residuary legatees in trust to carry out the purposes of the devise fails too; and a bequest over, where the prior bequest is defeated by contingencies other than those provided for by the testator, is also void. Administration, with will annexed, granted to next of kin in preference to residuary legatee, for the purpose of carrying out the intended charity.

THIS was a business of granting letters of administration (with the will annexed) of William Hall, deceased, promoted by Sarah Rudall, wife of Thomas James Rudall, the sister and only next of kin of the said deceased, against William Hall Warren, a minor (by Emma Badnell, his guardian lawfully appointed by the High Court of Chancery), claiming to be the residuary legatee named in the said will.

The deceased died on the 23d October, 1856. The will was dated in October, 1853; by it he bequeathed all his real and personal estate, of whatsoever kind, to William Unsworth and John Atkinson, "to be my executors of this my will; and I do appoint the said Messrs. Unsworth and Atkinson, their executors, administrators, or assigns, my executors or administrators to this my will." Mr. Unsworth predeceased the testator, and Mr. Atkinson renounced probate and execution of the will. The deceased died a widower without child or parent.

The clause on which the present question arose was as follows :—" I will that my freehold house, No. 71, Queen's Road, Bayswater, be given to the inhabitants of Bayswater to found a lying-in asylum for unmarried women, or poor married women, if there is more than three beds to spare. I will that there shall be no paid parson, priest, or chaplain, whose services is not given gratis, attend the said asylum. I will that the same be called 'Hall's Maternal Asylum for Unmarried Women.' I will that my said executors do call a meeting of the neighbours and inhabitants of one mile round the said house, as soon as convenient, to appoint a committee and trustees to carry out the same. I do appoint my godson, William Hall Warren, one of the said trustees, leaving to the inhabitants to make choice of as many more as they please. But in the event of the said inhabitants not appointing a committee, or not willing to carry out the same scheme, I then will that all my said property so given to said maternal retreat or lying-in asylum shall absolutely belong to my said godson, William Hall Warren; and I will that the deeds of the said house be given to the said trustee or trustees. I will that the said trustee or trustees be my residuary legatees to this my will."

The will proceeded to give further legacies—some to the legatees only for life, to revert " to my residuary legatee or legatees for asylum mentioned." There was no further disposition of residue.

It was agreed that the devise of the freehold house was void under the Mortmain Act.

*Deane*, for Mrs. Rudall, the sister and only next

1857.

May 25th.
June 4th.

RUDALL
v.
WARREN.

of kin of the deceased, contended that a personal bequest attached to a void charity as an endowment must fail with the principal: *Attorney-General v. Whitchurch*, 3 Ves. 141; and *Attorney-General v. Hinxman*, 2 Jac. & W. 270. In the latter case Sir Thomas Plumer held that a bequest of money in trust for the use of a schoolmaster was void as being connected with the devise of a freehold house as the residence of such master. Further, that when in such a case there is a gift over of the personal property, and the prior gift fails, not through the contingencies contemplated by the testator, but through an operation of law not foreseen by him, the gift over fails also: *Philpotts* v. *St. George's Hospital*, 21 Beavan, 131, where the Master of the Rolls concluded: " I wish that my view of the will should appear perfectly clear and distinct, viz., that the original gift fails by reason of its being contrary to the Statute of Mortmain, and that the gift over fails by reason of the events on which that gift over is directed to take effect not having arisen."

*Bayford, contrà,* contended that William Hall Warren appeared on the face of the will to be the residuary legatee; that it would be for the Court of Chancery to determine whether he was beneficially entitled or otherwise. He referred to *White's Law of Legacies, c.* 24, and prayed administration, with the will annexed, to be granted to the guardian of W. H. Warren, now a minor, the residuary legatee named in the said will; but if the Court should be of opinion that the said Warren was not residuary legatee, that this guardian should have administration as guardian to him, a principal legatee named in the said will; for he submitted that the Court was not bound by the statute, in the case of administration with the will annexed, to grant it to the next of kin; and that there were reasons in this case, as appeared by affidavits, why the Court should not grant it to Mrs. Rudall.

JUDGMENT.

SIR JOHN DODSON.

Considering the words of the will and the cases cited, I am clearly of opinion that the bequest attending the void devise fails, and the bequest over to Warren under these circumstances will also be of no effect. Neither does it appear from the whole will that Warren is residuary legatee or one of the residuary legatees, except for the purpose of carrying out the scheme for the charity; he has no beneficial interest in this character; and the next of kin is entitled to the grant. It has been contended that there are reasons in this case for the Court to depart from the ordinary rules it has laid down for itself in such cases, and to pass over the next of kin. It certainly appears that neither the deceased's sister nor her husband are very fit people to be intrusted with the administration of property; but as in this case they can only act under the direction of the Court of Chancery, no inconvenience can arise from that; and there is no sufficient reason to depart from the ordinary rules. I decree administration with the will annexed to the sister. Costs of both parties out of the estate.

CRUTTWELL AND OTHERS *v.* CLANCY.

*In the goods of* ALFRED BRETTLE *(deceased).*

Will—*Appointment of executors and trustees—Codicil
—Partial revocation.*

1857.

June 12th.

A., by will and first codicil, appointed four executors and trustees, and left them £500 each. By a second codicil he substituted B. and D. in the place of two of the original executors and trustees, and varied the £500 legacies accordingly. By a third codicil he revoked any codicil or codicils empowering B. to act as trustee, and appointed C. one of his trustees and executors. Held, on a view of all the papers, that the third codicil was a revocation only of C.'s appointment, and not of the whole codicil in which it was contained.

THE deceased in this case died on the 31st October, 1856, having made his last will and testament with three codicils thereto, and therein named executors and trustees, as follows:—

By his will, dated the 13th November, 1852, he appointed and named Francis Burdett, Esq., Charles Sedley Burdett, Esq., Thomas Cruttwell, and Robert Cruttwell, executors and trustees, and thereby bequeathed to them, as such executors and trustees, the sum of £500 each.

By the first codicil, dated the 18th April, 1855, the testator bequeathed certain pecuniary legacies, but did not alter the appointment of the executors and trustees of his said will.

By the second codicil, dated the 24th July, 1856, the testator appointed John Clancy, the younger, Esq., and William Augustus Sadler Pemberton, joint trustees and executors of his said will with the said Thomas Cruttwell and Robert Cruttwell, in lieu and in place of the said Francis Burdett and Charles Sedley Burdett, whose legacies he thereby expressly revoked, and gave the same to the said John Clancy and W. A. S. Pemberton, as a compliment for undertaking the trusts and executorship of his said will.

The third codicil, dated 21st October, 1856, in the testator's own handwriting, was in the following words :—

"I, Alfred Brettle, residing in Paris, at number Ninety-one, Champs Elysees, declare that I revoke any codicil or codicils to my will empowering John Clancy, Esq., to act as one of my trustees to the said will. And I appoint Colonel Francis Burdett, mentioned in the said will, one of my trustees and executors of the same.

" ALFRED BRETTLE.

"Witness, ROBERT BURDETT.

"Witness, WILLIAM WILLIS.

"Paris, 21st Oct., 1856."

Annexed to the affidavit of scripts was a letter from the deceased to Mr. Pemberton, as follows :—

"91, Champs Elysees, Paris, 9th Sept., 1856.

"MY DEAR PEMBERTON—I wish you to receive this communication with a strictly professional view. I will thank you if you shall have prepared for my signature, before your expected arrival in Paris, a codicil to my will (in your possession), composed of a few words, stating that I entirely cancel the appointment of executorship on the part of John Clancy, Esq. (identification following), to my said will, and that I appoint in his stead Francis Burdett, late lieutenant-colonel in Her Majesty's service (identification to follow), to act in concert with the two executors named by me in a previous will executed by me, to wit, Thomas Cruttwell, solicitor, of Bath, county Somerset, and Robert Cruttwell, solicitor, of Bath, county Somerset, and with William Augustus Sadler Pemberton, Esq., of

1857.

June 12th.

CRUTTWELL AND OTHERS v. CLANCY.

No. 8, Southampton Street, Bloomsbury Square, London, solicitor, appointed by me in a subsequent will co-executors with others, the said W. A. S. Pemberton, now holding possession of the same, so that the executors of my will shall be as follows:—

" THOMAS CRUTTWELL, Esq.

" ROBERT CRUTTWELL, Esq.

" WILLIAM AUGUSTUS SADLER PEMBERTON, Esq.

" FRANCIS BURDETT, Lieutenant-Colonel.

" The above mentioned to receive the sum of £500 sterling each from my estate."

These instructions were never carried out by Mr. Pemberton, owing to the unexpected illness and decease of the testator, and were only embodied in the above recited third codicil drawn by the testator himself.

On the 3d of September of Hilary Term, *Robarts*, as proctor for Thomas Cruttwell, Robert Cruttwell, W. A. S. Pemberton, and Francis Burdett, alleged them to be executors named in the said will and codicils, and prayed probate thereof accordingly.

An appearance was given for John Clancy, Esq., alleging to be one of the executors named in the second codicil, and praying he might be joined in the probate. The usual steps were taken till the second session of the present term, when a proxy of renunciation under the hand and seal of Mr. Clancy was exhibited, and it was declared that he proceeded no further.

Accordingly *Deane* moved the Court to decree probate of the will and three codicils of the deceased to be granted to the said Thomas Cruttwell, Robert Cruttwell, W. A. S. Pemberton, and Francis Burdett, the executors named therein. The only difficulty was, whether the words of the third codicil did not entirely revoke the whole of the second codicil. From the letter to Mr. Pemberton it was clearly the testator's intention only to revoke so much of the second codicil as contained the appointment of John Clancy, and to substitute Colonel Burdett. He submitted that, under such circumstances, a testamentary Court would not shut out any duly executed paper, but grant probate of it, and leave it to the Court of Chancery, if necessary, to determine its operation.

SIR JOHN DODSON granted the motion as prayed.

1857.
——
June 12th.
——
CRUTTWELL
AND OTHERS
*v.*
CLANCY.

*In the goods of* JONAS WELCH (*deceased*).

## On Motion.

1857.

June 12th.

*Will—Codicil—Date of will misrecited in codicil.*

A. made a will in September, 1854, another in February, 1855. In a codicil of the 12th February, 1857, the latter will was referred to as of September, 1854.

Held, under the circumstances set forth, to be an error of the clerk who drew the codicil, and probate of the will of February, 1855, granted.

JONAS WELCH, of Banbury, made a will dated the 4th September, 1854, prepared by his solicitor Mr. Aplin, of Banbury. On 14th February, 1855, he called at Mr. Aplin's office with this will, and instructed him to make certain alterations therein. Mr. Aplin finding that the testator only wished to substitute one executor and trustee in the place of another, and to make slight alterations in some pecuniary legacies, did not make a draft of a new will, but with a pencil made the alterations in question on the original will of the 4th September; and from this will so altered a new will was then and there engrossed and executed by the testator. A codicil was at the same time drawn up and executed, giving a legacy of £50 to Mr. Forbes, but no draft was made. The will and codicil were then inclosed by Mr. Aplin in an envelope, and taken away by testator. Prior to this 14th February, 1855, the testator told Mr. Brickwell (his most intimate friend) that he had appointed him his executor and residuary legatee, and shortly after the 14th February, 1855, the testator told Mr. Brickwell that he had made another will, and he then gave him an envelope sealed up, which he said contained his will; and Mr. Brickwell, by his desire, placed

1857.

June 12th.

In the goods of
JONAS WELCH
(deceased).

it in a tin box containing the testator's private papers; he at the same time gave Mr. Brickwell a paper writing, folded up, which he said was his former will, and told him to burn it, which Mr. Brickwell then and there did in the testator's presence, but he did not open or read it. On the 12th February, 1857, Mr. Aplin, by desire of Mr. Welch, called on him at his house and found him very unwell, and he then directed Mr. Aplin to prepare a codicil to his will bequeathing a legacy to his servant Elizabeth Burnham. Mr. Aplin being very busy, told his clerk, John Barton, to prepare a codicil to Mr. Welch's will to the above effect for immediate execution. Mr. Barton searched the papers in Mr. Aplin's office for the former will, and finding the draft will of the 4th September, 1854, and none of a subsequent date, and not remembering that the testator had made a will of later date, he presumed that to be the date of testator's will, and accordingly described such codicil as a codicil to the will of the testator, dated " on or about the 4th September, 1854." The codicil thus prepared was taken at once by Mr. Aplin to the testator, who executed it in the presence of Mr. Aplin and two of his clerks. Prior to the execution Mr. Aplin read the codicil over to the testator, and asked whether the date of the will was correctly recited, to which the testator answered, " Yes; it's all right;" but did not refer to the will. This codicil was left with the testator, and after his death delivered by his servant to Mr. Aplin, and by him to the executor's solicitors. Mr. Welch died on 20th February, 1857; Mr. Brickwell was constantly with him during his last illness, and Mr.

Y 2

Welch then told him that at his death his will would be found in his tin box, and that there was a codicil giving £50 to Mr. Forbes, and told him to take charge of the box at his death and gave him the key. Mr. Brickwell heard of the execution of the last codicil, but did not see it until after testator's death, when, on opening the tin box, Mr. Brickwell found the envelope sealed up as he had placed it there, and on opening it, found the will and codicil of the 14th February, 1855, but no other testamentary paper. He made a careful search among all the testator's papers and repositories, but has not found the will of 4th September, 1854. Mr. Aplin searched his papers with a similar result. These facts were verified by the affidavits of Mr. Aplin, Mr. Barton, and Mr. Brickwell, who further swore to their belief that the reference in the said codicil to the date of the will, as being the 4th September, 1854, was an error, and that the testator meant and believed it to be a codicil to his will of 14th February, 1855, and that from illness and presuming the date must be correctly recited, he did not refer to his will or discover the error.

*Deane* moved for probate of the will of 14th February, 1855, and the two codicils.

SIR JOHN DODSON.

I have no doubt that the reference in the second codicil to the will of 4th September, 1854, is an error of Mr. Barton, caused by the draft of that will remaining in Mr. Aplin's office and unnoticed by the testator at the time of executing the codicil, and decree probate as prayed.

*In the goods of* PETER RAINIER, ESQ. *(deceased).*

*On Motion.*

*Administration with will annexed—Administration bond—Inventory and account.*

1857.

June 20th.

Application to the Prerogative Court of Canterbury to confirm and allow an account of administration with will annexed, and to declare the administration bond null and void, on suggestion that the property under the will was fully administered.—Held, that the Court had no authority to declare the bond null and void.

PETER RAINIER died in April, 1836, having made a will and codicil, and therein named his widow Elizabeth Crow Rainier, John Rainier, and John Bowler, executors and trustees.

After giving certain legacies to his wife and executors, the deceased dealt with the residue of his personal estate in moieties:—As to one moiety, he bequeathed the interest thereof to his wife for life; and after her death, the principal thereof absolutely to his daughter Caroline Rainier, now Caroline Jones, widow, on the condition of her surviving her mother, and attaining the age of twenty-four years, which events happened. The other moiety of the residue the testator bequeathed to his executors, in trust to pay the interest and dividends to his said daughter Caroline for her life; and on her marriage, in trust to settle the same for her separate use for her life, and after her death to and among her children, subject to certain provisoes.

Mrs. Rainier, the widow, alone proved this will and codicil, and acted in execution of the trusts thereof.

Mrs. Jones married in July, 1841, her late husband, by whom she has four children, minors,

1857.

June 20th.

In the goods of
    PETER
RAINIER
(deceased).

now living.    By her marriage settlement, Mrs.
Jones, with the consent of her husband, assigned
the moiety of the residue, to which she would
become absolutely entitled on her mother's death,
to the trustees therein mentioned, in trust for the
benefit of such of her brothers and sisters as should
survive their mother, and they were Peter Rainier
and Ellen Catherine, afterwards wife of William
Yolland.

No mention was made in that settlement of the
other moiety, bequeathed to Mrs. Jones and her
children ; but Mrs. Rainier, as the acting trustee of
the said estate, continued to hold such trust funds
until her death, in October, 1852.

In May, 1853, letters of administration (with the
will and codicil annexed) of the goods of the deceased left unadministered by Mrs. Rainier the
widow were granted to Mrs. Jones, on her exhibit-
ing an inventory and her sureties justifying to the
amount of a moiety of the deceased's unadministered estate; and the usual administration bond
was given by her husband and by William Pottinger and Archibald Weir, as her sureties.  Messrs.
Pottinger and Weir, the solicitors of the parties,
having required some security from Mr. Jones to
cover their responsibility as to the sureties to the
administration bond, Mr. Jones, by indenture in
April, 1854, directed, limited, and appointed an
estate called Knolton Hall, with its appurtenances,
belonging to and vested in him, to Messrs. Pottinger and Weir, to hold them for a term of 1000
years, upon trust, and as an indemnity for any
losses they might be put to by reason of such their
suretyship, with the proviso that, upon the per-

formance of such trusts, the term should cease and determine.

In May, 1855, on the petition of Mr. and Mrs. Jones and the other parties interested, an order was made by the Court of Chancery, appointing R. P. Jones and the Rev. Ambrose Jones trustees of the estate of Peter Rainier, Esq., deceased. The estate left unadministered by Mrs. Rainier consists of the stock and moneys set forth in the inventory thereof made and sworn to by Mrs. Jones, and about to be exhibited to the Court ; the moiety thereof passing under the deceased's will to Mrs. Jones absolutely, she has paid over to her brother and sister, pursuant to the covenants of her marriage settlement, and the other moiety she has paid over to the new trustees of the deceased's estate appointed by the Court of Chancery, to be held by them in trust for her and her children, as directed by the will, so that the deceased's estate has now been fully administered ; and by an indenture of release, dated 26th May, 1855, those parties have respectively acknowledged to have received the sums of money and stock therein and in the said inventory stated, forming together the deceased's estate heretofore unadministered, and have discharged Mrs. Jones as administratrix therefrom, so that the deceased's estate has now been fully administered, and Mrs. Jones has duly made and sworn to an account, setting forth such her distribution thereof.

Mr. Jones died in January of the present year, having duly executed his will, and therein named his wife, Mrs. Jones, executrix, who has since proved the will in the Prerogative Court.  As such

1857.
——
June 20th.

In the goods of
PETER
RAINIER
(deceased).

1857.

June 20th.

In the goods of
PETER
RAINIER
(deceased).

executrix she is desirous of selling the estate of Knolton Hall, and it has been advertised for sale ; but for the purposes of a beneficial sale thereof, it is of great importance that the term of 1000 years, created therein for the benefit of Messrs. Pottinger and Weir should determine, and be reassigned to attend the inheritance of this estate ; but it appears that they declined to reassign it, on the ground that the bond to which they became sureties is still in force.

*Phillimore* moved the Court that the accounts of the administration on oath by Mrs. Jones might be allowed and confirmed by the Court; that Mrs. Jones might be discharged from further suits in respect thereof; and that the bond given by her husband and his sureties, on such administration being granted to her, might be declared null and void, and of none effect. He admitted that, as to pronouncing the bond null and void, he could find no case precisely in point as a precedent, but cited *Younge* v. *Skelton*, 3 Hagg. 782, and *Archbishop of Canterbury* v. *Tappen*, 8 B. & C. 151, as showing by analogy how the testamentary Court deals with administration bonds. He submitted that all the conditions of the present bond had been complied with, and that, as there was nothing remaining for it to operate upon, the Court would be warranted in declaring it null and void.

SIR JOHN DODSON was of opinion that, as to declaring the bond null and void, he had no power or authority so to do; and it was impos-

sible to say that no questions should hereafter
arise under the administration. As to the account, it was very inconvenient to allow and
confirm it merely on the *ex parte* statement of
the administratrix herself, and without the parties interested being cited. However, when he
should be satisfied that all these were before
the Court, or cited, and that the account was
correct, he should have no objection to confirm
and allow it.

N.B.—In this case, the trustees appointed by
the Court of Chancery appeared by a proctor,
who exhibited a proxy under their hands and
seals, and acknowledged that they had received
the several sums of money and stock in the be-
fore-mentioned inventory account and deed of
release.

1857.

June 20th.

In the goods of
PETER
RAINIER
(deceased).

ALFORD *v.* ALFORD *(by her Committee).*

*Intestacy—Administration—Widow and next of kin
—Committee of lunatic widow.*

1857.

July 6th.

A. died intestate, without child or parent, leaving his widow, his brother, and others entitled in distribution, him surviving. The widow became lunatic, and a committee of her person and estate was appointed by the Court of Chancery. On the question of grant of administration, it was Held, that the ordinary preference exercised by the discretion of the Court in favour of the widow would extend to such committee, unless the next of kin could show special cause to the contrary.

PHILIP ALFORD died intestate, without child or parent, on the 11th February in the present year, leaving him surviving his lawful widow Eliza Alford, his brother James Alford, three sisters, and two nieces, children of a deceased brother; so that the widow would be entitled to five-tenths, the brother to one-tenth, the three sisters to one-tenth each, and the two nieces to one-tenth between them of the deceased's personal property. The present question was to whom the grant of administration should be made? It appeared that shortly after the husband's death, it was thought necessary to remove the widow to a lunatic asylum; and by an inquisition under the authority of the Court of Chancery, dated 21st March, in the present year, Eliza Alford, the widow, was found to be a person of unsound mind, and not competent for the management of herself or her estate; and Charlotte Elizabeth Parsons, the widow of a deceased brother of Mrs. Alford, now living as housekeeper in a gentleman's family in Portland Place, was appointed committee of her person and estate. The deceased's personal property was under £4000 in value, principally consisting of leasehold houses. James

Alford, the brother, had been coachman in several gentlemen's families, and was now a cab or fly driver.

The grant of administration was claimed for the use and during the lunacy of the widow by Mrs. Parsons, as the committee of the person and estate of the lunatic widow, fully representing her, and so preferably entitled according to the usual practice of the Court in the exercise of its discretion under the Act, 21 Hen. 8, c. 5, s. 3, by James Alford, as one of the next of kin, and holding the proxies of the rest entitled in distribution, on the ground that the lunacy of the widow would determine the discretion of the Court in favour of the next of kin. The personal qualification of the respective parties was also matter of discussion.

*Addams* and *Spinks* for the committee of the widow.

*Deane* and *Swabey* for the next of kin.

It was admitted in argument, that there was no decided case exactly in point; but it appeared from the statement of the deputy registrar, that it is the practice in the registry to grant administration on the application of the committee of a lunatic widow without citing the next of kin.

JUDGMENT.

SIR JOHN DODSON.

The first question is, whether the Court has any power of choosing between the parties. I think the result of the discussion that has taken place at the bar is, that it is in the discretion of the Court to grant the administration to either of the applicants. It appears that the practice in the registry is to make the grant to the committee of the widow without citing the next of kin; the Court, however, is not bound by that practice, but may, where the next of kin appears and shows sufficient reason, grant administration to them. I am inclined to hold the committee of the widow entitled preferably, as the widow herself would be, unless good cause is shown by the next of kin; and on a full consideration of the special circumstances of the present case, I see no sufficient reason to deprive the committee of the widow of that preference. I grant the administration, limited till the lunacy of the widow determines, to her committee. I make no order as to costs.

## MADDOCK *v.* ALLEN.

*Will—Unattested paper—Reference to, by subsequent
duly executed codicil.*

1857.

July 9th.

THIS was a cause of proving the last will of Anne Allen, formerly Foote, widow, wife of Joseph Emanuel Allen, late of New King Street, in the city of Bath, deceased; promoted by Sir Thomas Herbert Maddock, one of the executors named therein, against Mr. I. E. Allen, the husband of the deceased. The will, in the handwriting of the deceased, was dated 1st December, 1851, and attested by only one witness, and so by itself invalid. The codicil, dated 13th September, 1856, the day previous to the testatrix's death was duly signed and attested by two witnesses. The question was whether, under the words of the codicil and the circumstances of the case, the informal will was so sufficiently referred to and identified as to acquire validity from the due execution of the codicil. Her property was just over £2000. The papers were propounded in an allegation given in on behalf of Sir Thomas Herbert Maddock, which pleaded—1. The settlement on the marriage of the deceased with Mr. Allen, under which she was empowered to dispose of certain property by will. 2. The custody of the original indenture. 3. A

*A. signed a paper intended for her will, in 1851, which was attested by only one witness. In 1856, on the day before her death, she duly executed a codicil " to my last will and testament." The paper of 1851 was not produced at the time the codicil was executed, but was found after A.'s death in a locked chest in her room; the codicil in a drawer. On a view of the two papers, and on evidence of the circumstances attending the factum of the codicil—Held, that the paper of 1851 was sufficiently identified as the last will and testament referred*

to by the codicil, and that it required validity from the due execution of the codicil.

copy of such indenture in supply of proof and the identity of the parties. 4. The factum of the will, that it was written by the deceased herself on the day it bears date, and was signed by her in the presence of F. W. Hoare, who in her presence, and at her request, subscribed and attested the same. 5. That the codicil was drawn up by her directions and instructions, and duly executed and attested on the day on which it bears date. 6. That since 1846 she had lived apart from her husband, Mr. Allen, since which time she had assumed her maiden name of Foote, and had been generally known by such name and no other (the will and codicil were signed by her in that name). 7. That after separating from her husband she declared her intention of benefiting her relatives by will, and frequently spoke of Sir Thomas H. Maddock as the friend who would manage her affairs in case of her death, and that since 1851 she spoke of having made her will, and of having appointed Sir Thomas an executor. 8. That the testatrix, in executing her aforesaid codicil to her will, meant and intended to confirm and give effect thereto, and that by the words " This is a codicil to my last will and testament" appearing written at the beginning of the said codicil, the testatrix meant and intended to refer to her aforesaid will as being such will. 9. That the testatrix having been in a state of ill health for some short time before her death, became seriously ill on the 8th September, 1856, and on the following day was attended at her residence in Bath, by Mr. F. Field, a surgeon, who visited her daily from that time until her death, which took

1857.

July 9th.
———
MADDOCK
v.
ALLEN.

place on the 14th of the same month ; that on the
morning of the previous day the testatrix being
desirous to make a codicil to her will, spoke to Mr.
Field on the subject, and in direct allusion to her
will, addressing him, said, " I wish you to do something for me in respect to my will," or to that effect;
and Mr. Field having consented to comply with her
desire, proposed visiting her again in the course of
the same day, and he accordingly did so, when
testatrix entered on the subject of her riches,
and stated that she desired to leave something to
her servant, and also some other trifling legacies to
friends; and added, " I wish to do this by a codicil
to my will."   From the dictation of the testatrix
Mr. Field then proceeded to write the codicil, and
on reaching that part in which the testatrix desired
that her servant Eliza Baker should have as much
furniture as her executor might deem sufficient for
furnishing a sitting room and bed room, he inquired
of the testatrix who was the executor of her will,
when she immediately replied, " Sir Thomas Herbert Maddock," and at the same time said there
was another executor, but did not mention his
name, and added that Sir Thomas Herbert Maddock
would be the acting person.   That the codicil
having been completed and executed as pleaded in
the 5th article, the testatrix on being asked by Mr.
Field where the will was deposited said, " Oh, my
will is in safe keeping."   And then by her direction
the codicil was placed in a chest of drawers in the
testatrix's bedroom, and locked up therein.   10.
That on the occasion pleaded in the next preceding
article the testatrix was very ill, and was fully
aware that her life was in danger, and that her

death might occur in a very short time; that in allusion thereto she requested Mr. Field immediately on her death to apprise her friend Sir Thomas Herbert Maddock, whose address she gave him, of the event; and at the same time directed the servant Eliza Baker to take charge of her keys, and not to give them up to any one except Sir Thomas Herbert Maddock. 11. That testatrix had in her possession several Indian trunks, two of which, bearing an inscription on a brass plate, " No. 1, Mrs. A. Foote," and " No. 2, Mrs. A. Foote," were exactly similar in size and appearance, and were kept locked in testatrix's bed room; that about a week before her death the trunk No. 2 was removed from such bed room into a bed room adjoining and communicating therewith, and was so removed to make room for a sofa for the use of testatrix. 12. That testatrix died on Sunday, 14th September, 1856; and that Mr. Field immediately communicated the fact to Sir Thomas Herbert Maddock, who shortly afterwards arrived at Bath, and repaired to the testatrix's residence, and caused a search to be made for the will and codicil, and that in a small box in the Indian trunk No. 2 was found, with other papers, the will now marked A, and propounded in this cause, inclosed in a sealed envelope, with indorsement, " Mrs. Anne Foote's Will;" and that in a drawer of the chest of drawers in the bed room of the testatrix was found the codicil now marked B; that diligent search had been made as well in the Indian trunks Nos. 1 and 2, as in all other depositories of the testatrix, and all due inquiry made with regard to testamentary papers, and that no other paper of a testamentary character

1857.

July 9th.

MADDOCK
v.
ALLEN.

of the testatrix, save the will and codicil pleaded, had been discovered. 13. That the testatrix, when she alluded to her will and declared that Sir Thomas Herbert Maddock was an executor thereof, and further declared that such will was in safe keeping, meant and intended the very will so found in the Indian trunk, No. 2, and, with the aforesaid codicil propounded in this cause, as the last will and testament and codicil thereto of the testatrix.

The will, dated 1st December, 1851, left pecuniary legacies to certain persons of the name of Drew, her brothers and nephews, and certain articles of jewellery to friends, and appointed " the Rev. — Wood, Curate of Christ Church, of Bath, and Sir Thomas Herbert Maddock, executors thereof." The codicil was as follows:—" This is a codicil to my last will and testament. I bequeath to my faithful servant Eliza Baker, now residing with me at No. 29, New King Street, in the city of Bath, the sum of one hundred pounds, with as much of my furniture as in the opinion of my executor will be sufficient to furnish a sittingroom and a bedroom; I bequeath the sum of one hundred pounds to Nicholas Drew, residing in the city of Worcester, tailor. This legacy is to be duty free. I bequeath one hundred pounds to Edward Drew, of the city of Bristol, brightsmith. This legacy to be duty free." The Drews seemed to be two of those to whom legacies were left by the will. The codicil went on to bequeath certain articles of furniture and dress—some to Mr. and Mrs. Taylor, friends and neighbours of testatrix, who were in the room at the time of its execution.

The codicil was subscribed by Mr. Field and

Thomas Hull, an inmate of the house in which
testatrix died.

The evidence of F. W. Hoare, the subscribed
witness to the will of Eliza Baker, of Mr. Field,
of Mr. and Mrs. Taylor, and others, sufficiently
established the plea, and they were not cross-
examined.

*Phillimore* and *Deane*, for the executor, contended
that the executor in this case had discharged the
requirements which the principles applicable to such
references and decided cases laid on him: first, to
show that the paper or document referred to was in
existence at the time the duly executed paper was
drawn up, which was not disputed in the present
case; secondly, that the reference must be distinct,
and such as to leave no reasonable doubt on the
mind of the Court as to the identity of the
paper described; thirdly, to give reasonable
negative proof that no other document is in existence answering to the description.

*Jenner* and *Twiss*, *contrà*, argued that on the face
of the papers the reference was not absolute or free
from doubt, and that since the Wills Act the Court
would be very cautious in admitting parol evidence
to supply the formal execution required by the
statute : *Smart* v. *Prujean*, 6 Ves. 561; *Utter-
ton* v. *Robins*, 1 Ad. & Ell. 431; *In the goods of
Lady Durham*, 3 Curt. 57; *Ferraris* v. *Lord
Hertford*, 3 Curt. 468—on appeal, 4 Moo.
P. C. C. 366; *Ingoldby* v. *Ingoldby*, 4 N. C.
493; *Sheldon* v. *Sheldon*, 1 Robert, 81, were
cited.

JUDGMENT.

SIR JOHN DODSON.

1857.

July 9th.

MADDOCK
*v.*
ALLEN.

The Court certainly has not the same extent of liberty as it had before the Wills Act in dealing with testamentary papers. Then the intention of parties, however arrived at, was the polar star to guide the Court in coming to a conclusion. It is now more strictly tied; but I have yet to learn that the executed paper must, on the face of it, refer to the other, so as to leave no possible doubt, and that no evidence of circumstances can be received. The sole question in this case is, whether the codicil so sufficiently refers to the unduly executed will as to make it a component part of itself. The contents of the instruments have been referred to as supporting one another. Certain legacies are increased by the codicil in accordance with her declarations as established in evidence. [Here the Court went at some length into the evidence, especially that of Mr. Field.] As to the discrepancy of her talking of Sir Thomas Herbert Maddock as her executor and as the person to manage her affairs, while in fact another executor was absolutely named in the will, it is clear that she did look upon Sir Thomas as the person whom she wished to act, and was likely to do so if he survived her. The will was not then before her, and had been made some years back. The request to Mr. Field to write immediately on her death to Sir Thomas, explains her view of the matter. On the whole, I have no reasonable doubt that the will of 1851 was the document referred to in the codicil. There is no trace of any

z 2

other document. Eliza Baker mentions a still earlier will made in favour of deceased's sister, but she also distinctly states that that was destroyed after the sister's death. I cannot think that the Court is so barred of its discretion as not to be free to consider the circumstances under which the codicil was made. In the *Marquis of Hertford's case* there were several codicils, some duly executed and others unduly executed, and it was held that the expression in the last duly executed paper, "I hereby confirm all my wills and codicils," would only apply to the duly executed codicils, because such papers were in existence to satisfy the strict meaning of the word. Here there is nothing before the Court but the one unattested paper. I decree probate of the two papers as together containing the last will and testament and codicil of the deceased. Costs out of the estate, as the suit was occasioned by the deceased's own act.

## CONSISTORY COURT OF LONDON.

ANONYMOUS.

*Impotency of wife—Decree for inspection.*

*Jenner* and *Phillimore* in support of the petition.
*Addams* and *Twiss contrà.*

DR. LUSHINGTON.

I am of opinion that this case is brought before me, not upon any misapprehension of what the Court did upon a former occasion, but upon an expectation of what the Court would do, without the slightest foundation for any such expectation. I admitted the allegation of the wife after it had been twice reformed, because I was of opinion that if the facts pleaded in that allegation were proved the suit of the husband would be barred. Upon this admission of the allegation the proctor for the husband prayed a monition against the wife for a personal examination. The Court said nothing. Then the proctor for the wife prayed to be heard on his petition against the issuing the decree. The Court was surprised at that prayer, which appeared to be perfectly superfluous. Now, to my astonishment, comes before me a minute from the registry, in which the Court is made to say what it never did say or intended to say. The only question which I have to decide is, whether I

1857.

Aug. 13th.

ANONYMOUS.

*Judgment.*

This case, the particulars of which are reported *antè*, 750, came before the Court on act on petition against the issuing of a decree for a monition against the wife to submit to a personal examination.

shall order the inspection at once, or wait till after publication. I have no hesitation now, as I should have had no hesitation before, in refusing the monition for inspection at present; and in so doing I am only doing what I am bound to do in sparing the feelings of the wife, where it is not absolutely necessary that she should submit to an examination. The husband will not be prejudiced by the delay, should it be necessary to have recourse to this inspection hereafter.

# ARCHES COURT.

1857.

April 23d.

DENISON
v.
DITCHER.

## DENISON v. DITCHER.

*Clerk in holy orders—Limitation of time in criminal proceedings under 3 & 4 Vic. c. 86.*

Held, that a "suit or proceeding" under 20th section of 3 & 4 Vic. c. 86 is commenced by the service of the citation on the party

THIS case came before the Court of Arches on appeal from a sentence of the Archbishop of Canterbury, acting for the Bishop of Bath and Wells, under 3 & 4 Vic. c. 86, pronounced at Bath, in Oct.,

accused, to appear at a certain time and place, before a competent Court, to answer certain definite charges; that from the service of such citation the two years limited by the section must be reckoned; that a commission to inquire, issued under the statute, and intermediate steps between the report of such commission and the citation, form no part of the same suit or proceeding.

1846, by which the Venerable G. A. Denison was deprived of the Archdeaconry of Taunton and of the Vicarage of East Brent, in the County of Somerset and Diocese of Bath and Wells, for advisedly maintaining and affirming doctrines directly contrary to the twenty-eighth and twenty-ninth articles of religion, referred to in 13 Eliz. c. 12. The point here determined did not go at all to the merits of the case, but was raised on the question of lapse of time since the last offence charged on the construction of 3 & 4 Vic. c. 86, s. 20.

This point was argued by *Phillimore* and *Deane* for the Archdeacon. They contended that the case was clearly within the limitation of the 20th section; that the commission of inquiry was distinct from the suit or further proceeding; that though notice of the issuing of the commission and of its sitting was required by the statute to be given to the party accused, yet that the commissioners had no power to compel his attendance, or to inflict any punishment; that on the report of the commissioners neither Archbishop nor Bishop had power to punish without the consent of the party accused; that the filing the articles whether in the registry of Bath and Wells, or in the registry of the vicar-general of the Archbishop, and notice thereof given to the Archdeacon, did not call upon him to answer at any given time or place before any persons authorized to adjudicate; that such notice, the necessary commencement of a suit, was only effected by the requisition to appear at Bath, served on 10th June, 1856.

*Bayford* and *Spinks*, *contrà*, argued that the issue of the commission to inquire was the commencement of the suit or proceedings mentioned in the Act; or, if not that, at least the filing of articles in the registry of Bath and Wells, or the service of the copy of these on the Archdeacon; that the cases cited had come before the Arches Court by letters of request, which distinguished them from the present proceedings, and made them inapplicable as precedents.

*Sherwood* v. *Ray*, 1 Moore, P. C. C. 98; *Bishop of Lincoln* v. *Day*, 4 N. C. 299; *Brooks* v. *Cresswell*, 4 N. C. 429; and *Bishop of Hereford* v. *T——*, 2 Robert, 595, were cited.

The judgment contains a sufficient statement of various previous proceedings in the cause.

JUDGMENT.
SIR JOHN DODSON.

This case come by way of appeal from a sentence pronounced by the Archbishop of Canterbury, sitting *pro hac vice* as and for the Bishop of Bath and Wells, under the provisions of the statute the 3 & 4 Vic. c. 86, commonly called the Church Discipline Act. The proceedings in the case, so far as it necessary to state them for the present purpose, are shortly these. The Reverend Joseph Ditcher, Vicar of South Brent, in the County of Somerset, in the Diocese of Bath and Wells, having, on the 20th of October, 1854, made complaint to the Archbishop that there

1857.

April 23d.

DENISON
v.
DITCHER.

was a scandal and evil report against the Venerable George Anthony Denison, Archdeacon of Taunton, and Vicar of East Brent, in the same county and diocese, for having offended against the statute of the 13th of Elizabeth, intituled, " An Act for the Ministers of the Church to be of sound Religion," by advisedly preaching and publishing doctrines repugnant to the articles of religion agreed upon in convocation in the year 1562. The *præsertim* of the charges against the Archdeacon being that, on the 7th of August, 1853, and on the 6th of November in the same year, 1853, and on the 14th of May, in the year 1854, he had preached three several sermons in the cathedral church of Wells, containing unsound doctrine, and that he had afterwards published the same. And Mr. Ditcher thereupon prayed that his Grace would grant a commission of inquiry into the grounds of the scandal; and it was agreed by the consent of counsel on both sides in the case that the time of the alleged offence having been committed should be limited to the first two sermons.

The sentence appealed from related only to the first two sermons. The reason being, I presume, that there was not proof of the preaching and publishing of the third sermon in the Diocese of Bath and Wells. Upon the 31st of October, 1854, a commission of inquiry issued by direction of the Archbishop. The commissioners accordingly met, and notice of such meeting having been given to the Archdeacon, he attended thereat. In January, 1855, the commissioners reported to the Archbishop that there was a sufficient *primâ facie* ground for

1857.

April 23d.

Denison
v.
Ditcher.

instituting further proceedings against the Archdeacon. The Bishop of Bath and Wells was then applied to to sign letters of request to the Arches Court; but he again declined to do so. Articles against the Archdeacon were then prepared and deposited in the registry of the Diocesan Court of Wells; and also in the registry of the vicar-general of the Archbishop in London. The printed papers in this case contain the proceedings in this cause; I find it set forth at length:—" The commissioners having made their report to the Archbishop of Canterbury, and the Bishop of Bath and Wells having been again applied to, and asked to take proceedings upon this report by sending the case to the Court of Arches, and having declined to do so, articles were prepared and deposited both in London and in Wells, on the part of Mr. Ditcher, and the Archbishop was pressed to constitute a Court, and to hear the case under section 11 of 3 & 4 Vic. c. 86. The Archbishop declined to proceed further in the matter, upon which steps were taken in the Court of Queen's Bench to compel him to proceed. The following are the dates of the several steps taken." This is a matter which has been dwelt upon very much in the argument, therefore I have stated it in the words of the book itself. Now, the dates were these. The rule *nisi* was applied for and obtained on the 22d of November, 1855. The rule was made absolute on the 24th of January, 1856; and peremptory on the 19th of April. The citation issued on the 5th of May from the Archbishop to the Archdeacon, summoning him to appear in London upon the 27th of May, 1856. The return to the rule was quashed

1857.

April 23d.

DENISON
v.
DITCHER.

upon the 26th of May, application having been made to the Court of Queen's Bench, and that Court considering the return insufficient. An appearance in London was given to the citation upon the 27th of May, 1856. Upon the 5th of June, 1856, a requisition issued to the Archdeacon to appear at Bath, and this was served upon the Archdeacon on the 10th. Eventually a Court was formed by the Archbishop to sit at Bath. The notice or requisition to appear at Bath is in these terms:—" I, John Bird, by Divine Providence Lord Archbishop of Canterbury, Primate of all England and Metropolitan, in pursuance of a *mandamus* issued to me, and dated the 26th day of April, 1856, by her Majesty's Court of Queen's Bench, do hereby require you, the Venerable George Anthony Denison, a clerk in holy orders of the United Church of England and Ireland, Archdeacon of the Archdeaconry of Taunton, and Vicar of the Vicarage of East Brent, both in the Diocese of Bath and Wells, and the Province of Canterbury, to appear before me either in person or by your agent duly appointed at the Guildhall, in the City of Bath, within the diocese aforesaid, at eleven o'clock in the forenoon of the 22d day of July, 1856, then and there to make answer to certain articles filed in the registry of the diocese aforesaid by the Reverend Joseph Ditcher, clerk and Vicar of the Vicarage of South Brent, in the said Diocese of Bath and Wells, the party complainant, and whereof a copy was served upon you on the 4th day of August, 1855. Given under my hand, this 5th day of June, 1856.—J. B. CANTUAR." The requisition issued on the 5th; it was served upon the 10th of June; and on the 22d of July the Court was opened at Bath, the Archbishop and his assessors forming the Court as required by the Act. Witnesses were examined upon the occasion, and counsel were heard. A protest was given in on behalf of the Archdeacon, and that was argued and overruled. I think an application was made to hear that in the first instance, and it was argued and overruled by the Court. And upon the 12th of August, in the year 1856, the Archbishop pronounced the doctrines set forth by the Archdeacon to be contrary to the twenty-eighth and twenty-ninth articles of religion; and called upon him to retract upon pain of deprivation; time being however allowed him for that purpose until the 1st of October thence next ensuing. The Archdeacon not having made the required retraction, the Court met upon the 21st of October to deliver its sentence. But a statement in writing, and also a further protest having been offered on behalf of the Archdeacon, application was made to be further heard thereon, which was granted. But the Court not deeming the same to be satisfactory, pronounced a sentence of deprivation, from which sentence the present appeal was brought to this Court.

Application has also been made to this Court by the learned counsel for the Archdeacon to be heard on the protest in the first instance, before entering into the principal case. It appeared to the Court, from the statement of the learned counsel, that one part of the protest, if well founded in law, might possibly dispose of the whole case, and it allowed that point to be first argued.

Now, that portion of the protest which the Court

allowed, and which was assented to on all sides should be first argued, is to be found in the printed papers. I will read it, for it is quite necessary that I should do so. It is the fifth paragraph of the protest, and it is in these terms: " That the suit or proceeding (if any) now pending before his Grace the Archbishop of Canterbury was commenced or instituted by the service upon the said George Anthony Denison, on the 10th day of June, 1856, of a certain instrument in writing or citation under the hand of the said Archbishop, dated the 5th day of the said month, and calling upon the said George Anthony Denison to appear at the Guildhall, in the city of Bath, either in person or by his agent duly appointed, at 11 o'clock in the forenoon of the 22d day of July, 1856, then and there to make answer to certain (pretended) articles therein alleged to have been filed in the registry of the Diocese of Bath and Wells, and of which (pretended) articles it is therein also alleged that a copy was served upon the said George Anthony Denison on the 4th of August, 1855; that the said pretended articles do not set forth any alleged offence, which was the subject of inquiry before the said commissioners, as having been committed by the said George Anthony Denison, within two years of such the commencement or institution of this suit, according to the provisions of the hereinbefore cited Act, and therefore the party accused cannot be called upon to make answer to the said articles." That was the ground of the protest, and it was founded upon the Act of Parliament, which has been referred to, the Church Discipline Act, and the 20th section I think of that Act, the 3 & 4 Vic. c. 86.

The question, then, which was thus raised, and which the Court is called upon to decide, depends upon what is the true construction of the statute, the 3 & 4 Vic., and especially of the 20th section of that Act, as applicable to the dates and circumstances of this case. Now, by the 20th section of that Act, it is enacted, " that every suit or proceeding against any such clerk in holy orders for any offence against the laws ecclesiastical shall be commenced within two years after the commission of the offence in respect of which the suit or proceeding shall be instituted, and not afterwards." Then follows a proviso, which I think does not apply directly to the present case; but it is that part of the 20th section to which I have already referred, namely, that proceedings or suits are to be commenced within two years after the offence alleged, and not at any subsequent time, " not afterwards."

Now, then, the question is as to when this, whatever it is to be called, whether it is a proceeding or whether it is a suit, commenced against the Archdeacon—whether it was within the two years, or whether it was not; and what I have to consider is, what is the commencement of the suit or the proceeding? On behalf of Archdeacon Denison it is contended that the commencement of the suit or proceeding is referable to the service of the requisition or citation on the Archdeacon to appear before the Court at Bath, that being the only Court which, under the circumstances, had authority to adjudicate between the parties. To that requisition I have already referred. That, the Archdeacon contends, is the first time that he is called upon in any suit or proceeding binding upon him, and therefore that the commencement is to be dated from that period. On the other hand, it is said, for Mr. Ditcher, that the commencement of the suit or the proceeding, whichever it is to be called, was first, the issuing of the commission by the Archbishop; and if that was not the commencement of the proceeding or suit, then it must be considered that the suit commenced at the time of the filing of the articles in the Consistory Court at Wells, and also at the Vicar-General's Court in London; and if the mere filing of the articles was not the commencement of it, then it must be taken that the service upon the Archdeacon of the articles must be the commencement of the proceedings; because they contained a charge against him, they were served upon him, and therefore that time must be held to be the commencement of the suit or the proceedings in the cause.

It is between these two conflicting statements as to what is the commencement of the cause or proceeding that the Court is now called upon to decide. With respect to the issuing of the commission of inquiry, whether that is to be held as the commencement of the cause or proceeding, or whether the requisition or the citation to appear at Bath is to be held as the commencement, is a very important point in the case. I must remark, in the first instance, that there is a very wide difference indeed between the issuing of a commission to inquire, and a proceeding against a party by way of punishment. The object of the commission, in the first instance, is to inquire whether there are sufficient grounds to make it advisable that " further proceedings"—as in one part of the statute

1857.

April 23d.

DENISON
v.
DITCHER.

it is stated—in another, that "proceedings" should be instituted, or that "a suit" should be instituted or that "a suit" should be instituted against the party. Now the commissioners, though they have the power to inquire, to examine witnesses, and so on; and though they are to give notice to the party who is charged with the offence, in order that he may attend if he thinks proper, have no power to compel his attendance, and they have no power whatever to inflict any punishment upon him, whatever the evidence may be that is given against him in the course of the inquiry which they have pursued. Neither has the Bishop, nor the Archbishop, nor any other person, any authority to punish for any offence that may be proved upon the evidence that is produced before the commissioners of inquiry, unless by the consent of the party himself. If the party defendant thinks proper to say, "I submit to the report of the commissioners, and I am willing to take any punishment that the Archbishop or the Bishop may award," then the Archbishop or the Bishop may give sentence against him. But it is by consent only; they have no power whatever of themselves to do so. Then, upon their report all that can be done is to institute proceedings regularly against him, either in the Court of the Bishop himself, who is to sit there with certain assessors, or the bishop may send the case, by letters of request, to the Court of Appeal of the province; and then the proceedings are regularly commenced, and regularly go on, as in any suit instituted against an offending party.

Then, as to the articles being filed in the registry of the Court below, that would be no sufficient notice to the party. The serving of the articles upon him, which is required by the Act, is, to some extent, a notice given to him of the proceedings that are going on against him. But it is a very imperfect notice. He is not bound to take any steps whatever in consequence of it. He is not called upon, as in a citation in a cause to appear before any particular judge, or at any particular time or place. There is no citation of that sort. He need take no notice of it whatever, unless the parties think proper to take further steps. He is not bound to move merely because articles have been served upon him. He has no knowledge of where he is to appear, or before whom his case is to be adjudicated. It is wanting in all the requisites of a citation making the party the defendant in a suit. It is deficient in these respects, and, therefore, it cannot be said that that would be binding upon him, unless this service of the articles be followed up by a citation.

It is said in this case, that great hardship was imposed upon Mr. Ditcher, the prosecutor, in consequence of the delay of the Court, or the Archbishop, or whoever is to proceed in this matter, to adjudicate upon it; that it is a great hardship upon him that he should fail, merely because the proper steps have not been taken by the Archbishop. But suppose they have not—and suppose the Archbishop was to blame for not having proceeded with due celerity in this case—is it a reason why the Archdeacon should be punished, contrary to the tenor of the Act, which expressly provides that the suit or proceeding shall be commenced within two years; if, through the default of Mr. Ditcher himself, ⟶

1857.

April 23d.

DENISON
v.
DITCHER.

or of any other person, no such proceedings are taken? If the Archdeacon is not convened before the proper court within the time required by the law—that is within two years—it is expressly provided that he shall not be proceeded against afterwards; these are the terms used in that 20th section of the Act. And I apprehend, whosoever fault it might be, if fault there was, that the cause was not carried on with due activity, the Archdeacon is not the person to suffer upon that account.

I think it is hardly necessary to go through this Act, which has been commented upon at considerable length by the learned counsel in the cause. But it may be as well just to observe from the recital of the Act, that its purview is this:— " Whereas the manner of proceeding for the correction of clerks requires amendment." It is as to " causes for the correction of clerks," that this statute is particularly directed. And then the Act provides this court of inquiry, in a later section, for the purpose of making inquiry as to the grounds of such charge or report; that is what the commissioners are to do. They are to inquire into the ground of such charges or reports, and to see whether there is any necessity for further proceedings. In one or two of the sections the term " further proceedings" is used. For instance, in the 4th section they are to inquire and to see whether " further proceedings" are to be instituted; and again, in the 6th, " any further proceedings." And after that, throughout the Act, the words are, for " instituting proceedings" after the inquiry; that is what they are to do. They are to inquire

1857.

April 23(

DENISO(
v.
DITCHEI

whether there is ground for the scandal, and whether there are grounds for instituting proceedings, that is, for bringing a suit in point of fact—for it can be by a suit, and a suit only, that the party can be proceeded against and punished, unless he shall think proper, voluntarily, to consent to the punishment assigned by the bishop or archbishop upon the evidence which is given upon the inquiry. But beyond that he is not liable; and it appears to me, therefore, that these terms, that no suit or proceeding shall be instituted after two years, are confined to legal proceedings in the nature of a suit or proceeding. " No suit or proceeding," or " proceeding or suit," are terms which are to be reckoned precisely the same. There is no difference. Then I apprehend that the Act must mean the suit, and not the preliminary inquiry, whether there should be a suit or not. That is " in itself no suit or proceeding." Here, undoubtedly, is a suit, but not within the two years; and, consequently, as it appears to the Court, the charge brought against Archdeacon Denison does not come within the period required by the statute.

There have been some cases determined upon this point, several of which have been referred to by the learned counsel in the course of the argument. I think the first of those cases was one decided by Sir Herbert Jenner Fust, and is reported in the 4th vol., Notes of Cases, p. 304. The case to which I am adverting is that of the *Bishop of London* v. *Day.* The learned judge, in the course of his judgment upon that case, made some remarks as to the inconvenience of delay. He says, " But supposing there are reasons for the delay, it must be admitted that great inconvenience results from such delay. The jurisdiction of the Court is limited to a period of two years, before the commencement of the proceedings; and it might happen that the report of the commissioners of inquiry would be applicable to a different state of things, where seven months intervened between the report and the commencement of the suit. The Bishop issued his notice on the 7th of August, 1844, and what offences may have been proved before the commissioners, independently of these before the Court, I have no means of ascertaining. It would appear that any offences committed after the 25th of September, 1842, might have formed the subject of inquiry before the Commissioners, whereas this Court can only inquire into offences committed after the 10th of May, 1843. This clearly shows the importance of allowing as little delay as possible to occur between the report of the commissioners, and the commencement of proceedings in this court." So that he clearly held that this Court could not proceed in regard to offences committed at a greater distance of time than two years, although the court of inquiry, from its sitting nearer to the time of those offences, might have inquired into them. If they had been inquired into, and it was found by the court of inquiry that they afforded grounds for further proceedings, or for instituting a suit against the clerk, the learned judge was of opinion that he could not take notice of those charges; though the commissioners of inquiry might do so, he could not do so, if more than two years had elapsed from the time. And this is a case in which the learned judge expressed himself very strongly and very clearly upon the subject.

1857.

April 23d.

DENISON
v.
DITCHER.

Then it is said that this can only apply to cases where the suit is brought by letters of request; and it is admitted that if the suit is brought by letters of request (I do not know whether it was admitted merely for the purpose of argument, or whether it was admitted distinctly and absolutely), that that indeed constituted a new proceeding and a new suit; and, therefore, that the Court sitting in consequence of those letters of request, could not inquire into prior acts; but that if the bishop or archbishop who had granted the commission of inquiry had himself proceeded, and the further proceedings or suit had been before him, that then such proceedings might have included all the facts that were charged before the commissioners, and found before the commissioners; whether those facts were within the two years or not. But I really cannot see any difference between the two modes of further proceeding. If the one is a new suit; if that which is brought by letters of request is a new suit, why, surely the other must be a new suit likewise! How does the matter stand? When the commissioners have reported, it is competent to the bishop either to proceed in his own court with certain assessors, or to sign letters of request. Whether he does the one thing or the other, either is a proceeding entirely free and distinct from the report of the commissioners of inquiry, whether there should be proceedings instituted, or not. It seems to me, therefore, that the opinion of the learned judge, as expressed here, is quite clear; and, also, that it would be the same whether the case were by letters of request or not.

There was another case of *Brooks* v. *Cresswell*, which was also before my predecessor in this chair.

The case is reported in 4 N. C., p. 432, and the learned judge said—" It has been also objected that " a specific charge laid in the third article, relating " to an occurrence in October, 1842, is out of time, " being beyond the limit of two years prescribed by " the Church Discipline Act, as the citation was not " returned till the 7th of November, 1844; whereas, " it was contended on the other side that the com- " mencement of the proceedings was the taking out " and service of the citation, which was served in " August, 1844, and consequently within two years " of the offence. This point might have been raised " in the case of *Lincoln* v. *Day*. But in that case " it was not necessary for the Court to determine " the point, as it held the offence charged not to " have been established. The Court, however, was " then inclined to hold that the commencement of " the proceeding dates from the return of the cita- " tion, and upon further consideration, the Court " is now prepared to hold that the commencement " of the proceedings is to be dated, not from the " time the citation was extracted, but from the time " of its service upon the party." Then he goes to the case of *Sherwood* v. *Ray*.

There is also another case, but that is not so important, because that was decided by myself; but it was in conformity with the decision of Sir Herbert Jenner Fust, and in fact it was founded very much upon his judgments, and upon what was considered to be the practice of the Court, and the doctrine of the Court upon this point. I refer to the case of the Bishop of Hereford against a person whose initial is T. I do not know what the name was; that is not important. It is reported in 2 Robertson.

1857.

April 23d.

DENISON
v.
DITCHER.

Now, what fell from the Court upon that point is as
follows:—"Hitherto, then, I do not consider that the
"objections raised would warrant me in dismissing
"the reverend gentleman; but one more objection
"remains to be considered, and that the most im-
"portant one; namely, the question of time. The
"offences are charged to have been committed
"between the months of March, 1850, and June,
"1851, but the decree was not issued until the 20th
"of September, 1852; therefore the offences may
"all have been committed more than two years
"prior to the institution of this suit, since it is not
"stated that they were continued to June, 1851.
"Now, by the 20th section of the statute, it is
"enacted ' that every suit or proceeding shall be com-
"menced within two years.'" I need not go through
that section of the statute. Then, I say:—"Here is
"a positive enactment which is strengthened by the
"following negative words, 'and not afterwards'.
"By this section, literally as it stands, it is clear
"that the person cited cannot be proceeded against
"for the offences charged, as they are not, as I have
"observed, alleged to have been committed within
"two years of the commencement of this suit. But
"it was said, that this section is not to be taken
"alone, it is to be construed with reference to other
"parts of the statute." Then I proceed to comment
upon the several sections of the Act, and I state
"that the term 'further proceeding' is used in
"other parts of this Act; and it is said that the suit
"in this court is not an original proceeding, but a
"continuation of the first proceeding, namely, of
"the commission of inquiry, which was instituted
"within the two years." So that in this case, as in

one of the cases which had been decided by Sir Herbert Jenner Fust, there had been this commission of inquiry, and the question was whether it was to be considered as a continuation of that, or whether it was a new suit or proceeding. "I cannot "adopt that view, though I allow that there is a "want of distinctness in some sections in reference "to the precise meaning of the words 'proceedings' "and suit. The words of the 20th section, already "cited, are plain. I cannot, then, attempt to explain "any words that are distinct by words which are "to some extent ambiguous. Even if a doubt could "exist, as to the meaning of the 20th section, it "would be my duty, as this is a criminal proceeding, "to give the individual cited the benefit of that "doubt; but the truth is, I have no doubt respect-"ing the meaning of the Legislature; the 'proceed-"ings' or 'the further proceedings,' when sent to this "court, are to be 'heard and determined according "to the law and practice' of this court," and so on.

This must, therefore, be considered as the doctrine of the Court, right or wrong, as to the course that has been pursued, and from which I am scarcely at liberty to depart, unless it should be made clearly to appear that there has been some great error committed upon the point. I say I am not at liberty to depart from that doctrine, unless there has been such error clearly made out, or unless there has been some decision of a superior court, to which, of course, it would be the duty of this Court at once to bow, and to correct the error which it might have committed. But in this case I do not find that there is any decision by any superior court that at all militates against the doctrine here laid down. It is quite

1857.

April 23d.

DENISON
v.
DITCHER.

true that the Archbishop and his learned assessors came to a different conclusion, and certainly I should bow with deference and respect to them; but I have been taught in this case that the Archbishop was only sitting upon the present occasion, not as an archbishop, but as and for the Bishop of Bath and Wells; and that it is to be considered an inferior court, and that from that inferior court the appeal lies to this court. I must therefore adhere to the doctrine that has been laid down by my learned predecessor, and which has been followed by myself, and the only conclusion to which I can come is this, that this suit or proceeding, or whatever it is to be termed, has not been brought within the time required by the statute, that more than two years have elapsed from the commission of the alleged offence; and it is, therefore, the duty of the court, I think, in this case, to pronounce for the appeal, to reverse the decision appealed from, and to dismiss the Archdeacon from all further observance of justice in this suit. I make no order as to costs.

# INDEX

# PRINCIPAL MATTERS.

---

## ADMINISTRATION.

To the Crown's nominee decreed but not extracted, revoked at the instance of a creditor without a fresh warrant; and administration granted to the creditor, with the consent of the Queen's proctor, and upon the original decree and advertisements on behalf of the Crown. *In the goods of Ellen Steinorth.* 270

Granted to simple contract creditor in preference to a judgment creditor, the debt of the former being the largest and the majority of interests in his favour. *Ernest v. Eustace.* 271

The Prerogative Court has no power to declare an administration bond null and void. *In the goods of Peter Rainier.* 317

To committee of a lunatic widow in preference to next of kin. *Alford v. Alford (by her committee).* 322

Refused to assignee of creditor, assignment of the debt having been made after deceased debtor's death. *Baynes v. Harrison.* 15

With will annexed; form of grant in Scotland varied as to the effects of the deceased in England. *In the goods of Diana Mackenzie.* 17

To the guardian of minor residuary legatees, in preference to an executor and residuary legatee in trust named in will, the appointment of the latter as executor having been revoked by a codicil. *In the goods of John Poyer Poyer.* 184

With will annexed, of effects of a father granted to the widow of

the son, as administratrix of
her husband, whilst living the
sole executor and universal
legatee in the will—the father
and son having been found
drowned together. *In the goods
of James Shilling.*    183

L. appointed R., her daughter,
sole executrix and residuary
legatee; R. predeceased L.,
leaving issue and her husband
her surviving; the husband died,
having appointed A. and B.
his executors; A. alone proved
the husband's will, power being
reserved to B. *Held*, that B.
must be cited as well as A.
before administration with the
will annexed of L. could be
granted to a legatee. *In the
goods of Sarah Leach.*    294

## ADULTERY.

*See* CONDONATION.
IMPOTENCY.

In a suit brought by A. against
B. for adultery, B. pleaded her
virginity and recriminated. A.
admitted that he had not consummated the marriage, and
the medical evidence proved
the virginity; *held*, that B. was
not guilty of adultery, and was
entitled to a separation from
A. on the ground of his adultery, which was proved. *Hunt
v. Hunt.*    121

Where there is proof of attachment, criminal intention, and
opportunity, the presumption
is, that adultery has been committed. *Davidson* v. *Davidson.*    132

In a suit for divorce by reason of

adultery, brought by husband
against wife, she was not allowed to plead a verdict for
the plaintiff in an action
brought against the husband
for board and lodging of, and
money lent to, the wife, which
the husband had attempted to
defend by trying to prove the
wife's adultery. *Jenkyn* v. *Jenkyn.*    268

Cannot be pleaded by the wife in
an allegation contradicting the
husband's libel for divorce by
reason of her impotency. *Anon.*
295

## ALIMONY.

The husband cannot deduct from
permanent alimony sums paid
by him on account of debts incurred by his wife before the
allotment or payment of alimony *pendente lite. Harmar* v.
*Harmar.*    282

## ATTESTATION.

Attesting witnesses need not
subscribe in the presence of
each other. *In the goods of
Jane Webb.*    1

Names of attesting witnesses on
first sheets of a will but not on
the last, on which the testator's name appeared singly,
*held* to be no attestation. *Ewen
v. Franklin and others.*    7

Attesting witnesses subscribed
their names in the next room
to that in which the testator
remained after writing his, the
door being open, but he was
not in such a position as to
have been able to see them;
*held* to be no attestation. *Norton v. Bazett.*    259

## BOND.

The Prerogative Court has no power to declare administration bond null and void, though the estate in hands of the administrator may have been fully administered up to the time of the application. *In the goods of Peter Rainier.* 317

## CLERK, IN HOLY ORDERS.

A "suit or proceeding" against, under 3 & 4 Vic. c. 86, s. 20, is commenced by the service of the citation on the party accused, and from the service of such citation the two years limited by the statute must be reckoned. *Denison* v. *Ditcher.* 334

## CODICIL.

*See* EXECUTOR.
WILL.

A. by will and first codicil appointed four executors and trustees, and left them £500 each; by a second codicil he substituted B. and D. in place of two of the original executors and trustees, and varied the £500 legacies accordingly; by a third codicil he revoked any codicil or codicils empowering B. to act as trustee, and appointed C. one of his trustees and executors. *Held,* on a view of all the papers, that the third codicil was a revocation only of B.'s appointment, and not of the whole codicil in which it was contained. *Crutwell and others* v. *Clancy.* 310

Date of will misrecited in, *In the Goods of Jonas Welch.* 314
Unattested will referred to and made valid by a duly executed codicil. *Maddock* v. *Allen.* 325

## CONDONATION

Is connubial intercourse with full knowledge of all the facts. *Campbell* v. *Campbell.* 288
Innocency and condonation are inconsistent pleas, but may be pleaded together. *Ibid.*
To establish condonation the Court must have undoubted proof of conjugal intercourse. *Ibid.* 289

## COSTS.

In matrimonial suits, the ordinary presumption is that the husband must bear them; and when the wife has no income, however great her demerits, whether she be plaintiff or defendant, the husband must pay the whole costs; even of vexatious appeals. But where the wife having an independent income of sufficient consequence is the plaintiff the Court will hold its hand till the termination of the suit, and give costs as in ordinary cases between parties not husband and wife. *Fyler* v. *Fyler.* 175
Executor propounding will of a testator who had been under insane delusions, and the East Company intervening as residuary legatees in trust, condemned in costs. *Dyce Sombre* v. *Troup and others* (Arches). 120
On appeal in the same case, the

Judicial Committee varied the above decree as to costs; gave no costs against the appellants (the executors and East India Company), but allowing them one set of costs only, including the costs of the appeal.  *Ibid.*

A next of kin unsuccessfully opposing a will made in the English form by a British subject domiciled in France, not condemned in costs.  *Bremer* v. *Freeman and Bremer.*      257

Two executors having taken probate in common form, the probate was called in by one of the next of kin—one of the executors, the brother of the next of kin, declared he did not propound the will, but appeared by a separate proctor, and cross-examined the witnesses of the next of kin—his interest in fact being identical with hers ; condemned in £50, *nomine expensarum. Ibid.*      258

## DOMICIL.

A., a British born subject, left England many years before her death, resided in Paris for the last 15 years of her life, and died there; assumed for many years an Italian name, and described herself and was described in legal documents as the widow of an Italian. There was no evidence of the fact of marriage ; and the statements made by the deceased in respect to the marriage were contradictory.  She had real property in India, the bulk of her personalty in England, and made her will in the English form, disposing of her property, with the exception of four small legacies, amongst English persons.  *Held,* that by the law of nations, deceased was domiciled in France, but that as she had not been naturalized, nor obtained an authorized domicil according to and as required by the law of France, she might by the French law make a will in the English form, and that such will was entitled to probate in this country.  *Bremer* v. *Freeman and Bremer.*      192

A British born subject domiciled in Spain, made his will according to the law of Spain—probate granted in England.  *In the goods of Thomas Osborne.* 4

## EVIDENCE

Of adultery need not go to particular time and place when criminal attachment and opportunities of indulging it are shown.  *Davidson* v. *Davidson.*      135

Of a single witness in Ecclesiastical Courts requires corroborative evidence of some sort.  *Ibid.*      137

Facts stated in interrogatories will, under circumstances, be assumed as proved. *Ibid.* 138

The doctrine *falsus in uno falsus in omnibus* has not been received in English Courts as a general principle ; each case must stand on its own particular circumstances.  *Ibid.* 141

*Vivâ voce* in Ecclesiastical Courts. *Campbell* v. *Campbell.*      285

## INSANITY.

Where insanity, though confined to certain one or more delusions, has once existed, and the evidence shows the deceased to have been instructed to conceal the continued existence of such delusion or delusions, and the evidence to prove perfect recovery of capacity is at least doubtful, the will made by a person so affected, though rational and rationally instructed, is not entitled to probate. *Dyce Sombre* v. *Troup.*     22

## LUNATIC.

Where a lunatic widow is entitled to administration of her husband's effects, and a committee of her person and estate has been appointed by the Court of Chancery, the ordinary preference exercised in favour of the widow will be extended to her committee, unless the next of kin can show special cause to the contrary. *Alford* v. *Alford* (by her committee).     322

## MARRIAGE.

*See* IMPOTENCY.

## PAUPER.

A surgeon recently discharged under the Insolvent Debtors Act denied on oath that he had any income at all, or that he had had any patients since his discharge, and was allowed to continue his suit as a pauper—difference in this respect between a professional man and a skilled artisan. *Spratt* v. *Spratt.*     276

## PROBATE.

*See* WILL.

Of a joint will granted. *In the goods of Sir J. H. Tracey.*     6

Of several papers (one written after the death of the deceased) granted as together containing his will, on proof of the law of the domicil. *In the goods of Thos. Osborne.*     4

Of letter written on actual military service. *Herbert* v. *Herbert.*     10

General probate of a will limited to take effect only in certain contingencies. *In the goods of P. A. Cooper.*     9

## WILL.

*See* DOMICIL.
ATTESTATION.

A testatrix in a will bequeathed to her sons, A., B., C., and D., "articles of plate, set down under their respective names in the annexed schedule." On the same sheet of paper were lists of plate, with the name of each son attached; there was no evidence to show whether the lists were written when the will was executed. *Held,* that the lists were entitled to be included in the probate. *In the goods of A. M. Ash.*     181

A., the day before her death, cut off the last sheet of her will, and desired her servant to burn it, as being of no consequence —this the servant refused to do; the deceased then made alterations in the body of her will, and sent for her solicitor to execute a new one, but died on the next day, before anything could be effected; *held* that the intention to revoke the first was dependent on the execution of a second will, and that the first was entitled to probate. *In the goods of C. Cockayne.* 177

General probate decreed of a will expressed "to take effect only in the event, etc." *In the goods of P. A. Cooper.* 9

Probate decreed of draft copy of a codicil burnt by testatrix's order with intent to revoke, but not in her presence; 20th sec. Wills Act.
*In the goods of Ann Dadd.* 290

A will signed by the testator and two witnesses in the margin of the first four sheets, but in the fifth sheet the signature of the deceased only appeared; *held* that the witnesses had not subscribed the will. *Ewen* v. *Franklin and others.* 7

Probate granted of a *joint* will, which is a distinct thing from a *mutual* will. *In the goods of Sir Josias Henry Stracey and Diana Stracey.* 6

Made by British born subjects domiciled in foreign countries —in France. *Bremer* v. *Freeman and Bremer.* 192

—in Spain. *In the goods of Thomas Osborne.* 4

The two subscribing witnesses were the only ones produced in support of a will—one of them was discredited; there was no evidence of instructions; will pronounced for on the evidence of the single witness, corroborated by the probabilities of the case. *Farmer* v. *Brock.* 189

Probate of will granted in the absence of proof of instructions or knowledge of contents, and the attesting witnesses not recollecting any of the circumstances of the execution of the will. *Foot* v. *Stanton.* 19

Duly executed will in February, 1847, "it being my intention by a separate paper to allot my plate." A codicil in January, 1851. After testatrix's death in 1855 there was found with the will and codicil a paper in her handwriting purporting to dispose of plate, pictures, etc.; it was dated 26th April, 1847, and signed by testatrix. The attesting witnesses to both will and codicil deposed that they saw nothing of this paper at the execution of either will or codicil. Probate of the will and codicil granted without the paper of April, 1847. *In the goods of Emma Hakewell.* 14

Will made in India on actual military service, 1 Vic. c. 26, s. 11. *Herbert* v. *Herbert.* 10

Execution of, by virtual acknowledgment in the presence of two witnesses. *In the goods of W. Jones.* 3

A. signed a paper intended for her will in 1851, but it was attested by one witness only. In 1856, on the day before her death, she duly executed "a codicil to my last will and testament;" the paper of 1851 was not then produced, but was found in a locked chest in her room after her death—the codicil in a drawer. *Held* that the paper of 1851 was sufficiently identified so as to acquire validity from the duly

### WITNESS.

*See* ATTESTATION.
WILL.

END.

BUMFIELD & JONES, PRINTERS, WEST HARDING STREET, FETTER LANE.

# ERRATA.

Page 310, in last clause of side-note, *for* " C.'s appointment " *read* " B.'s appointment."

 ,,  15, at line 8, *for* " February " *read* " April."

 ,,  295, in place of first part of side-note, *read* " L. appointed R., her daughter, sole executrix and residuary legatee; R. predeceased L., leaving issue and her husband her surviving; the husband died, having appointed A. and B. his executors; A. alone proved the husband's will, power being reserved to B."

 ,,  333, case of *Denison* v. *Ditcher.* This case was accidentally misplaced.

Lightning Source UK Ltd.
Milton Keynes UK
18 March 2011
169413UK00005BA/5/A